The Tome of the Unknown Actor

a memoir by

Christine Ozanne

Nick ~
"Pigeons on the grass, alas"
Ah ~ memories !

much love *Christine*

Ⓞ
AVOCADO BOOKS

Avocadobooks.com

First published by Avocado Books in 2016

© Christine Ozanne

ISBN: 978-0-9935658-5-4

Author asserts the moral right to be
identified as the author of this work

A catalogue record of this book is
available from the British Library

Cover artwork and formatting:
Matt Trollope / JaxEtta.com
© Avocado Books, 2016

Front cover images: Chrstine Ozanne is pictured (clockwise) in
Upstart Crow, 2016, with Tom Conti in *Present Laughter*, 1988, with
John Inman in *Take a Letter Mr Jone*s, 1981, with David Jason in
Comedy Playhouse, 1974 and in *Carry on Nurse*, 1958

The author will be happy to rectify any omissions at the earliest
opportunity.

For licensing inquiries contact the publisher through the website
Avocadobooks.com

For: my fellow 'unknown' actors and
for anyone whose mirror does not
reflect 'drop dead gorgeous'...

...you know who you are!

RUNNING ORDER

Programme Notes

A few years ago I co-wrote a book with my partner, theatre and screen director Patrick Tucker, entitled *The Actor's Survival Handbook,* which at the time I felt fully qualified to write. Having 'survived' as an 'unknown' actor, I have looked further into my records to find out where the instinct to act came from, and who else was involved in my acting career. These questions and many more are asked and, hopefully, most are answered in this account of what life has been like for me, and all those hardworking, wonderful actors whose careers parallel mine and are similarly unaffected by fame.

We may have a few fans among our nearest and dearest, but mention our names to the general public and they wouldn't have a clue. When strangers discover I am an actor they often seem quite sure they have seen me in something, but if I ask them to name a part or a show I have appeared in, they never can; and they usually think I am somebody else, anyway. The 'big breaks' do come along occasionally, but moments of great promise can often be thwarted by bad-timing or incredible misfortune. I myself have been to the edge and looked over, and have worked and socialised with many 'famous' people and observed their lifestyle. So, when I look back at all the work and travelling I have done, and the friends I have made along the way, I realise what a privilege it is to be part of the acting profession, and my life could hardly be better.

My father's encouragement to "go and collect some memories" when he saw me off on my way to *RADA (The Royal Academy of Dramatic Art)* never left me, but writing this memoir was eventually inspired by my being thrown unexpectedly into a job at a moment's notice. In 2013, at the age of seventy-seven and for the 15th time in my career, I replaced an actress who had already been contracted to play the part. These are detailed in the 'Replacement' accounts throughout the book. They include ten theatre jobs, two commercials, one television show, one long-playing record and this most recent feature film.

When I made a list of all these events and decided to write them up, I took myself on an exhaustive trawl through old diaries, programmes and note books, which proved to be an intriguing search. I then realised that there had been other kinds of 'replacements' in my personal life, and this started to look like the beginnings of a memoir which I hope, for you dear reader, will be an amusing trip and, for me, a voyage of discovery.

Memories, of course, can often play tricks on us and are not always truly reliable. In this memoir I have made every effort to be truthful and accurate, and I apologise for any mis-reporting, which may unintentionally crop up in these recollections of my rather long life.

I was in Riga, the capital of Latvia, roughly halfway through my 78th birthday when I started to type up these notes. Patrick, who was directing the pilot for a Russian sitcom, came back to our room and said: "I've got good news and bad news, which do you want first?"

I plumped for the bad news.

"We only get to see your hands and feet."

"And the good news?"

"You're playing 'The Grandmother'."

The background to this short piece of dialogue is chronicled later in the book. The description of the hotel room alone is worth the wait.

Curtain Up

There are three things you should know about actors...

1. They are always hungry.
They will attend functions, receptions and fundraisers, and happily agree to meet local dignitaries and fans, responding to the inevitable 'How do you learn your lines?' question with a wry smile, in order to consume a plate full of sandwiches and vol-au-vents from the free buffet. And who could resist the 'Full English', sitting in a steamed up location catering bus on a cold winter morning? Then the famous bacon butty at elevenses, putting inches on their waistline and giving the wardrobe mistress an almighty headache? It was Mel Brooks who summed it up perfectly in *The Producers* when a character is asked:

"Why are you so rude to the actors, they're only human?", to which he replies:

"Have you ever eaten with one?"

2. They have all imagined winning an Oscar.
They will have planned some witty remark to get them 'rolling in the aisles'. My favourite acceptance speech was delivered by the Great Gambon who, knowing he was about to win yet another 'Best Actor' award, must have planned something eloquent to say. When his name was announced, and the audience was

expecting something clever and original, Michael lolloped up to the podium, grabbed the microphone, swung himself round and, with a big grin, uttered the immortal phrase:

"Well, fuck me!"

3. Even famous actors were 'unknown' once.

In 1959 I had rented a large flat in St John's Wood which I shared with many fellow actors. Even before mobile phones were dreamt of, the merest hint of a bottle party at '22' would spread like wild-fire and the world and his mother would turn up. At one such beano, pre-*Lawrence of Arabia* Peter O'Toole arrived with his regular drinking mob, and not far into the evening he managed to drop a glass beer tankard down the lavatory pan, leaving a large hole just above the waterline. Chaos ensued, and the local pub on the corner of Queens Grove, known affectionately as 'Rose's', was our bolthole for the next few weeks until my landlord could be persuaded to cough up for a new loo. Mr O'Toole liked a drink or two in those days. Mind you, I did end up in his bed, and I had a very comfortable night. Oh, he wasn't in it at the time! It was some 50 years later, when we were both cast in the new *Lassie* film being shot on the Isle of Man. They put me into the five star hotel bedroom Peter had vacated just for the weekend, and I'm happy to report that the lavatory was intact.

By 1965, after two more addresses, I had settled in Randolph Avenue, Maida Vale, a property I was now sharing with Patrick. We had a spare room for a lodger, and we heard that a young National Theatre actor needed somewhere to stay. So Tony moved in. He was another one who liked a drink or two, and one evening he threw a bottle of red wine at the wall - not quite as inconvenient as breaking the lavatory - so we swept up the glass and decided that the stain looked rather Bohemian, and left it there as a memento. After all, he had thoroughly entertained us with his impersonations of fellow actors at the 'Nash' and, who knew, one day he might be famous? About a year after he moved out, I took a phone call from a woman who said:

"I'm trying to track down Anthony Hopkins."

"I'm sorry," I said. "He doesn't live here anymore. You could try the National Theatre."

"This IS the National Theatre," she said.

Scene 1

My First Entrance

Apparently there was great rejoicing among the extended Smith family when news of my arrival on the 28th of July 1936 reached them. I was the first girl to be born on my father's side for three generations, some 92 years in fact, when my great-grandfather's older sister Henrietta was born in 1844. My three-year-old brother, Gordon, was taken to stay with his grandparents, while my mother walked a mile to the midwife's house where my birth certificate states I was born at No 5, Thorsby Street, Leicester.

I googled 'what day of the week was 28.7.36?' In a flash 'Tuesday' came up. I visualised a little man in an anorak, looking like the dishevelled Dustin Hoffman in *Rain Man*, answering these questions with the lightening speed of a brilliant mathematician who's wired up wrong. But who needs the remarkable 'memory man' when we have computers? Mind you, I googled myself once (as you do) and a picture came up of a HORSE!

About a month before I was born, my mother lost her footing and fell all the way down the stairs with my brother in her arms. I used to tell people this story, but after a while the predictable response of, 'that explains a lot' didn't amuse me any more, so this is a rare outing. With no telephone, she stayed very still until my Dad came home from work. Gordon was obviously not hurt, but it must have been very traumatic for her. Anyway, I stayed in the oven till I was fully cooked, and she always said I must have been a very strong baby...aaahh.

So, a 'female' at last. This tiny baby girl had finally put an end to the long male dynasty, and this could be said to be my first 'replacement' job. Tuesday's child, so the ditty goes, is full of grace. No, not full. Not even large quantities and, thankfully, my parents resisted any temptation to give it to me as a name. Audrey was what they had in mind, until my grandmother intervened (bless her heart) and strongly suggested Christine, which I am very thankful they settled for.

*****

Note to self: must make 'notes to self' as I go along, detailing my discoveries.

*****

The War Effort

The war for me was between those delicate ages of three and nine and I recall very little in the way of visual entertainment to show me how it was done. The beloved radio in the back room with a loud speaker extension into the front room was, apart from a piano, the only luxury in our house. We doted on ITMA - *It's That Man Again* - starring Tommy Handley, and my mother would later claim that he and Winston Churchill "got us through the war". Then there was *Children's Hour, Monday Night at Eight, Workers'*

Playtime, PC 49, Saturday Night Theatre and *Mrs Dale's Diary*, among many others. My absolute favourite thing, though, was when Gordon and I were allowed to sit alone in the back room with the light out, in front of a one bar electric fire, listening to the great radio detective *Paul Temple*, with the most memorable signature tune, *The Coronation Scot*. Marjorie Westbury played Steve, Paul's wife, and I adored her. I loved her voice, and had a really strong picture in my mind of what she looked like; beautiful, of course, slim and smartly dressed. Then one day - some years later - her photograph appeared in a magazine, and I was totally shocked. This beloved actress was short, dumpy and plain.

*****

Note to self: nobody has to be drop dead gorgeous on radio.

*****

I was dead keen to learn how to talk like the posh people on the *BBC*, and spent hours in my bedroom copying them. I suppose I didn't want anyone to hear me imitating announcers and newsreaders, but I must have thought that it would be a necessary asset some-time in the future. Heaven knew when or where this would be of any use, but I very much wanted to speak like them. There was no childhood theatre going that I can remember, apart from a concert party show at Bridlington during our last holiday for six years, in 1939. I was only three, but I can still see the comical man who sang a song with the line, "Shall I buy a tin of blacking or throw me shoes away?" and I still remember the tune.

Otherwise, I remember the gas mask, air-raid drill at school, outdoor Anderson shelters, our indoor Morrison shelter in the front room, which doubled as a bed for me and Gordon, and the base for Dad's brilliant, hand-made model railway, ration books, a 'map of the world' on the wall, with little flags of countries pinned to it showing the war in progress, Dad's ARP (air-raid patrol) fire-fighting equipment, consisting of a bucket and stirrup pump, and blackout boards, each one slotting nicely into the window frames with little wooden pegs to hold them in place. Then there was the dreaded siren, warning us of an impending bombing raid, the doodle bugs which droned overhead, then cut out, the fear in Mum's eyes, then the relief of the 'all clear', and the air-raid over Coventry - only 23 miles away - which lit up the night sky. Occasionally we spent the night in a neighbour's garden shelter. On one occasion a landmine hit Dad's factory, at the same time blowing our front door open. Dad's allotment and back garden, which kept us supplied with vegetables to add to our meagre rations; the rabbit he brought home one day from work - the gift of a friendly colleague, and watching Mum skin it - a job she clearly didn't relish; and the garden railings disappearing – "for the war effort", they said; the young Princesses, on the radio, talking directly to us children, and Mr. Churchill's call to, "fight them on the beaches".

Something to look forward to each Christmas was the food parcel from Australia sent by my Mum's younger brother, Uncle Major (yes, that really was his Christian name) who had emigrated there in 1929, well before the war broke out. The large box would include a rich fruit cake, a huge tin of peaches, and an enormous block of Cadbury's chocolate - made in Birmingham. It was always fun to think of the journey this chocolate had made on the high seas going out to Australia, dodging the submarines - and back - subjected to the same dangers, to bring us our Christmas treat made just 40 miles away.

The lead up to Yuletide was always exciting - Mrs Bramford, Teddy's mum, halfway up a ladder to clean her bay window, singing 'I'm dreaming of a white Christmas'; pinning up the paper decorations; listening to Handel's *Messiah* from Huddersfield and the sublime Carols from King's College, Cambridge on the wireless; then Christmas Day itself. A pillow case at the bottom of the bed with a Rupert Book, a Post Office set, a board game, a metal puzzle and an orange - Oh, frabjous joy! Then, after our only chicken dinner of the year, The King's Speech.

Interlude
The only time we ever had a turkey was when my number came up in a raffle at work, but Mum couldn't get it in the oven without rearranging half the kitchen furniture. In the end she had to saw the thing in half and cook it in relays. Yummy.

During the war a 'Neighbour's League' was set up, which involved all the families in our section of the road. A wonderful idea, bringing together the collective skills from a variety of people to help each other survive the many restrictions the war threw up, with imaginative recipes and sewing patterns. With severe rationing of food, even after the war we were restricted to one bar of chocolate a week, and with clothing coupons, I barely remember having anything new to wear as a child. Even

17

in my teens, all my clothes were hand-me-downs from mum's friend 'Aunty' Gladys, who thankfully had pretty good taste in two-pieces suits and twin sets; perhaps this is where Charity Shop seeds were 'sewn'? ...boom...boom.

Interlude

Because I am rather short, clothes have been the bug-bear of my life. Off the peg garments are always too long somewhere, and although I've had a few things made for me, these can be jolly expensive and don't always fit well, consequently my wardrobe is pretty well full of mistakes. Mail ordering is a disaster; I never learn, and order and send things back with monotonous regularity. I give clothes away, often before I've worn them, and when I see a garment I really love, chances are it is on somebody else who, more often than not, "found it in a charity shop several years ago". I clearly inherited this need to look 'well dressed' or 'smart' from my mother, but attempting to achieve this has been a life-long headache.

*****

Note to self: when shopping for clothes, serendip-ity is your only friend.

*****

One strange phenomenon all through those years of great neighbourhood camaraderie, was that the grown-ups always addressed each other as Mr and Mrs. There was genuine politeness and respect and a rather touching innocence about it all. Looking back

I realise the naivety of Mr and Mrs Dickman who named their only child, Everard. Poor Everard Dickman, he must have had a terrible time at school and so, perhaps, he discovered the magic 'name changing' trick, even before I did?

Appearances Are Everything: (aged 9)
For the 'Victory in Europe' celebrations in 1945 (VE Day) the Neighbours League organised a fancy dress parade for the children. My brother looked terrifically handsome as the Sheik of Araby, with a white sheet draped over his head and a coloured scarf twisted round and pressed firmly down on top of it; my mother clearly had a 'thing' about Rudolph Valentino. Nothing glamorous for me, though. I was dressed as a char woman in a long skirt and old woolly jumper, with a square scarf round my head, tied up in a big bow on top; a large canvas bag round my shoulder with the words CAN I DO YOU NOW, SIR? printed on the front. Yes, I was 'Mrs Mopp' from the BBC radio show *It's That Man Again*. It seems I was destined to be a 'character bag' even at the age of nine. But (could this be a clue?) I won first prize! Maybe I wouldn't always be an 'unknown'. I don't remember Gordon's reaction to this, but it must have been a tough pill to swallow.

After the war I was taken to the traditional Christmas Pantomime at The Opera House in Silver Street - a real thrill each year - plus the odd amateur concert, but the radio still came first. Little did I suspect that one day I would actually work with some of those great radio entertainers of the war and post war years such as Charlie Chester, Eric Barker, Vic Oliver, Maurice Denham, Harry Worth, Sandy Powell, Jimmy Jewell, Dick Emery, Richard Goolden,

Peter Jones and Jimmy Edwards.

Early Stages

In 1945 I trod the boards for the first time as part of *The Dream Ballet* in Leicester's 73rd May Festival at the De Montfort Hall. I still have the programme for *The Tale of a Crown*. 'A Fantasy, presented by the Leicestershire and Rutland Band of Hope Union'. I wasn't mentioned by name, but proudly appeared in yellow butter muslin and pranced around dutifully as instructed by our leader, Mrs Mason. These large extravaganzas were a huge 'happening' in the city after the Second World War, and the songs still echo in my memory.

The Big Picture

Not long after the war I discovered the cinema. I would be allowed to go to 'the pictures' twice a week. The programmes at the local 'Evington' and 'Trocadero' changed on a Thursday and showed a main feature, a 'B' picture, a 'newsreel' and a 'short interest film', as well as trailers and adverts. You could go in at any time and stay as long as you liked - well, until Mum made the most dreaded of announcements:

"Come on, ducky, this is where we came in."

I adored 'the pictures' and in 1947 an important 'replacement' occurred in my life when *The Rupert Book* at Christmas gave way to the *F Maurice Speed Film Annual*. I studied the film stills so diligently all year that they are, even now, imprinted on my brain. My mother told me that it took much longer to make a film than the time it took to watch one, so I studied the other pictures, too; the ones which showed how films were made. Looking at photographs, where stars like John Mills in full period costume would be acting a scene with the camera almost on top of him, and lots of people standing round with microphones and things, I began to get the hang of what it must be like to perform in front of a camera. I could see that there was a lot going on round the actors that you couldn't see when you watched the film. I was 11-years-old when Mum took me to see a film called *Caravan* and I really hated the scene where Dennis Price sank in a quicksand. So, to alleviate my fear, I tried to think of how it was done, and imagined him standing on a stepladder with his head and shoulders poking through a layer of sand, and slowly stepping down till his head disappeared and he was able to walk to his dressing room. Well, that was good enough for me. I was quite happy with that image. I would even walk down the street pretending that there was a camera on me, and that it was my audience looking in on my private world.

Mum got involved in acting at her Women's Meeting, and we would all troop off to see her in a play with nervous anticipation. All went well until the dreaded moment when Mum 'dried'. The prompt came, and *we* all heard it, but for some ghastly reason *she* didn't. The deafening silence was broken only by her one chirpy word. "Pardon?"

We all died. Mercifully, after a second prompt, she picked up her line and all was well again. She was mortified, but it became a repeated anecdote never to be forgotten, as I prove here and now.

Mum clearly had a flair for performing and always took great pride in her appearance; she never went to the local shops on her bicycle without wearing a hat. Dad, who had no ambition whatsoever to act, could crack a joke with a well-timed punch line. I certainly took on the vanity from her, which annoys me, and the neatness from him, which annoys other people, but maybe I inherited something theatrical from both of them with my desire to 'show off' and a pretty good sense of comedy timing.

Mark My Words

Miss Pilkington, my long-suffering schoolteacher, who could stifle a yawn and talk at the same time, wrote just two words on my end of year report: 'Incessant chatterer'. Sadly, I was forced to ask my mother what she meant.

"You talk a lot, ducky," she said.

No bad thing in the long run, I suppose, since talking was going to be the central part of my work load as an actress, but I knew precious little about that at the age of twelve. Oh, by the way, I use the word 'actress' here deliberately, as I only became an 'actor' when some pedantic know-all decided that we 'actoreens' should all have the same title (except in *The Spotlight Directory* and at Awards' Ceremonies, of course). I remember the total thrill on leaving *RADA*, being able to say: "I am an actress." We wouldn't have dreamt that one day we would be lumped together with men.

I never made any conscious decision to become an actress...I believe I always was one...it was simply a question of opportunity and timing. I 'act' for an audience, which could consist of one person, and often does. From childhood I was always able to do something to make people laugh, mainly with facial expressions, and later with jokes or phrases (usually hijacked from somebody else) but getting the required reaction just the same. "She's been on this earth before," a neighbour remarked, to a reaction I got when I was about four (but, was I an 'unknown' in that life, I wonder?). I have to say, though, that this ability works best with complete strangers, since their reaction is spontaneous and natural. I really dislike watching a show where the audience is stuffed with friends and relations of the cast, producing forced laughter and unwarranted applause. Worst of all are standing ovations and people whistling as if they were hailing a taxi.

That, however, was all very much in the unchartered territory of the future when, at the age of 14, my schooling came to an end and I was thrust out into the world looking for a job. I began work as an office junior in what I thought might be a life-long job with the *Automobile Association* (*AA*) in Charles Street, Leicester. This was my home town and it sported, what we now know to be, one of the best and most flourishing of the 'Little Theatre' companies in the country, and this was to become my stomping ground and basis for my acting career for the next five years. Earlier than that, of course, was my childhood, where there must surely have been signs of the entertainment gene lurking beneath the liberty bodice and leggings of my wartime wardrobe.

Scene 2

Growing Pains

The Mirror Image
As I grew into adolescence - well, that was just the problem, I didn't grow very much and once I hit four foot eleven, I stopped. My brother had grown to a respectable height, so I was predictably referred to as 'Titch'. Looking at myself through the angled mirror of my mother's dressing table I saw that my nose had developed a bit too much and, realising that I had a rather prominent profile, became distraught. I seemed to have inherited my mother's nose, which didn't sit happily on my round face and rather receding chin. My mother apologised to me; ah, bless; how could she be responsible for that nose being more suitable for her than for me? It clearly hurt her to see me so upset. I was also becoming overweight, so Gordon added 'Pudding' to his list of nicknames for me, whereby I resigned myself to being unattractive to boys. This was borne out in reality as I spent many a mournful hour as a wallflower at the Palais de Danse in Humberstone Gate (cue violins).

I would have intense crushes on young men. The first was a choir boy who I could sit and watch for ages from the congregation. Then in my mid-teens an older boy from the youth club. Next the centre forward from the mixed hockey team I played for, but with no reciprocation, just shed-loads of unrequited love - oh, so painful. I was rescued from this misery by the realisation that I could always make people laugh and this sustained me for many years, until I met Patrick, in fact, by which time I was 29 years old.

Interlude

I sometimes wonder if there is any significance in the fact that I was the 'backstop' in rounders, the 'goal-keeper' in hockey and the 'wicketkeeper' in cricket? Hmm? Was I defending something else in my personality, I wonder? I seem to remember my mother referring to girls who chased boys as being "a bit forward"!

Speech Patterns

My mother, having spotted my tendency to "talk a lot", especially with adults, encouraged me by treating me to elocution lessons (sadly a thing of the past) where I could develop my *BBC* English. Dad was a stickler for good grammar and Mum would never mind being occasionally corrected, but I am really puzzled as to why I was the only member of my family who wanted to develop a standard English accent. Why was it so important to me before I had any professional aspirations? Maybe when we were listening to *Paul Temple* in a darkened room, Gordon would get involved in the plot and I would imagine myself as 'Steve' living an exotic life in Half Moon Street, Mayfair, with a car in the garage and a manservant called 'Charlie'. Yes, that must be it…I wanted to live that life.

Herbert Mason, a local speech expert helped by correcting me each time I said "look" instead of "luck" and "braykfast" instead of "breckfast", and many other regional variations on 'standard English'.

My early teens were very active. I cycled everywhere, played hockey in the winter and cricket (for Leicester Ladies) in the summer. I also had piano lessons, and by learning to read music and discovering a voice, Mum, Dad, Gordon and I would sing quartets together - rather well, actually. I joined *The Leicester Girls Choir* who tried to emulate *The Luton Girls Choir* which had become a national institution. Our modest success was enough to give me great pleasure, though, as well as plenty of self-confidence.

As children, Gordon and I never had religion thrust upon us, but belonging to a church or chapel was part of most people's way of life in those days. My parents first caught each other's eye in Leicester Cathedral, as members of an augmented choir. Dad was 'C of E', but Mum's background was more 'chapel'. The consequence of this was that, in their new home on the other side of the City, they were situated equal distance between the two. The division took Mum towards her new friends at the chapel, while dad, when he felt inclined, would either put in an appearance at St. Chad's, or visit village churches round the Shire.

Dammit, I'm a Girl
Gordon and I joined the Scouts and Guides and all these extramural activities were fun and fulfilling, but I did experience my first real taste of sex discrimination in early adolescence. For a while, Mum switched her allegiance to St Chad's and joined the choir, because Dad, having shown his abilities in sight-reading music and an extensive familiarity with Hymns Ancient & Modern, became the choirmaster and Gordon a boy soprano and regular soloist. But I could sing - we were a quartet - but I was not yet confirmed, and being a girl, was not allowed to enter the chancel.

I was forced to sit with some adult or other in the congregation, and I rebelled.

During one Sunday Evensong, I feigned illness and Mum was summoned from the choir stalls. She sat on the porch steps with me and I told her that the sound of the organ made me feel sick. She took me home and I never went to another service there again. My parents, being eminently sensible people, must have realised how desperate I found the situation and left me to find my own way to continue church going, which I dearly wanted to do. Eventually, when Gordon's voice broke and Dad relinquished the position of choirmaster, Mum went back to her chapel and Gordon and I found a lovely village church, just a bike ride away. We went twice every Sunday until he joined the Navy to do his National Service, and I went off to London to train at *RADA*.

Learning By Failure

I once heard it said that there were three main necessities in life...'identity', 'security' and 'stimulation'. My blissful childhood certainly contained all three, and was marred only by my failure to pass the Eleven Plus. It didn't seem a big deal to me. It was almost as if I didn't expect to pass and I don't remember being particularly upset, mainly because my parents showed no great disappointment, even if they felt it. All I do remember is Mr Hughes, my form teacher, walking rather menacingly towards me as I sat at my desk on the front row, and saying: "You should have passed - why didn't you pass?" before thumping me hard on the back several times. I then felt ashamed that I hadn't passed and wondered if I had deliberately failed for some reason, because I had come third in the overall class marks that year.

If my parents had been from a different breed, maybe they would have complained to the school - not so much about the unjustified beating (although, can you imagine the outcry these days?) but that, coming near the top of the class, there was a possibility that the marks might have been miscalculated or even 'adjusted' in some way. Nothing was done, however, and I realise now that my life would most probably have taken a completely different route had I gone to a Grammar School, as my brother had done. I did envy him, though, having a school 'master' to call 'Sir', since I was destined to be in an all girls school with all female teachers, having to call them 'Miss'.

My life at Bridge Road Secondary Modern was alright, but I was bullied, chiefly for being 'different'. I was considered 'posh', and I was chastised by one of the teachers for wanting to sit next to her on the bus, rather than sit with the other girls. Obviously my 'improved' speech had caused some segregation, but it clearly didn't bother me too much. There was only one girl in the school who spoke 'posher' than I did, and I clung to her like a leech. She rejoiced in the name of Mildred Looms, and together we battled the storm. Then, after three years at Bridge Road, an incredible thing happened. A school had been built right opposite my house and I was eligible to go there for the last year of my school life...AND...it was to be co-educational. MIXED! "Thrilled" was not the word. I was ecstatic about it, and couldn't wait for term to start in the autumn of 1950. It was to be called Crown Hills Secondary Modern School and my first form teacher was to be Mr Mayes. At last, a 'Sir'.

Kenneth Mayes was something of a genius. He brought joy and music into our classroom, which had a piano installed, and we began every morning by singing a song. And he taught English...I just loved him. There were about 15 of each, boys and girls, in my form and these were undoubtedly the happiest days of my life. Then, just before the Christmas holidays...CATASTROPHE. It was announced that next term, for some unaccountable reason, there would be a change in the class arrangements, and my new form teacher would be Miss Wheeler! This was a 'replacement' that shook me to the core, and, as if leaving the beloved Mr Mayes was not bad enough, my new classmates would be ALL GIRLS. I cried for three weeks, all through the Christmas holidays. My mother was at a loss. I was inconsolable. And I remained in Miss Wheeler's class until I left school, just one day before my 15th birthday.

Entering The Workplace

So, what sort of work might I be encouraged to go for. I can't remember what my classmates did, but there were plenty of factories in Leicester taking on 15-year-olds, either on the shop floor, or in the offices. I really wanted to go into the 'Wrens'. A result of watching all those war films, no doubt, and my cousin Christopher's naval uniform (more of him later) but I discovered that you had to be over five foot four. This was my first taste of discrimination against anyone vertically challenged. My desire to lose my local accent and develop better communication skills had pretty well ruled out working in a factory, as I thought I would be 'sent up' for being too posh yet again.

Whether it was through the influence of my parents or the school I'm not sure, but I was encouraged to find a job in an office rather than a factory. In fact, I don't recall factory work ever being considered. With no academic qualifications, my job opportunities were somewhat restricted. I had an interview at The Information Bureau, who gave me a spelling test, which I failed, but was taken on by the *AA*. Dad was thrilled about this, although we would never have a car, because I'd be dealing with maps. This was my passion too, since he taught me to read them, even before words. Wherever I am (apart from Tokyo) I know which direction I am facing, because I see my surroundings in the form of a street map.

Interlude

I was just three years old on holiday in Bridlington when, after settling into the digs, we went for a walk on the promenade and somehow I got separated from my parents and six-year-old brother. Somewhat frantic, the family returned to the digs to get help, only to find me sitting on the landlord's knee, as I had found my way back to the digs entirely on my own. So, a good sense of direction and courage were there right from the start, and have rarely let me down.

En route

Beginning as a junior at the *AA*, I was required to open the morning post and distribute it to the various departments; the same with the tea and coffee making duties, and also to operate the telephone switchboard. This was an 'up-to-date' apparatus with plugs and cords and sockets and little numbers that winked at you when an extension was picked up. I loved it, and felt very grown up being in charge, and making 'long distance' calls to our Head Office in Birmingham, where I would hear in a strong Brummy accent, "Allow, Lister" on the other end.

It was the norm for office juniors to learn shorthand and typing at night school, and eventually

I progressed to Home Touring, my absolute favourite department. I was in my element, surrounded by maps and working out routes, mainly for holiday destinations, and making them up into neat little packs. One day I answered the phone to a man who wanted "a rout t' burry vere dirby." (a route to Bury via Derby, in case you're wondering). Maybe this inspired me even further to lose my Leicester accent.

Interlude
As a test (for females only) place your hands flat on a table. If your ring finger is longer than your index finger, you are most likely to be a good map-reader! Something to do with testosterone, I believe.

Around about this time I discovered the Saxon Players Repertory Company at the Theatre Royal, and the upper circle became my world almost every Saturday night for the next five years. For one and ninepence and a threepenny programme I would sit on a backless bench 'up in the gods' and worship the actors. They were heroes to me, but probably 'unknown' in the wider reaches of the profession, and performed a different play twice-nightly at 6pm and 8.30pm every week until the theatre was closed and finally demolished. CALAMITY. I adored everything I saw there, and learnt more about playing for an audience than I could ever have realised at the time.

*****

Note to self: inspiration and help is close at hand, although you may not realise till much later.

*****

Scene 3

Relative Values

Major Surprises

Ever since the wartime food parcels arrived from my uncle Major in Australia I had hoped, one day, I might be able to thank him personally for his wonderful gifts, but it seemed most unlikely. He was three years younger than my mother and had emigrated to Australia soon after my parents married in 1929. I still have a few photographs of him at their newly built house. One on a spiffy motorbike and one in a snazzy little open-top car, so he clearly had a flare for travel and expensive looking accessories. There was an exchange of letters after my grandparents died in 1950, but they contained no mention of him having any family of his own.

Then, one Saturday afternoon (me aged 19) a car pulled up outside our house. This was a particularly rare occurrence, since nobody had a car in our section of Gwendolen Road. I was standing in the front room and I noticed the driver, who was on his own, adjust the mirror and smooth his hair back with his hands. Then he leaned over and looked at our house, as if to check the number, and at that very moment, I knew it was my uncle Major. I had never met him in my life, of course, but from photographs it was clearly him.

He got out of the car and as he walked up the path to the front door, I went to open it.

Standing before me was this rather nervous, slightly gaunt middle-aged man who, with a soft voice and unfamiliar accent, gently enquired: "Is your mother in?", then added: "You must be Christine." I was inches from the bottom of the stairs, so I called up: "Mum, Mum, you'd better come down."

All I could think of was that, without any warning whatsoever, my mother's brother had turned up unannounced, after 30 years, and she was going to get the shock of her life. Being totally unprepared for what was about to happen, she emerged from the bedroom where she'd been what she called 'titivating', and I saw to my horror that she still had curlers in her hair. She would never get over it.

Halfway down the stairs she saw him and, for one brief shining moment, she forgot her curlers, threw caution to the wind and her arms round her brother's neck. There were tears, too. Dad, who'd been enjoying a quiet pipe in the back room, emerged and joined in the greetings. When the dust settled and someone put the kettle on, we learnt that Uncle M had sold his business and decided to come back to England to see us, look up old haunts and, maybe, visit some exciting European cities. The truth, which emerged some weeks later, was that he had terminal lung cancer and this was his 'farewell' trip.

We heard a little more about his life and work, but the big bombshell was to come. For some years now, he told us, he had been married. Mum was very surprised and slightly hurt that she'd been left in the dark for so long, but there was more to come. The wife was on the trip with him, and he would like to bring her over that evening to meet us all. He said her name was Betty, she was Australian and they had no children. As calmly as we could, we dealt with this amazing news and rustled up some supper, while Uncle M went off to prepare Betty for the meeting ahead.

My uncle was only 51 and had apparently been quite a ladies man in his time. He had sent a few snapshots of himself on Bondi Beach when he was youthful and handsome, surrounded by a bevy of beauties all in trendy 1930s swimwear, but we had precious little to prepare us for what might turn up that evening. After a tentative tap on the front door knocker, Mum and I went to greet just about the most unlikely couple we could have expected to be our guests that evening.

It sounds unkind, but 'old crone' would best describe Betty as she emerged into the light of the hall, with a bent back, wrinkled face, dyed hair - the colour of nicotine stains with dark grey roots. She had old withered hands with long red painted talons, but wearing expensive clothes and jewellery. She must have been pushing 80 (probably an exaggeration to my youthful gaze) and with a strident Australian accent, her appearance only added to the mystery of this inexplicable marriage. They didn't stay for supper and after about half an hour they left. I never saw her again, except in the mirror, when attempting to replicate that image on stage some years later.

I did see my uncle twice afterwards and was able to thank him again for those wonderful food parcels. From his longed-for tour of Europe, he brought back two presents from Copenhagen. One was a small bronze replica of the famous Lure Blowers statue, and for me a beautiful silver filigree bracelet which he had gone without several meals to buy. I treasured it.

Fresh Blood

One of the greatest influences during these teenage years was my first cousin Christopher. His father and mine were brothers - and there is no doubt that he had a great deal to do with my future career and lifestyle. He had been evacuated from London to a Leicestershire village during the war, and had attended the Wyggeston Boys Grammar School, after which he went on to a career in the Navy. One day the rarest of things occurred, a telegram arrived which took us almost an hour to decipher. It read...

PROPOSE DESCEND 2030: CHRISTOPHER

By the time the penny dropped that 'twenty-thirty' meant 'half past eight'...there was about five minutes left to prepare for his arrival. Christopher was from a different world. Brought up in Beckenham with middle class professional parents, he spoke in a way my mother had described as 'bay window'. He introduced Gordon and me to classical music and took us to symphony concerts at the Royal Festival Hall, and big cricket matches at Lords and the Oval. We were already loyal supporters of our beloved Leicestershire, and now found ourselves following Middlesex and the great Denis Compton. Cricket at Grace Road in the summer and football at Filbert Street in the winter to watch 'City' play were major events in our lives.

Who would have thought that this more or less 'unknown' team would one day be regarded as the surprise football champions of all time? It is wonderful for Leicester, recently made famous by the discovery of Richard the Third's remains turning up in a city car park, but it does feel strange that I cannot identify the players as men of Leicester. I can still recite the names of the entire team that played for 'City' when they reached Wembley in the 1949 Cup Final. I realise that Jamie Vardy, today's star goal scorer, is a local hero, but he too was 'unknown' outside the football world until this freakish elevation to worldwide fame.

So, the '49 Cup Final, against Wolverhampton Wanderers, was a huge event for everybody in Leicester. Although I was too young to go to Wembley itself, Gordon, being three years older than me, was invited to Beckenham for the weekend. My aunt and uncle had a tiny television set, and he would get to SEE the match…live! I was so jealous, only being able to hear the radio commentary, and when he came home I was full of: "did you see it…what was it like…what about that goal…did it look 'off side' to you?" I was bubbling over.

"Oh, we only saw a bit of the match," he said. "We got bored and went for a drive."

I have never quite forgiven him. Anyway, *he* would never have been bored watching 'City', but I suspect that he would have gone along with the suggestion of a drive to be polite, secretly dying inside. Once, as a child, I beat my brother at chess and I don't think he has ever quite forgiven ME. For the record we lost to Wolves 3 - 1. It was TRAGIC.

Playing Away

Being invited to Beckenham for a long weekend, especially when Christopher was there on leave from the Navy, was truly the most exciting thing in the world for me. Uncle Eric would meet me at St

Pancras and escort me through London to catch the train either to Beckenham Junction or West Wickham, and I relished these journeys through the leafy London suburbs. On Saturday morning we would drive into Bromley or Croydon and have lunch…in a restaurant. Then, after a bit of shopping, it would be back to Wickham Way for 'high tea'. Aunty Evelyn was like no-one I had ever known before. She was the daughter of a Church of England vicar - later canonized, and since her maiden name was Ball, much humour was drawn from his new title. She had strong Indian Raj connections among her relatives, and numerous amounts of silver and carved wooden objects around the house reflected this.

In the evening we would play cards. Although I was used to games where you had trumps and took tricks, Bridge was not on my radar, and they all exercised extreme patience in an endeavour to teach me the rudiments of building a 'contract'. I wasn't completely cack-handed and held my own pretty well, only to be utterly deflated at one vital moment by the look on Aunty Evelyn's face as I triumphantly trumped my partner's Ace. But she was immensely kind and, because she had been a teacher, was willing and able to broaden my cultural horizons. On Sunday morning three of us would be sitting in the car with the engine running, impatiently waiting for Christopher, who would be standing at the front door with a cup of tea in one hand and a piece of toast in the other, determined to finish his breakfast, at the same time making us all late for church. The Smiths were ALWAYS late for church. A pew, near the front, would be left empty for The Smiths to fill during the first hymn.

Home for Sunday roast, then in the afternoon, oh

bliss, my favourite thing…a game of croquet. Their lawn was rather too long and thin for this vicious game, but who cared if a few flower beds suffered? All three of them were completely ruthless. I was quite shocked, but I loved the game because it was quite simply a thing of beauty and a 'class' act to boot.

Sometimes on Sunday evenings we would drive up to Waterloo to wave goodbye to Christopher, so handsome in his Naval uniform, as he left on the night train to Portsmouth. It was very romantic…quite *Brief Encounter*-ish. I could almost hear Rachmaninov's *2nd Piano Concerto* in the background.

Christopher also taught me to drive, because he was so impressed that I had a provisional driving licence. Although no-one in my family had learnt to drive, I was determined that, one day, I would live in his world. I'm afraid he was not the best person to start me off on this road (so to speak) as he had a somewhat cavalier approach to the whole thing. Aunty Evelyn drew the line, when she spotted several smashed plant pots in the front garden as a result of my trying to turn into the driveway and bring their precious motor to a halt, only inches from the garage door.

One day, abandoning the car, Christopher threw caution to the wind and plonked me on the back of his motor bike. With absolutely no protection, I just clung on to him as we raced, it seemed to me, through the Kent countryside. Villages came and went and I only remember feeling shattered as I dismounted to discover that I had been sitting on the top flap of his pannier bag which he hadn't even noticed was open. I had trouble walking for several days!

In 1953 (aged 16) I went up to London especially to see the coronation. Christopher and I were planning to sit out all night on the pavement in Trafalgar

Square, where we knew we would be able to see the procession three times. Then it rained and rained and never stopped raining. Aunty Evelyn said: "NO." So that was that. They had a nine-inch console model television set, though, a luxury we wouldn't see in our Leicester home for another 15 years, so we watched it all on 'the box' in good old black-and-white. In the evening we drove up to London and watched the magnificent fireworks, and that was good enough to last me a lifetime.

Seeing Stars
It was on these visits to Beckenham that I was introduced to the wonderful world of the West End theatre. Sitting in the 'dress circle', handing round a box of chocolates and waiting for that magic moment when the curtain would go up to reveal a beautiful set, with elegant furniture and (usually) the telephone ringing to start off a sophisticated drawing room comedy, was my idea of heaven. I remember being taken to see Alistair Sim in *Mr Bolfrey*, Ralph Richardson in *A Day by the Sea*, Sybil Thorndike and Edith Evans in *Waters of the Moon*, Celia Johnson and Anna Massey in *The Reluctant Debutante* and the adorable Virginia McKenna in *I Capture the Castle*. This undoubtedly opened me up to an astonishing array of great actors, and increased my desire to go on enjoying the thrill of theatre visits. The idea that, one day, I would stand on the stage as a professional actress never entered my head, but I now realise that those experiences enriched my knowledge and under-standing of acting.

Scene 4

Beginners, Please

My introduction to acting began when my mother came home from her night-school drama group and said that the class might have to close unless they could get more people to join.   Mum had a joyful outgoing personality and relished the opportunity to act, but a local Am/Dram would be her only experience. She begged me to go along with her the next week to make up the numbers and, since it was at my old school, I agreed to go.

Such groups would take a whole term of 11 weeks to rehearse and perform a one-act play. I remember being given a script to look at for the following week, with a particular part marked out. I turned up seven days later with the complete part memorized and performed it straight through without a prompt. The director just let it run on to the end when there was a total silence, and I noticed everyone staring at me as if they knew something I didn't. Then it dawned on me. It was that one moment in my life when I thought, oh, that's what it is I can do…it's called acting. Of course, I had no idea at the time that I might actually 'do acting' for a living, but as long as there were amateur companies around putting on plays, I had found my niche. It felt the most natural thing in the world. I just seemed to know how to do it. How to stage myself, not be masked, not 'pull focus' until it was 'my turn'. I didn't know the terms for any of these things, but my instincts were trustworthy.

Interlude

Drama students have it constantly drummed into them that they must be real and truthful, but I wonder if this is so. In real life we often hide our true feelings from others, but as actors, we are required to expose our character's true feelings to the audience. That's why it's called 'acting', and making it appear believable, rather than truthful would be nearer the mark. After all, when you are acting, you know what is coming next; in real life, you don't.

My Amateur Debut

Amazingly, our little evening class drama group was considered good enough to be entered for *The British Drama League Festival* at the Little Theatre, and we did this for three years running. The first of the three plays was called *Dark Brown*, a quaint old Victorian melodrama in which I was cast as the middle-aged spinster shopkeeper, 'Miss Tasker'. Remember, I was just 16-years-old. I recall how natural it felt to let the audience see me full on, recounting a scene which had taken place off stage, and how I seemed to know exactly the trick of waiting for the laugh to subside before continuing. It's called 'timing' and it was in my blood. Three plays were performed each evening for a week, then on Saturday night, after the last play, the adjudicator did his summing up and awarded the prize for the winning play, and the best performance. This was a moment I have remembered vividly all my life.

Oh, I know what you're thinking, that I won the Best Performance prize. Well, I did and I didn't. I can see the adjudicator now, standing on stage in front of a full house, debating with himself, literally, how to decide between ME and a man in the final play. This man, it is true, was very good. He was a mature, experienced actor who, we discovered later, had once been a professional, a thing absolutely not allowed in *The British Drama League Festival.* Apparently this information had not filtered through, and after much dithering, he said he felt he had to give the award to the man. Afterwards, people appeared astonished to find out that 'Miss Tasker' in *Dark Brown* had been played by a 16 year-old, and much praise followed. The last thing I had ever expected was to win such a coveted prize anyway, so all I really remember is that it meant I had an opportunity to audition for the *Leicester Drama Society (LDS).*

*****

Note to self: never expect an award.

*****

A natural progression from my elocution lessons, over the next four years, was to take up *The London Academy of Music and Dramatic Art (LAMDA)* examinations. These were primarily for non-professionals who want to improve their acting skills, and I achieved success in all six grades, followed by the bronze, silver and gold medals. I was accepted by the LDS and the next four years were wonderful. My first part was the straight juvenile 'Sella' in Andre Obey's *Noah*. Directors were called 'producers' by amateurs in those days, and Geoffrey Burton, the wonderful man who had cast me in my first part, was really special. Being a leading light at 'The Little', it was a privilege to work with him, and I felt totally at home and welcome in this place and my prospects for continuing membership were good.

Then, one morning, we woke up to the terrible news that an arsonist had set fire to the building and destroyed the main auditorium. It was a devastating blow, after my first outing as a proper actress, for the theatre to be suddenly destroyed by the whim of a ne'er-do-well. Fortunately, there was a large space directly underneath the auditorium called The Moira Hayward Hall, which was miraculously undamaged, and became the 'replacement' theatre for the next few years. I was rehearsing for the next play at the time of the fire. It was another juvenile part, 'Delia Duffy' in *The Whiteheaded Boy*, and a shocked cast rallied round and stoically performed it on schedule in the new venue. I worked on 'wardrobe' for *Tobias and the Angel*, played 'a peasant' in *To Live in Peace*, was prompter for *Private Lives* and (aged 18) was promoted to my first middle-aged character part as 'Mrs Rummel' in *Pillars of the Community*, which I absolutely adored playing. I felt completely comfortable with this, and my subsequent castings over the next two years with the *LDS* bore this out.

The Empress Intervenes

I was 19-years-old, still mapping out routes at the *AA* and performing for the *LDS* in the temporary hall, when things were about to change dramatically for me, although I didn't know it at the time. In *Anastasia* I was playing another of my speciality character roles, 'The Baroness Livenbaum', lady-in-waiting to

'The Empress', who was being played by Rita Barsby, a formidable woman of great stature. She was a kind person, nonetheless, who observed my acting with some interest. One evening she said:

"You love this work, don't you?"

"I live for it," I said.

"Well, they're always looking for character actresses in the West End," she said. "Why don't you try for *RADA*?"

I was already familiar with the West End, and had noted such artistes as Athene Seyler and Fabia Drake playing these kind of roles but, although I wasn't too sure what she was suggesting, I appeared to make the right noises. I had a friend in the company, Freda Dexter, who had tried her hand at *PARADA* (*RADA*'s Preparatory Academy) so I sought her advice:

"Go and find the address in the telephone book," she said. "At once!"

It hadn't really occurred to me that I would be making a life-changing decision. To stay at the *AA* and work my way up to Head of Home Touring; continue playing character parts at the Little Theatre, and possibly find a new place to live, marry and have babies. Well, I don't remember pondering these thoughts for a moment because my 'entertainment gene' needed to be exercised and that's all I cared about. Apart from anything else, my overwhelming desire to live in London would be fulfilled and my spirit of adventure would be stretched by new experiences. I had to go for it.

Without telling my parents, I sent for a prospectus. This came back with an audition application form, which required the payment of £2.00. I furtively borrowed a pound each from two family friends, and by return of post I received a booklet full of audition pieces with a suggested date. Now, I had to come clean with the parents who, thankfully, were delighted and full of encouragement. I'm not sure how or when I was able to repay the £2,00. Thinking about my parents now, I wonder if they may have discussed my future, in the light of my ability to express myself verbally and physically. Mum may have (slightly) invented the need for more people to keep the class going in order to get me involved in acting. I'm pretty sure she also raised the £2.00 to pay back the kind friends.

Interlude

Mum would occasionally manage to send a ten shilling note with her regular letter to me, when she could scrape it together. Once, when she knew I was down to a few pence, a £5.00 note arrived. It just about saved my life. She only revealed, some years later, that she had sold a 'gold' bracelet to a man at the door for that exact amount.

If my Dad was ever asked what he would do if he came into some money, he would say:

"I'd go and get myself educated."

He was a semi-skilled draughtsman and would clearly have yearned for a chance to improve his prospects, but the need to keep a family going during the war on an extremely modest salary with no easy way to move on, thwarted his ambitions. He must have realised, that through my blossoming talent, I would be able to take advantage of the opportunity for further education that was denied to him.

Having The Nerve

On Saturday the 30th of June 1956, at 10.45am, I took the *RADA* audition in what was then The Little

Theatre in the Gower Street building. This one was even 'littler' and seedier than the one where I had made my mark in Leicester, so I felt supremely confident on the stage. The pieces set out in the prospectus ranged from Shakespeare to Lewis Carroll, the latter of which I chose simply because all the others looked completely unsuitable or totally boring. This was a piece of narrative, which included a conversation between Alice and the Caterpillar and offered a duologue for variation. The piece of my own choice was a favourite one I had used for my LAMDA Gold Medal: 'Mrs Grigson' from *Shadow of a Gunman* by Sean O'Casey. It was an amusing speech delivered by a middle-aged character woman with an Irish accent; the sort of part I had become used to playing back home, and if memory serves, produced a few titters from the panel of judges. Maybe it was my choice of 'an old frumpy' part, which amused them, after seeing an endless stream of 'Violas' and 'Juliets'.

*****

Note to self: for auditions - do what you are good at; not what others are good at.

*****

I was able to get a glimpse of the competition as I watched from the wings and saw the girl just ahead of me. She was young and pretty, but appeared to me to have very little experience or, for that matter, talent. I would even suggest that it gave me confidence, along with my record of success in the past, to go on and perform well. I didn't feel the slightest bit nervous, in fact I thought of it more as going out there to entertain.

A couple of weeks later, back in Leicester, I received a letter saying that, although my marks had not been quite high enough for an immediate place, would I be able to take one at short notice? I don't remember being greatly disappointed, after all this was the *RADA*, and seeing the ingenue types lined up at the audition, I thought it probable that my 'characterful' appearance might have counted against me. I said "Yes", of course, although I had no belief that anyone offered a place would pull out, so I went on a group walking holiday in Surrey and contemplated what my future roles might be with the local 'amdrams'.

Towards the end of the holiday I ran over some rough ground and turned my ankle, spraining it badly. One of the holidaymakers who happened to be an osteopath, distracted my attention, and clicked a bone back into place. I yelled, but it did the trick and with a bandaged foot, he gave me a lift all the way home, on his way to Todmorden in Yorkshire. How does one remember these things?

As I hobbled up the garden path I saw my mother at the window, frantically waving a letter. As she opened the front door, I saw that it had *Royal Academy of Dramatic Art* printed in red on the envelope. Why had they written to me after all this time, I wondered? I opened it and discovered, to my astonishment, that I had been offered a place to begin as a student in three week's time, on Monday the 1st of October!

This was undoubtedly the biggest challenge of my life. The prospect excited me a good deal, but for now Sunday had to be faced on tenterhooks, since nothing could be done about anything until Monday morning. What really gave me a sleepless night was the fact that my parents had also been away on holiday, and that the letter had been sitting on the hall floor for a week! Would the *RADA* place still be available?

A phone call to London first thing on Monday morning confirmed that it was. The next thing was to ring the *AA* office to tell them about my sprained ankle, and that I would not be able to get to work, probably for a week. Since the unpromising audition result, I had made no approach to the Leicester City Education Department to put the wheels in motion regarding fees and subsistence, so rather nervously I rang and told them that I had suddenly been given a place at *RADA*. I was quite astonished at their reaction; they were impressed and congratulated me, and would not require me to take any further test for them. When the money came through a week later they had awarded full fees of £66.00 per term, plus £7.10s (£7.50p) a week in term time. My weekly wage at the *AA* was £2.00 less than this, so I was quids in.

I went back to work after a week's recovery and faced a 'mixed reception' when I announced that I would be leaving the office in two weeks time to go to London and train to be an actress. Everyone in the office knew of my devotion to acting at the Little Theatre, but training in London to become a 'professional'? That was a tough pill for them to swallow, and their reaction was cool to say the least. Since most of them were resigned to being in an office for the rest of their working lives, I can understand their feelings of...well, let's be kind and say...envy. Some of them didn't make it easy for me in my last two weeks although, interestingly enough, the actors at the Little Theatre were completely thrilled and proud of my *RADA* place.

The complication of how the *AA* paid their employees in those days is worth recording. When I began working for them in 1951 my salary was 35 shillings (£1.75p) a week, which was paid fortnightly, in advance. At the end of the first week I was handed two week's money, then at the end of the second week I received another two week's money. This meant that when I left after five years I had to work my two weeks notice for nothing. Worse than that, *RADA* had asked all the new students to foregather in the Gower Street building on the previous Friday afternoon for an introduction to 'The Academy' and to familiarise themselves with all the facilities. When I faced my boss with the news that I would need to leave on the Thursday, he said that I would have to give back a day's pay, the princely sum of 16s. 8d. (sorry, I can't work that one out). How mean of them? Although I had the consolation that leaving would take me away from such small-minded people.

Interlude

In an attempt to discover what caused my life to take such an unpredictable journey, I am puzzled as to why my brother and I chose such very different paths. Gordon stayed in our home town and, as a local government officer, working on finances for the education department, kept the same employer almost from the start, to his retirement. It occurs to me that he was influenced more strongly by my father's dedication to family life and a love of transport. He has brought up two children (my lovely nephew and niece). He has built up an intricate model railway in his attic and clearly loves holidaying abroad (though rarely to countries of a distinctly different culture).

I, on the other hand, took on much of my mother's more extravert, theatrical personality, which inevitably took me away from my roots, and into a wider mix of cultures. Otherwise we share the same genes, childhood and love of cricket and music (although long, health-giving hill walks are more his passion than mine). So it must be the parents' individuality which was initially responsible for our diversities. Like most siblings I imagine, we agree to differ on certain subjects, but atheism seems to be the one thing we share which, interestingly, neither of our parents initiated. Where did that path come from?

Major Developments

The sequence of events in 1956 involving my uncle's return from Australia, and my life-changing experience of getting into *RADA* are a bit misty, but I do remember him meeting me in Gower Street after my audition, and taking me for an elegant tea somewhere, before seeing me off on the train back to Leicester. By now he was living (with his wife) in London, but this was the last time I would see him. I stayed with my aunt and uncle in Beckenham for the first three weeks of term and during that stay I received a letter from Mum telling me that Uncle Major had died. I was dreadfully upset and rang my mother to console her. Tearfully she told me that she had received a phone call from 'the old crone' who, in her broad Aussie twang, had said:

"I thought you'd like to know your brother died today."

She then added that if Mum wanted to go to the funeral, it would be "at Golders Green next Tuesday at noon". Of course my mother wanted to go, and managed to get there on her own. It was as sparse a turnout as could be imagined, just Betty and three men, one of whom was a solicitor, who was reasonably kind to my mother in her plight and somehow guided her back to St Pancras. There were no refreshments laid on after the cremation and Betty never spoke to her at all. There was no follow up, no mention of 'a will', no legacy...nothing.

My treasured bracelet was stolen from a dressing table in the flat I was sharing with a large group of young actors in Vauxhall, shortly after leaving *RADA*. I guess it would have been worth a bit, certainly a few weeks rent for a down at heel actor...but it broke my heart. I had only myself to blame, of course. As 'Angelo' soliloquises in *Measure, For Measure:* "The Tempter, or the Tempted, who sins most? ha?"

*****

Note to self: you can lose things, but you can always hang on to memories.

*****

Scene 5

Learning The Ropes

It was a dank, autumnal morning as I stood on Leicester, London Road Station waiting for the arrival of the train that would take me to a new city, a new world and a new life. I was 20-years-old and about to become a student at *The Royal Academy of Dramatic Art!* Only the day before, I had cleared my desk, said goodbye to my office colleagues after five years, and cycled home. Less than an hour before, I had left that family home, which the parents had bought new in 1929 for the princely sum of £550. The mortgage was to take all of Dad's working life to repay, but it afforded a small bay window in the front room where Mum was standing as I turned and waved goodbye. Her proud smile was, I am sure, tinged with a little sadness as I had disappeared from view. Dad, of course, had accompanied me to the station.

As the train appeared like a ghost, puffing a head of steam, and noisily arriving at Platform 3 with the evocative sound of slamming doors, our conversation was inevitably limited to railway timetable trivia, the awkwardness of 'goodbyes' being thankfully avoided. I boarded a 3rd class carriage, quickly found a window seat, and returned to the door, pulling up the thick leather strap to lower the window where Dad was standing, nonchalantly checking out the rolling stock.

"Glad you got a good seat," he said.

"Yes, great," I said. "Cheerio then. See you at Christmas."

Then, as the train shuddered, signalling its intention to pull away, he looked at me with just a trace of envy in his smile, somehow finding a wonderful phrase to see me on my way.

"Go and collect some memories," he said.

One of the requirements of *RADA* was to turn up with a 'Complete Works of Shakespeare'. Apart from the few purple passages I had learnt by heart, copying my brother who was actually being taught the classics at his Grammar School, I had no knowledge of Shakespeare's plays. Thank goodness there was a 'Complete Works' in the house; a beautiful leather-bound, gilt-edged book, which we had inherited from Grandpa Smith, Dad's father, and Mum had no qualms about me taking it.

"Wouldn't grandpa be proud that his Shakespeare was going to *RADA*?" she said.

"Umm," I added with a twinkle. "And possibly his granddaughter, too?"

Inside the Gower Street entrance to *RADA* was Rainbow Corner. This was an array of coloured cards slotted into a large board representing each class for every day of the week. There were 76 pupils in my first term, and they were divided into three groups: A, B and C. My group 'C' was 27 in all, and our first class was 'Mime' with Miss Phillips. This was a discipline I had never encountered before, and I was a little apprehensive. When we were asked to choose a partner I stood timidly in a corner. Then, from across a crowded room, Nicholas Kepros was walking straight towards me. Nick was a gentle American, just a little older and wiser than I was, and he gave me the amount of confidence I needed to take this whole new experience on board. We have been close friends ever since and meet up whenever I visit New York, where he lives and still works. I also have a small 'coven' of very close friends from my *RADA* days, which I cherish. Looking round the first year's group I saw no sign of the pretty girl who had auditioned ahead of me on that day way back in June. Her name would remain 'unknown' to me, and the rest of the world most probably.

*****

Note to self: maybe good looks aren't everything.

*****

Our second class was 'Make-up', something I must have used in a modest way as an amateur, but this was advanced stuff. We were encouraged to buy numbered sticks of greasepaint, especially 'Five and Nine', which I soon learnt was the general phrase applied to all theatrical make-up. 'Five' was a dark cream and 'Nine' was a tan/orange colour, and the two mixed together and spread all over your face, formed the base for whatever role you were playing. In my case, playing regular 'character' parts, I would make a mix of 'lake' (a dark purple) and 'grey' in my palm and apply, with a thin brush, to form the various lines, which had not yet appeared naturally on my face. We used to say it looked like Clapham Junction, but I learned a subtle way of blending these colours and highlights. I would need this skill for many years in repertory, or 'rep' as it is widely known in the industry, since I usually played way above my own age.

'Voice Production' training was paramount at *RADA* and we learned how to speak 'on the breath' and use our 'inter-costal, diaphragmatic muscles'. It certainly helped me to sustain the breath over longer phrases, and improved my stance. I still use this method, which also helps relieve nervousness. 'Movement' with Miss Boalth gave us a certain amount of grace, but 'Fencing' with Mr Froeschlen, proved nothing but a joke for me. I got more laughs in this class than any other. I bent my knees and thrust the foil full-length in front of me, and with the tutor's repetitive phrase of "down, down lower, sit", caused infectious giggling, leading to mild hysteria and, finally:

"Can we get on with some serious work here, please?", which led to my removal from the class-room.

We looked forward to our 'Acting Technique' classes, because we were all rather in awe of Mr Barkworth. Peter Barkworth was already making his name as a West End actor and was appearing in *Roar Like a Dove* while using his daytime to teach we young and impressionable hopefuls. I think it would be fair to say he specialised in subtle comedy, and he watched and critiqued our various performances. After graduating, he insisted that we call him Peter, but that felt over-familiar, and to this day we all still refer to him affectionately as 'Barkworth'.

A major influence in my third term was being directed by the great veteran actor, Richard Ainley - son of the famous Victorian matinee idol, Henry Ainley. Richard, who had been badly injured in the war, with one arm out of action and a distinct limp, could no longer perform professionally, but emerged as an inspirational teacher and director.

A Midsummer Night's Dream would be my introduction to Shakespeare. There would be two casts due to the largeness of the class, and in the first one I was to play 'Hermia', BUT...only as far as the Interval, missing the great quarrel scene. In the second cast I would only play one of Titania's fairy attendants, but when Mr Ainley suggested that my 'Cobweb' should be a 'boxing' fairy, all was forgiven, and my usual comedic appearance produced the regular hysterics from my fellow actors, as I hoped it would from the audience. Then, Mr Ainley was spotted coming through the pass door from the auditorium. Standing in the wings for our first entrance we asked him if there were many people out front. His deep, booming voice was heard loud and clear: "Only three," he said. "Two dwarfs and a lesbian."

To this day, I still use this delicious remark when describing a very small audience, no pun intended.

In the fourth term Ellen Pollock came into my life. She was to direct my group in *The Constant Nymph,* a classic romantic comedy, which had originally starred Nöel Coward. His character had to be an excellent pianist, so this large cast play was not often performed, although it was ideal for drama students. Fortunately, our group contained two such pianists in Robin Ray (later well-known on television for his extensive knowledge on *Face The Music*) and Basil Moss, who earned extra pennies in the evenings, tinkling the ivories in a hotel bar. In both casts, Philip Voss and I played 'The Leyburns', who are invited to entertain at a soiré organised by the 'lady of the house', where he has to accompany her on the piano.

As Philip could play well enough to accompany me, an 'Indian love lyric' was decided upon and *The Temple Bells Are Ringing* was the chosen song.

When it came to discussing costume, our director went round the room with ideas and suggestions, but when she came to me, she placed her finger under her chin, narrowed her eyes, pursed her lips and pondered for a moment, then she released the expression and said:

"Just surprise me, dear".

It just so happened that, among my collection of odds and sods, I had taken possession of a rather beautiful 1930s long black velvet evening gown, thrown out by an elderly relative and rescued by my mother. It came adorned with a matching cape, which had a caramel lace yoke, adorable and just perfect for 'Mrs Leyburn'. With my straight hair parted in the centre and covered at the sides with plaited earphones, I looked every inch the part.

Towards the end of the song there is a moment when she appears to have finished, but there is a bit more to come. I reacted to the premature applause with shock and horror, as I determinedly ended with a deep contralto, but quivering voice. The 'turn' Philip and I did was a show-stopping moment, and is remembered (by some) to this day. Philip and I always recall it as a moment of magic whenever we meet. Robin, told me that his father (Ted Ray, one of my favourite radio comedians) had come to the show a second time, just to see 'The Leyburns' again! Clearly that little cameo had caused the desired effect.

The morning after this performance we had a technique class with Mr Barkworth, and I had prepared the first 'Chorus' speech from *Henry the Fifth*.

"O For a Muse of Fire," I began, and continued with relish, copying the way I had learnt it from my brother when I was about 12-years-old. I finished and sat down. I knew that our illustrious tutor had seen my 'Mrs Leyburn' and looked forward to his comments:

"Oh, Christine," he said. "I just don't know how you can be so good one day and so terrible the next."

From then on I assumed that Shakespeare was not for me and this situation remained unaltered for the next 15 years, only changing after I met Patrick.

The peak of my days as a student came with the casting of *Rookery Nook* by Ben Travers, one of the Aldwych Farces made famous in the 1920s. The play takes place in a country house and the obvious 'character bag' role was that of the daily woman, 'Mrs Leverett'. Our director was Hugh Miller, him- self a farceur of great renown. Once again, due to the large number of students we were to present the play with two different casts, but being the sole character bag, I was to play Mrs L in both of them. This was a wonderful opportunity to work continuously with Mr Miller, but after a while he sent me away; not in disgrace, I hastened to add, but because I was in danger of being over-rehearsed.

"You just need an audience," he said.

Although the play had a rural setting, I decided not to give Mrs L an accent since the lines were loaded with eccentricities, but I did give her a funny walk which gave the impression of an afflic- tion of some kind. All I actually did was to go up on one toe as I moved about. This proved to be a talking point...even many years later. In fact, Derek Fowlds ('Bernard' in *Yes, Prime Minister*) who was a term or so below me, mentions it whenever we meet. Once, when I was having a cup of tea in the canteen with his classmates who had seen the play, they enthused and said:

"Oh, go on Chrissie, do that limp for us again."

"What limp?" I said, and 'limped' away, as if I was permanently afflicted. They never forgave me.

Interlude

Mrs Brazier, a large, robust woman, ran the *RADA* canteen and provided the full, midday meat and two veg, plus pudding at a very low price, doing nothing to reduce my weight, but maintaining my Midlands tradition of dinner at lunchtime.

Beyond Belief

My progress through *RADA* was steady and enjoyable, but at the end of the fifth term (of six) another envelope arrived in the post with the *RADA* logo on the front. My first reaction was that I had been thrown out, or kept down to do the same term again, as this happened to a few students at the end of every term. Why else would they be writing to me?

My fears turned to disbelief as I read: "You have been awarded *The Fabia Drake Prize for Comedy*" and learned I had bagged the princely sum of £3.00. This was for playing a nun, 'Sister Josephine', in *Bonaventure*, which was a serious drama about a convicted murderess. Naturally, I was thrilled to bits, especially since it meant that the great Fabia Drake had seen my performance and noted my comedy skills.

In my last term I entered a competition entitled *A Quick Grasp of Character and Situation*, and was awarded *The Athene Seyler Prize*, which she had personally judged. Then, for my performance in

Rookery Nook I won *The Gilbert Prize* and a cash award of £5.00, for *The Best Female Student in Comedy and Farce*. I never knew who 'Gilbert' was, but the delight of being recognised for my comedy by the two actresses I had admired so much in the West End, was the very pinnacle of my success at *RADA*.

I was a real fan of Fabia Drake and, reading her book *Blind Fortune*, I discovered that she was originally named Ethel, which was my mother's name! Further research revealed that these two 'Ethels' were born on exactly the same day, January the 20th, 1904. I loved that. Athene Seyler was pretty much the reason I went to *RADA*. She was exactly my type of actress and appeared in many West End plays, sometimes three or four in one year. That was my ultimate aim in an ideal world, but an over ambitious one as things turned out. When I won her book, she wrote inside, "For good work in my competition" along with her signature. I stupidly leant it to someone at the *Royal Shakespeare Company (RSC)*, which was never returned to me. Many years later I was taken to meet Miss Seyler in her flat overlooking the river in Chiswick. She was 99-years-old, and I brought along another copy of her book, which she graciously inscribed: "Christine, to wish you happy fruitful days Athene Seyler". What a treasure!

Not all good news

At my graduation in 1958 an Honours Diploma had been introduced for the first time, and I was one of only four recipients. Altogether this was a pleasing prospect for the future. At my final interview with the Principal, John Fernald, his praise for my work came with a note of caution:

"Being a character actress," he said, "you may have to wait until you're 30 to get noticed, but one day your name will be a household word."

"Well," I said. "I could change it to 'Kitchen' now, and get it over with."

Interlude

I once worked with Michael Kitchen in a TV play, before he became famous as Foyle. Aha...Kitchen /Foyle! Making doubly sure are we, Michael? But I spared him my anecdote. Maybe I'll send him this book. Well, he does come from Leicester.

John Fernald's opinion is shared by many who believe that character actors have to wait a while to 'come into their own', but I have discovered, through bitter experience, that younger leading actors make their name first, then later grow into the juicy character parts. What a surprise!

What's in a Name?

On the subject of name changes my family name was Smith, but I felt that my life was changing direction and a new name would help that process. At the end of my first term I spent the Christmas holidays back home in Leicester, but I found it unsettling, having made such an enormous leap into a new world. I discussed my name with the parents, and searched through the family tree for anything suitable to go with Christine. My mother's maiden name was Brouard - a Guernsey name - and I toyed with that before coming across her aunt Adele, who had married Ira Ozanne. Hmm? Christine Ozanne. It sounded pretty good. So the 'replacement' of Smith with Ozanne was registered at *RADA*, and most of my fellow students eventually forgot I was ever a Smith. One of them, Susannah Fletcher, sought my opinion on her choice of a new surname, since she knew I had gone through the process.

"What do you think about 'York'?" she asked.

"Sounds alright to me." I said.

Screen fame came to Susannah York within six months of leaving *RADA*, when she appeared with Alec Guinness and John Mills in *Tunes of Glory*. Did I mention that she was drop dead gorgeous?

*****

Note to self: jealousy'll get you nowhere.

*****

I will offer a few tips on choosing a new name should you not be entirely happy with the one you have. This could be for a number of reasons, but whatever they are, when it comes to any alteration, you might take note of the following.

1. Spelling: Try to choose names that are easy to spell and pronounce. I found that I needed to spell out my second name so often that I now do it automatically, and even my first name can be spelt several ways; with a 'K' or without an 'h'.

2. Rhythm: Any combination of four syllables is good. I got that one right. (Three separate names are a bit of a bore).

3. Separations: Another thing to be aware of is how the names join together. For example: if the first name ends with a consonant sound and the second name begins with a vowel sound, the consonant will 'bleed' into the vowel. My reason for pointing this out is simply through the experience of dealing with my own choice of name, Christine Ozanne. When I meet someone for the first time and I say my full name, it surprises me how often people respond by calling me Christina, because that is what they have heard. I have learned to separate the 'n' from the 'o' with a minute break, so I would strongly recommend that you check this point.

I Could 'Doolittle' About It

An incident towards the end of my last term at *RADA* was something of a learning curve. The opening of *My Fair Lady* at the Theatre Royal, Drury Lane was almost a 'happening'. The theatrical world awaited this musical transfer from New York with bated breath. *RADA* was asked to supply ten female students to sell programmes on the grand celebrity opening night. I was desperate to be chosen, simply because I wanted to see the show and this would be a fantastic opportunity. My friend Paul Huntley, (the now famous wig maker in New York) had played the LP recording for me several times but, when it came to *RADA*'s chosen girls, my name was not among them. Then, one of the favoured students was taken ill and I begged the registrar to let me 'replace' her. Without any explanation, a different student was chosen and I missed out once again.

I had to face it. I just wasn't attractive, not in the '*RADA*' sense of the word. Things are different now that I am old and the glamour days are over but, unlike most people, I cannot look back to when I was beautiful because I never was (cue violins again). Having spent two years among the 'beautiful people', as I called my *RADA* friends, it was easy to get laughs with my looks. That gave me a great deal of pleasure but deep down I wanted to be physically attractive too. Consequently, this tragic *My Fair Lady* episode confirmed that I was not, and never would be a pretty ingenue or leading lady; just a character bag from the age of nine, and only then did I really understand why I had missed out on the first selection of my entrance audition.

*****

Note to self: maybe it was talent after all that got me in to *RADA*. (cue, stop violins)

*****

Interestingly, *RADA* dropped the medals, prizes and diplomas regime some years ago, which added an element of competition for individual awards, as there is in the profession. Instead, they adopted the BA system, making it equal to a University Degree, and enabled the students to apply for grants, and become qualified for teacher training. Consequently, all the students complete their three years with a 'BA in Acting', which would appear to be of no special benefit to them when it comes to casting, since talent and suitability for a part is a matter of opinion rather than qualifications. Talent will out, but I'm convinced that looks are still paramount, and a 'famous' name can definitely help.

Veterans beware!
The entertainment industry has changed so drastically in the past 50 years, and the conditions and expectations for actors now are unrecognisable and, therefore, incomparable. I have been mentoring final year *RADA* students for some time now, and I have seen some of them catapulted into instant stardom in theatre, television and films. Although many of them, due to the huge numbers leaving drama school every

year, have disappeared off the radar. Students bemoan the fact that there is no longer a repertory system where they can cut their teeth and show their versatility in a variety of roles. "You were the lucky ones," they say to us, and it is true that most of us worked for many years in 'rep'. But that was the trouble, we also stayed there for many years. As time went on, it became more difficult to break into films and television because there would be 'new kids on the block', and they would start to snaffle up the screen parts. We must use caution when offering criticism or advice, because we know what 'the business' was like when we started out, and we must be aware that today's graduates do not. It is a completely different ball game, and we should recognise that.

Some student productions these days require a whole range of talents that, in my day, we were never trained for. Musicals, for example, where actors today are required to sing and dance...no lessons for that. Now, most of the students I see can act, sing and dance amazingly well. I watch shows at *RADA* and I know that my contemporaries would have come nowhere near being able to perform with such dexterity. We were simply trained for stage acting. The completely different craft of screen acting was never referred to.

One of the greatest changes between then (when you were physically categorised) and now, is that new, young professional actors these days are offered a plethora of juvenile character parts in plays, musicals, serials and sitcoms, which do not require you to be 'drop dead gorgeous'. There were fewer than ten drama schools in the 1950s, and each would take in about two hundred graduates a year. Now, there are over 300 countrywide training courses, and university programmes, turning out 'wannabe' actors, so the numbers flooding on to the market is positively frightening. I know that *RADA* has to work its way through 2,000 applications before selecting the final 30 or so each year. So in 1958 (aged 22) as a successful *RADA* graduate - with prizes - I had reached the top of the ladder, only to find myself, within days, at the bottom of another one.

Interlude

In my new life in London, I dropped regular church going, refined my accent, and learned to smoke, because it looked bad if you couldn't do it properly on stage. I became hooked on cigarettes, of course, and continued this disgusting habit for the next eight years; the irony being that I never had to play a character who smoked. Sex was not yet on the agenda and I only drank alcohol at someone else's expense. I gradually expanded my range of foods to include dishes ending in 'i' and, having resisted subtitled films all my life, I was somewhat reluctantly dragged off to see *Les Enfants du Paradis* at The Academy Cinema in Oxford Street. Yes, I had finally grown up.

Scene 6

Doing The Business

It would be impossible these days for a young person to grow up without a computer, a smartphone and all the benefits of the internet and social media. In fact, they would barely be able to exist were these 'essential' items suddenly removed from their lives. In 1958, drama school graduates had none of the above.

I shared the No 22 flat (of Peter O'Toole fame) in St John's Wood with five others, where we had one 'pennies only' coin-box telephone fixed to the wall. Staying in, waiting for the phone to ring and taking messages for the others, was part of the life of a struggling young actor in those days. The thrice weekly visits to the Labour Exchange to 'sign on', and the trawl round the offices of the agents and casting directors, who dealt mostly with walk-on and extra work, were routine.

Not a great start to my career perhaps, but I could have been forgiven for thinking that it might have taken off immediately after graduation. My performance as the middle-aged woman in *Rookery Nook* had attracted the attention of an agent, who I only remember as Joan, who wanted to put me up for a West End part in *Auntie Mame*. A very funny little character, a side-kick to Mame, and 'just my cup of tea' you might think, but when I met up with Joan, she gasped and went a bit quiet.

"How old are you?" she asked.

"Twenty-two," I said.

She looked gravely disappointed.

"I thought you were a middle-aged woman, with full *Equity*," she said. "But there's no way I can send you for this part. They wouldn't even see you."

She clearly thought I was worth further promotion, though, because a few days later - it was a Friday, I remember - she rang me and said she had found the ideal small part and had already suggested me to the producers. It was a comedy juvenile (for a change!) in a new play called *The Amorous Prawn*. It was for a young woman in uniform, and certainly intended to look comical. She sounded so enthusiastic and read some of the script to me over the phone. "And then you say this...and then you say that..." she enthused, as if I already had the part. She said it would be coming straight into the West End, and she would ring me on Monday to talk more about it. The phone did ring on Monday, and it was her, but with the tragic news that the role had been cast at a party over the weekend. She had clearly forgotten that I would probably not be eligible for a West End part, anyway.

The options in 1958 were limited to weekly 'rep' theatres, summer seasons, special weeks, schools tours, national tours, and walk-ons or cameo roles in films and television. So this was how life went.

Special Agents

Finding an agent to take you on and put you up for jobs, generally promoting you and your particular talents to casting directors, was no simple matter. I would get to know many of the smaller agents, who might find me jobs on a casual basis, but it would be several years before I could expect to settle with a personal manager.

Quite simply, my problem was height...just four foot eleven. The legendary 'walk-on' and 'small parts' agent, Eric Blythe, sitting behind his desk in a seedy little office in Great Newport Street, with a cigarette hanging permanently from his mouth, would look at me over his half-rimmed glasses, shake his head for the umpteenth time and utter the dreaded, yet not unexpected line:

"There's nothing for you today, I'm afraid."

Then one day, as I turned to leave, he added:

"You see, Christine, the trouble is, you'd stand out in a crowd."

I always hoped he was only referring to my height.

Repertory Theatre (rep)

A season with a weekly rep company - even twice-nightly - was a fabulous, if exhausting job. I was long-ing to get into a rep company, ever since my years of worshipping the Saxon Players, but this 'height' thing - well, lack of it - proved to be a real bugbear for me. At my first attempt to get into a major rep company after doing their 1958 pantomime season in North-ampton, the Artistic Director completely destroyed my confidence by telling me that he wouldn't be able to cast me in more than one in eight plays. I was out of work for the next ten months.

Interlude

When Peggy Mount, an actress best known for play-ing 'Emma Hornett' in *Sailor Beware*, went from doing two different plays a week (twice nightly) to doing just one play a week (twice nightly) she quipped: "I had so much time on my hands, I took a job in Woolworths."

Summer Seasons
These, especially at the seaside, were highly sought after, since it usually meant you would have only one or two parts to play in repertoire, and a guaranteed long spell by the sea, with pay. Bliss. Unfortunately, they never came my way.

Special Weeks
These were offered, by rep companies dotted all round the country, to boost their regular company when a large cast play came up in their repertoire. It would usually consist of one week rehearsing (£5.00) one week playing (£10.00) and one return train fare but, you must find and pay for your own digs. Not a lot left at the end of two weeks, but a boost to the ego and time away from the temporary office work. I did a lot of these and loved them.

Tours
These were pretty good jobs for young actors as they were usually weeks running into months, with regular money, and saving up for the 'out of work' nonsense to come was imperative. I did a number of these, including *Oliver!* which I stayed with for a year.

The Spoken Word
A number of drama school graduates managed to make a niche for themselves in radio, and once they became established in this medium it was, what they call, 'a nice little earner'. Voiceovers, too, could be very lucrative, but it is surprising how many 'famous' people you hear backing television commercials, and narrating documentaries. I was once asked to give a

little talk to a group of non-theatrical women, so I began by asking how many of these voiceovers they recognised. Surprisingly they identified about six actors correctly, but I had spent the previous week listening to, and noting down, all those I recognised and it came to well over 50! This has always been the case; the big money earning actors would pick up some extra pocket money this way. Most annoyingly, when asked about their current work, they would list the visual stuff and rarely mention radio or voice over jobs, as if that didn't really count as 'work'.

I didn't get my foot in the door of Broadcasting House until 1976 (aged 40) after some 18 years in theatre and television. This was for the producer, Simon Brett (the now well-known writer of amusing crime fiction). He was putting together a team for a series called *The Half Open University*, with Timothy Davies, Christopher Emmett and Nigel Rees (of *Quote/Unquote* fame). I was the first female to perform in a comedy show on Radio 3. Six weeks later, Simon cast me in *Things Could Be Worse* starring Harry Worth, and one of the co-writers of both these shows was David Renwick (who later wrote *One Foot in the Grave* and *Jonathan Creek*, among many other celebrated TV shows). Then, two months later, again for Simon, I played a straight part in two episodes of *Strong Poison* in the *Lord Peter Wimsey* series on *Radio 4*, in which I had a long scene being interviewed by Peter Jones. When I listen to it now I hardly recognise myself, not just because it was a long time ago, but it was quite a big part and, dare I say it, competently done? Oddly enough, in spite of my looks not being an issue in this medium, I did no more microphone work, either in radio or voice overs, probably because I never quite took to non-visual acting, but...well, there's still time...

Book of the Week perhaps?

West End, Television and Films

Apart from possible 'cameo' roles, mostly in B Pictures, there was little chance of a beginner breaking into these mediums straight from drama school. I actually appeared once as a 'walk-on' in a 'live' hospital drama, *Emergency Ward 10*, when I was 'cued' to walk through the ward carrying a vase of flowers. 'Live', of course, meant that it was transmitted at that very moment, so you will be relieved to know that I didn't drop the vase. My mother went next door to watch me on her neighbour's tiny black and white telly. Nerve-wracking? Very. How the main actors dealt with it I'll never know, but I'm jolly glad the technology improved.

Joan, the 'unknown' agent, still kept up her endeavours on my behalf, and when she discovered that I could sing, invited me round to her flat in Knightsbridge, where she accompanied me on the piano and joined in the songs herself with gusto. Through another agent I soon got my first job, an eight-week season of rep in Sidmouth, but while I was there Joan procured a film part for me, just 'a one-liner', but it was to see me at Pinewood Studios before the year was out. When word went round that I had a film job so soon, one of my *RADA* mates said: "Oh, I suppose we'll have to pay to speak to you now?"

*****

Note to self: fellow actors aren't always overjoyed at your success.

*****

My professional debut: (aged 22)

My very first job was as 'assistant stage manager (ASM)/actor' for two months at the Manor Pavilion, Sidmouth. I was in seven of the eight plays, including the lead role in the very first one. 'Nanny' in *All For Mary* was a great character role, but one of my lines was in French (which I didn't speak). I shared digs with a fellow *RADA* student, Maggie Riley, who spent what seemed like hours drumming it into my head. Now, of course, it's the only line I can remember.

The company manager, a flabby man called Arnold, who had a single tooth in the middle of his top gum, which made eating a pickled onion quite a show stopper, came to me just before my 'debut' performance and asked me to make the curtain speech. Fortunately, from my many years of watching The Saxon Players, I knew what he meant. At the curtain call I duly stepped forward and thanked the audience...then announced the title of the next production, although I hadn't yet opened the script to see what I was playing!

Interlude

In this two-month season the men were payed £10.00 a week, and the women £8.00. Even on this pittance I managed to save £22.00...all I had in the world.

The lifesavers

On my return to London from Sidmouth I had absolutely nowhere to live, so I fell upon the mercy and kindness of Paul Huntley. He had a flat in Maida Vale, with only a rather uncomfortable couch for unexpected guests, but I was immensely grateful to him none-the-less. Then, as I was drawing a meagre £1.00 from my Post Office savings book, I met up with one of the actors from Sidmouth, who immediately offered me a mattress on the floor of a large apartment just south of the river in Vauxhall (they used to say they lived opposite The Tate Gallery) which he was sharing with a load of ex-*RADA* buddies.

Back to Joan and my film contract. Because of my 'no fixed abode' status and huge difficulty in communications, I almost missed out on this job. I had already been booked for chorus work in the Northampton pantomime, and the four filming days would be during our rehearsals. This meant that for my first 'shoot' day I had to travel from Northampton to London after a day's rehearsal, and get myself to Pinewood for an 8am make-up call the next morning. Trouble was, I had nowhere to stay overnight having given up the Vauxhall space for the duration of the panto.

Arriving in London, I had no alternative but to throw myself on the mercy of the desk sergeant at the Tottenham Court Road Police Station, who let me stay overnight in an interview room with only one upright chair and a small table. I might have preferred a cell, at least that would have had a bed of sorts, but my crime was clearly not grave enough for that. Eventually the day dawned and, although stiff and weary, I was on my way to make my film debut.

The instructions were to take the tube to Uxbridge, then a bus to The Crooked Billet...THEN...a mile long walk to Pinewood Studios. Boy, those were the days! The film was a follow-up to a very popular comedy called *Carry on Sergeant*, a series that became a screen phenomenon. My insignificant role in the epic *Carry on Nurse* has produced more demands for my autograph than anything else I have ever done.

On my first day I was to deliver my one line: "Do

you mind?", and after one 'take' they moved on to the next shot. I had delivered my three words in the right order, and that seemed to be all that mattered. Looking at it now, I am filled with regret. In fact, I think most drama schools still believe that if you are good on stage you'll be fine on screen, as if the craft is exactly the same. Common sense tells you that there has to be a difference, but I knew nothing of such refinements as a complete newcomer to film.

My title was 'Fat Maid', and while vacuuming the floor I got pushed to my knees by another ward orderly played by Harry Lock, whose broom handle struck me on the bottom. Then, in a close-up, I looked at him and uttered the 'famous' three words. I have since learnt a great deal about film acting, so I know I made two big mistakes. My vocal level was far too loud for a close-up shot, and I should have done a quick reaction before I spoke. But this was my first ever day on my first ever film, and a lot of actors playing small parts say that they feel pressured to speak as soon as they hear the word 'ACTION'. I know better now.

My little scene took place two feet from the end of Kenneth Williams' bed. I noticed he was watching my eagerness to do the right thing. After one 'take' I heard someone say: "Cut, check the gate," followed by Mr Williams' dulcet tones commenting on my performance:

"Of course, you're very inhibited, aren't you, dear?"

Happily, I later found that other experienced actors were more supportive than the snide inhabitant of that particular bed.

Otherwise, it was a delight and privilege to work with - what came to be - 'the Carry On team'. At the end of my first day, Joan Sims, who was appearing in

Breath of Spring at the Duke of York's, offered me a lift in her limo. When we arrived at the theatre she told her driver to take me wherever I wanted to go. I was tempted to say 'Northampton', but had to settle for Euston. When I finally reached my digs, which were in a large vicarage, the owners had gone away for the night leaving me to feed their pets. Alarmingly, the rather large dog was lying DEAD on the hall floor with some brown paper covering it, indicating that it had died before the owners had left, and the clearly traumatised cat 'turned on me' viciously, as if it was all my fault.

So, there I was, having just completed my first day's filming at Pinewood Studios, been treated like royalty by Miss Sims, and needing a good night's sleep, facing a dilemma of monumental proportions. Should I attempt to feed this disturbed animal and go to bed with the thought of facing the dead one again in the morning...or what? If I could have imagined an extension to the popular film I had just been part of, then this could have been the beginning of *Carry on Regardless*. Once fed, the cat calmed down, but the dog, alas, was still dead in the morning. So, leaving it under its brown paper shroud, I scooted off to the theatre to rehearse my 'third villager from the left', and was grateful that, by the time I got back for supper, the owners had returned and the dog had found its final resting place.

Interlude

It was during this panto season (1959 remember) that a homosexual actor, curious about another man in the company, asked me: "Is he gay?"

It was the first time I had heard the word 'gay' used in this context, but I somehow knew what he meant.

"I'm not sure," I said, ambiguously, letting both me and the other chap off the hook. I simply didn't want to appear ignorant. I could hardly have gone through *RADA* without recognising the obvious 'queers', as I'm afraid we called them then (although I was fooled by some) and the underground gay language 'polari' had not been popularised, as in the 'Julian and Sandy' sketches in *Round the Horn*, which didn't start until 1965.

How strange that a simple three-letter word had gone from describing lively and colourful behaviour, to a secret in-crowd code word, and today's playground insult. Hmm? We could never have imagined that, one day, this use of the word 'gay' would be accepted and used regularly in public and on worldwide news bulletins.

The Coven
In my recollections of life at *RADA* I referred to a particular group of fellow students. I would suggest that close, long-standing friendships are quite rare, and six of us later became widely known as 'The Coven'. With me, there was Flick, Jan, Jill B, Jill S and Maggie. The probable reason why we six grew into a specific group was because of my first flat in St John's Wood, commonly known as '22', which we all shared at some time or another.

The flat was made up of two bedrooms each with one double bed, plus one single-bedded attic and a large sitting room. Not only did we share one kitchen and one bathroom, which included the loo, but we shared the double beds. This arrangement was constant over a period of five years. There were rarely fewer than four sharing the flat at any one time, but it could go up to eight (chaps as well) with mattresses on the sitting room floor for the desperados. I believe I once counted up to 50 the number of people who had stayed there on a fairly casual basis. There must have been a shortage of keys because, after 50 years, Jan has recently informed me that she used to carry a knife in her handbag and opened the door by sliding it past the latch. If I've only just heard about this now, I wonder how many other things went on without my knowledge?

With no television and only occasional 'comps' for West End shows, the main entertainment back then was our local cinema, the Hampstead Playhouse. Through a friend who worked there, we collected some poster-sized, front-of-house pictures of many famous stars. We hung four or five in each room and their presence was a great talking point with visitors.

Well after the end of one of our famous bottle parties, attended by the equally famous Dennis Price (having survived the quicksands in *Caravan*), he found himself wandering round a flat which now resembled a warzone. As the dust was settling, he entered one of the bedrooms and, fumbling around in the dark, tried to get into the bed where my flatmate was sleeping. She woke with a start, switched on the light and came face-to-face with Mr Price, who politely responded with:

"Oh, I'm frightfully sorry, dear lady, do forgive me." Then, slowly leaving the room, he added:

"It's a very irregular club altogether."

We were all doing stints in various rep companies, and swapped clothes with each other since we had to provide our own for each role in those days. There was one neat little wine-coloured tweed suit, owned by Flick, which each of us climbed into from time to time. I wore it to play the race-going, butch spinster

'Miss Meacham' in *Separate Tables*, which gave birth to the constant cry:

"Is the 'lesbian' suit free this week?"

Inevitably, as the years passed, our gang moved out of '22'. Marriages and children came along (neither for me, I should add) and we saw less of each other. Maggie, for instance, married with three children, spent some years in far away places with strange sounding names, but the ties were never broken, and we would meet up individually all through these childrearing years.

'The Coven' still gets together for summer and Christmas gatherings. We're well past the age when the conversation turns inevitably to sex; now it's more hospital appointments and "what are you taking for that?" There has been divorce, widowhood and an (outside) gay relationship, but strangely, our busy and eventful lives are hardly touched upon when we meet as a group, and would probably come as a surprise were they to be revealed in a memoir. We shall see....

Briefly, after a youthful and successful acting career, Maggie went to live in Oxford and gained a 'first' in French at Brookes University. Jill S stayed in 'the business', and has worked tirelessly, over many years for the *Save the Children Fund*. Both she and Maggie are also passionate gardeners. Making a break from her acting career, Jan became a very successful ambassador for a breast cancer charity. Jill B became a writer and director, gaining an MA with the Open University, and after acting, Flick became an excellent stage manager, moving into politics, becoming a Liberal Democrat councillor for Camden, and was recently awarded an MBE.

Once the six of us had become a distinct group and had arranged more regular meetings, we made several short trips abroad to celebrate our various 50th birth-days. Our first was to Paris, which Flick and Jill B knew quite well and guided us to the most suitable areas and cafés. You can imagine, six middle-aged women behaving like fresh out of drama school actresses. We laughed so much we wet ourselves, didn't we, Jan? My favourite bit, in spite of the gorgeousness of Paris, was the cross-channel ferry (what am I like?) especially the return journey at night. Maggie and I went up on deck, chatting at length under a densely starlit sky. I had seen nothing like it since my childhood when there was little or no street lighting. You felt it bearing down on you; heavy, brilliant...full of wonder.

Then came Amsterdam, Bruges, Lille and our last, in 2009, Ghent. By this time Jill B was showing signs of frailty in her ability to walk, even gently, round the city's amazing sites, but she did enjoy the trip as we all did. Although I was aware that this might be the last 'Coven' outing the six of us would make together.

When Jill B became seriously ill and died in 2012, the five of us - which seemed strange - rallied round, helping as much as we could. We prepared a eulogy with contributions to reflect Jill's life and loves, where the strength of our friendship was evident for all to see.

1st Intermission

The First Replacements

I have often been asked under extraordinary circumstances to replace another actress who has already
been contracted to play the role. For various reasons
the part had been relinquished and a recasting sought.
This is not a 'stand-in' or a 'takeover' or an 'understudy', but something much more unusual.

Replacement No.1: (aged 26)

This happened during my four-month season of
weekly rep at the Assembly Hall, Tunbridge Wells in
1962. In those days actors were distinctly categorised
and I was expected to play landladies, maiden aunts,
friendly neighbours, servants, secretaries etc, but
never the leading lady. Then, after playing the main
role in every play for the first eight weeks, our leading
lady decided to ask for a rest, and suggested that I
might take on the lead part in the next play. The management agreed because the part was played originally
by Flora Robson in her late 50s. So I, at the age of 26,
found myself playing the central role in *Black Chiffon*,
of a menopausal woman who had been caught stealing
a black chiffon nightdress from a department store.

Fortunately in my amateur days I had acted many
middle-aged parts and, despite the enormity of the
role and the fact that there were no laughs, my forté

you might say...I thoroughly enjoyed the experience. The entire second act was the interrogation of this poor woman, which was the most dialogue I had ever had to learn in half a day. All right for the Inspector, who could have the 'questions' in his note book, but I had all the long explanatory responses.

I loved playing this part and felt quite at home in this really serious, tragic role. I remember a friend, more used to seeing me raising laughs, being very impressed and full of praise. My future career, however, stayed firmly in the comedy world.

Replacement No.2: (aged 27)

Before television entered living rooms and people became addicted to soap operas, they would love to go to their local theatre to watch the same troupe of actors perform different roles each week. If merited, they would applaud an actor when leaving the stage, or an 'exit round' as it was called, and once they got to know you, an 'entrance round' could even be earned. This happened for me at the Palace Theatre, Watford when Jimmy Perry of *Dad's Army* fame was running the weekly rep there, and he had cast me in several comedy or character parts.

Then, one Sunday evening he rang me at home with an urgent request. I was already appearing in the current production due to open the next day, and on Tuesday morning *Wuthering Heights* would go into rehearsal. Apparently the actress playing the 'glamourous young woman' from the neighbouring house, had been taken ill, so:

"Could you take it on, love?" I protested on the grounds of my lack of...well, 'glamour'.

"Nonsense," he said. "You'll be fine".

I had as much time as the previous actress to

prepare the role, and I was highly amused by the leading actor constantly referring to the house as 'Witherin' Eights'. They quickly ran up a gorgeous costume for me, with a really elegant hat. Still feeling inadequate for the role, I remember standing in the wings on the first night feeling worried, because I had my first entrance round the week before from the audience accustomed to me making them laugh. So, I closed my eyes and repeated over and over again:

"You're beautiful, you're beautiful."

This was a trick adopted by Dame Edith Evans, who was totally aware of her plain looks, before making an entrance as a young actress, and I thought, well, if it worked for her...?

I strode upon the stage and, mercifully...no applause, no laughs, not even a titter, and each time I left the stage I was, for once, grateful for no exit round. The show was popular and received with warm applause. Then, one night, another 'characterful' actress, Lucy Griffiths, who I much admired for her many cameo roles in British films, sought me out after the performance and was very complimentary, since I suspect she totally understood my plight. I must say that what began as a terrifying idea, ended up as quite a confidence booster, especially as I had spent the entire evening trying NOT to get laughs and had succeeded.

*****

Note to self: 'character parts' are much more fun than straight roles.

*****

Replacement No.3: (aged 28)

My next experience in this spate of weekly rep jobs came when my name was mentioned by a friend, Sheila Reid, to a director who was desperate to find a replacement for an actress who had fallen ill. The play was Christopher Fry's *Venus Observed*, and the part was 'Jessie Dill' - originally created in the West End by Brenda De Banzie. The company had played it for a week in Lincoln, but were due to play for a further week in Scunthorpe. I happened to be staying with my parents in Leicester for the weekend when the call came through on Sunday morning. Could I get to Lincoln that day, pick up a script and rehearse on Monday morning with the cast? We would then travel to Scunthorpe in the afternoon and play that evening.

With Dad's timetable skills and Mum's swiftly packed sandwiches, I arrived in good time to be fixed up in wonderful digs. I studied the lines as far as I could in the circumstances, and turned up to meet everyone the next morning. The cast were extraordinarily kind, no doubt relieved to see a familiar face, as I was known to some of them. Brigit Forsyth, Paul Chapman and Norman Jones totally understood my not being over-familiar with the lines. That wasn't all I was unfamiliar with. I didn't know the play at all and had no time to read it.

The part was split quite neatly into the three acts. I did manage to learn most of Act One by the time the curtain went up. There was a short scene where all the cast go up-stage into a conservatory, so I reckoned I could take my script out of my handbag and read the few lines without it being seen. Act Two saw the character with a writing case, which was big enough to conceal the script. Act Three was half a dozen lines, which I memorised in the second interval.

The result of not knowing the play lead to two alarming incidents which took me totally by surprise, both in Act One. At one point I was sitting downstage left, when Brigit, down-stage right, held up an apple, which had been pre-cut into several sections. Then, Norman (centre-stage) fired a gun at the apple which appeared to explode. A slice of apple shot across the stage and hit me full in the face. Surprised? You bet! The look on my face, apparently, was so funny that the whole cast 'corpsed'. Then, when we went up-stage to take our seats in the conservatory (me with the script in my handbag) all the lights went out…to watch a total eclipse! Nobody had thought to mention the 'blackout'. While struggling to read my script, Paul leant over and whispered the lines for me to repeat…more or less accurately.

Interlude
Just to explain the word 'corpse' in this connection. It is used when an actor is seen to be laughing at something which is not part of the play. It is simply that his character has 'died', so becomes, as it were, a corpse.

Beyond the Eclipse
The rest of the play went without a hitch, and by the second performance I was DLP (dead letter perfect). This is an old-fashioned theatrical expression you rarely hear now, probably because actors have much more time to learn their lines, but I love it. I was pleased that they had remembered to put a slip in the programme to indicate the 'replacement', but I turned

up as Christina Rozanni. (See: my tips on choosing a name at *RADA*).

*****

Note to self: always check your biography before the programme is printed.

*****

It was a week in Scunthorpe never to be forgotten. Some years later I learnt that the actress I had 'replaced' was not ill in hospital, as I had been told, but had suddenly died. On reflection, the cast dealt with that (and with my arrival) magnificently.

Replacement No.4: (aged 28)

In the early 1960s I was contacted by Farnham rep, again on the recommendation of Sheila Reid, about replacing an indisposed actress in a lead role. The play was *George and Margaret*, an adorable comedy set in the house of a middle-class family who have invited George and Margaret for dinner. The big joke being that they do arrive at the front door, but are never seen. Mother (my part) was clearly mature with three grown-up children and although I was still in my 20s at the time, it hadn't proved to be a problem in my provincial theatre rounds. Being two stone overweight meant I was totally acceptable in these 'mumsy' parts.

The daughter has brought her new boyfriend home to meet the family and the mother has one of my favourite lines in the play as she is setting the table for dinner…"Never get married if you're a woman, Roger," clarifying the distinct real life roles of men and women in those days. The line still makes me laugh, especially since I never became a wife or a mother; although I do set the table - for two - at dinner time!

Scene 7

I Closed A Theatre

The Ardwick Empire, 1961: (aged 25)

Actually, I closed three theatres. That is, I appeared in each of their very last productions. J. B. Priestley wrote a book called *Lost Empires* and 'Ardwick' was one of them. I was in a touring company and this was the very last show to be seen at this historic theatre. It had the exceedingly unilluminating title of *Divorce on Tuesday*, and two things stand out in my memory about this production. One: I, at the tender age of 25, was understudying the veteran actress, Chili Bouchier, who had been a silent movie star!..and Two: at this ridiculously advanced age of 25, I was playing an eleven-year-old child. I was also the assistant stage manager. In addition to the cast, there was one non-acting company/stage manager, and that was it.

On the opening night, during a moment in the play where I had to enter through the French windows, carrying a cabbage for some bizarre reason, I was alone on stage when the telephone was supposed to ring and the character, played by Miss Bouchier, had to enter to answer it. Unfortunately, the one person able to make the telephone ring - the stage manager - had decided to go out front to watch the show from the back of the stalls, leaving the prompt corner entirely unattended. Seeing me enter, he suddenly remembered the phone call and made a dash for the pass door, but on stage, I had to deal with a 'dead' scene. Playing a child actually helped as I sidled over to the desk and started to snoop around. Then I playfully picked up the receiver, and pretended to hear someone speaking:

"Hang on a minute," I said, then shouted (to anyone) offstage: "Someone's on the phone."

Miss Bouchier entered and the play proceeded. An unedifying beginning to the final week in the life of The (great) Ardwick Empire.

The Royalty Theatre, Chester, 1962: (aged 26)

My favourite 'closure' encounter was at this theatre, with a small group of actors doing a different play every week, performing twice nightly at 6pm and 8.30pm. The company was being run by a theatrical rogue who seemed able to keep himself just this side of the law.

Arthur Lane was well-known in the business for his dubious financial arrangements and cavalier attitude towards both plays and actors. One week he promised us all that he would treat us to a meal at the local café on pay day. Come Friday, an excited gang of 'hungry' actors (remember?) gathered round the largest table at 'the greasy spoon' in anticipation of a good blow-out before the first house. Arthur joined us and we all sat there, holding our knives and forks like spear carriers at the Old Vic, as he took a deep breath, and with a big, booming voice enquired of the waitress: "Tell me, my good woman, what can we have for one and three?"

Beans on toast it was…and we all ended up paying for ourselves. On another occasion, after he had entertained the company to a meal, he summoned the waiter and asked for the bill. When it arrived, he ostentatiously signed it with a great flourish. "There you are, my good man," he said, as he led the actors out of the restaurant. He never did pay up.

Arthur did make one concession, however, and thank goodness he did. The season, so far, had included such classics as *Hot and Cold in All Rooms* and *A Basinful of the Briny*, but for some extraordinary reason he broke the mould and announced that:

"Next week we shall be doing *Pygmalion*, for one performance only each night."

We had a wonderful stage manager in John Inman - yes, 'Mr Humphries' in *Are You Being Served?* - who was often called upon to perform when the casting demanded an extra actor. He was to play 'Freddy Eynsford-Hill' and I, at the age of 26, was to play 'Mrs Higgins', the mother of 'The Professor', which was being played by our 55-year-old director, who had a slight affliction in that he had one foot shorter than the other. The result was that he couldn't turn left, so to make an 'exit stage left', he would stand up, turn right, go round in a circle and then walk off stage. Quite disconcerting for those of us who, not used to him, thought he had set off in the wrong direction. Also, because he was directing the play, he would often make an entrance and rearrange the furniture if he thought it had been set in the wrong place...still, thankfully, saying the correct lines.

Various local people had been employed as backstage crew, and one of them was a delightful old gentleman well into his '80s, who was in charge of props for *Pygmalion*. The scenery in those days consisted of tall flats that were cleated together with rope. Sometimes if there was, let's say, a fireplace which jutted out into the room, there could be a gap behind this flat which would not be seen by the audience. Such was the case in *Pygmalion*.

At one particular performance (picture the scene)...'Mrs Higgins' is entertaining 'Eliza Doolittle' to tea. So, I am seated at a small table near the fireplace, and I'm in full flow pouring tea into each cup, when I hear: "Pssst! Pssst!" coming from the gap in the scenery close to my right ear. I try hard to ignore it, but the next thing I see is an ancient hand shakily waving a blue plastic spoon in my direction. Apparently, our dear old props man couldn't find the silver teaspoons when setting the tray so, rather than continue this farce, I took it graciously as if it was all part of the play. Huh...some hopes.

During the final scene, the denouement you might say, between 'Higgins' and 'Eliza', I am standing in the wings, just outside the living room door, waiting to appear for the curtain call, when suddenly the old boy sidles up to me and, proving conclusively that he does have a sense of humour, whispers in my ear:

"I wouldn't go in there just yet if I were you, they're 'aving a row."

The night a corpse, corpsed

Back to the regular twice-nightly routine, we were doing the inevitable Agatha Christie play. Believe me, you were grateful to get away with one in a season like this. We were performing *Verdict* in which I was playing the cockney daily woman...what else? The leading man has a dowdy, invalid wife confined to a wheelchair, but has a mistress who in the second act kills the wife.

Working with this kind of pressure, where you have two plays on the go at the same time, and performing twice every night, by the second act of the second house you tend to lose track of where you are, which act you're in, or even which play you're doing. And so it came to pass, on a midweek, second house performance of *Verdict*, that the inevitable happened. During the first Interval, I had been looking at my lines for the next week's play, which was a north country comedy, when I heard my cue coming up, so I prepared to make my Act Two entrance.

The poor woman playing the wife had been directed to die in a wheel chair, with her head pulled back and mouth wide open. Goodness knows how long she was expected to stay in that position, but while she is alone on stage, I had to enter and deliver quite a long chatty monologue before discovering the corpse. Unfortunately, I started to deliver my lines in a north country accent, having established myself as cockney, and simply couldn't get back. DISASTER. This poor actress tried desperately not to corpse, but failed. I had to go and stand in front of her to shield her from the audience, but our efforts to finish the scene were nothing short of disgraceful. It wasn't the first time I'd seen a corpse 'corpse', and I'm sure there will be others, but this was how the Royalty Theatre, Chester breathed its last.

Interlude

I was told of another occasion in (rep) where a character 'had died' and fallen behind the sofa. When the inspector discovered the body, he saw that the actor had unbuttoned his shirt to reveal the word CORPSE written on his bare chest, producing the intended catastrophic result. Unfortunately for the 'Inspector', the audience had no idea why he was 'corpsing'.

*****

Note to self: whatever the pressure - remember - it's only a play!

*****

The Lyric Theatre, Hammersmith, 1963: (aged 27)
I had been on tour in a play called *Domino*, this time in a role relinquished by Sheila Reid. It starred the delightfully interesting actress, Rene Asherson, who told me that when she and Robert Donat married, they bought a two-shilling wedding ring from Woolworths. Some ten years later I was to play 'Prossy' to her 'Candida' at the New Theatre, Bromley, where we continued our friendship as if we'd never left off. *Domino* also starred the beautiful, now grown up (boy) actor, Jeremy Spenser (*The Roman Spring of Mrs Stone*, among other feature films) and who was being understudied by Jeremy Conway, the now legendary theatrical agent.

I remember nothing of the role I played, but I expect it was yet another 'maid', and we ended the tour at the Lyric Theatre, Hammersmith, where this play was the last to be performed on that site. Many years later this theatre was demolished, although the Frank Matcham's interior was carefully preserved down to the last gaslight, and placed into a new exterior building. It now stands some 30 yards away from the original and is part of the Kings Mall Shopping Centre. Ours is not to reason why.

Scene 8

I Feel The Hand Of History

This complex story begins in 1962. During a season of weekly rep at Tunbridge Wells, the management decided to put on a play called *Distinguished Gathering*, which a lot of companies round the country were doing that summer. The veteran wartime radio comedian, Vic Oliver, had suggested to a number of rep companies that he could come and play the lead role in their production by arriving on a Monday, after the cast had worked on it for a week without him, and slot into the dress rehearsal before opening that night.

Just to explain the weekly repertory system briefly...Samuel French Ltd would produce a script from an original West End production, which would include moves, attitudes, gestures, the set design, furniture placings, a list of props, sound effects and lighting cues. All this would make life much easier for actors and stage management, with restricted time in which to rehearse and put on a play. These collections of scripts would do the rounds of the reps, with individual ones being 'marked up' for the various characters. Usually your character's copy would come heavily underlined with some nice helpful clues in the margin.

This process made it quite easy to accommodate

Mr Oliver and slot him in to our pre-rehearsed moves. All went smoothly and he was very friendly talking about his career. He made us laugh a lot and the week went splendidly.

The following year I found myself on tour in *Rain* by Somerset Maugham, with Sir Winston Churchill's youngest daughter, Sarah, playing the leading role of 'Sadie Thompson'. Sadly, by this time, she was known for her unruly behaviour as a result of excessive drinking, and she was actually in court on the morning of our opening night in Brighton. When not in this state, Sarah was the most delightful person; graceful, fun and good company.

The next time we met up was less than a year later, but by now Sarah was Lady Audley and had been to Switzerland to receive help for her condition. The play was called *Fata Morgana*, by Ernest Vajda. It was being directed by Ellen Pollock, my *RADA* teacher, who had cast me in this play to be aired at the Ashcroft Theatre, Croydon.

The play duly opened for a short run, and great excitement was generated when Sarah announced that her parents would be coming to the last Saturday matinee and that they would like to meet the cast! I arrived at the theatre on this final performance day and noticed that there was to be a musical concert that evening in The Fairfield Halls next door, and that the conductor was one, Vic Oliver.

This is where the plot thickens. In 1936, Sarah was appearing in a musical extravaganza at the Vaudeville Theatre where she met and fell in love with a certain Vic Oliver. Churchill did not like Oliver, an Austrian Jew, and would not entertain the idea of meeting him or agreeing to support their relationship. Sarah and Oliver eloped to New York and married there on

Christmas Day.

They were blissfully happy, but when the war came three years later, everything changed. Sarah went home to do her stint in uniform, by which time their marriage was ending and she went back to the stage. She was an enchanting 'Peter Pan' at the Scala Theatre in 1958.

Sarah and I must have discussed Vic at some time in the past, because when she learned of his presence in the adjacent theatre that day, she asked me if I had seen him. I hadn't at that point. Once the cast had all shaken hands with the 'great man', I swiftly took myself off to the bar to celebrate the event. The next thing that happened was the sound of a familiar voice from across the other side of the large half-moon shaped counter:

"Hello, Christine."

It was, none other than, Vic Oliver. I hurried towards him, as he extended his right hand and with it, he shook mine. Within minutes I had been the link between these two old and long-standing adversaries.

There was good coverage in the Sunday papers of the famous theatre visit, and I managed to contact *The Observer* on the Monday. As a result I procured a single picture of me, shaking hands with Sir Winston Churchill, which gave my mother the thrill of her life.

Scene 9

Busy Doing Nothing

Resting?

Most sensible people realize that actors are not in work all the time, and are tactful enough to ask: "Are you 'resting' at the moment?" rather than, 'out of work!' However, being out of work usually means that an actor is anything but resting. Alternative jobs, even careers, have to be sought, and other skills learnt or maintained. I know very few actors who earn their living entirely from professional acting jobs.

Suddenly, after a great start to my career, with a rep season, a feature film and a pantomime, the work dried up and I spent almost the whole of 1959 - a real scorcher of a summer - struggling to survive. I solved this by working for the actor Victor Maddern and his wife Joan. They had established Scripts Ltd in Wardour Street, and for the first time since leaving the *AA*, my touch-typing skills were to come in handy. I could barely believe it when I was given the scripts for *The Angry Silence* and *The League of Gentlemen* to type for the Richard Attenborough and Bryan Forbes team at Beaver Films. With a ten-year gap, I had followed Richard Attenborough into The *Leicester Drama Society* and then on to *RADA*, and now - his film company. He was always our local hero and I did get to meet him, some 45 years later at a charity event. I reminded him of some of those names from his days at the Little Theatre in Leicester and, as I expected, he remembered them all. What a charmer!

Auditions and Casting Sessions

Looking for work when 'resting' can be the busiest time of an actor's life, and going for an audition, especially when demoralised by unemployment, is particularly hard. My chums and I would be forever looking for original pieces to do for the many theatre companies we longed to join. There were several books available with collections of audition pieces, but most of them were hackneyed, old-fashioned and boring. If you were lucky, you would be asked to act out a section of the play you were being seen for, but for general auditions you would need to prepare two contrasting pieces, after which it was the luck of the draw.

The Northcott's First Company

For anyone who has never experienced the naked terror of an open audition, let me tell you...there are many things in this world I would rather do. Why? I want to act, so get up there and do some acting. If it were only that simple. You are face-to-face with a person - often several people - you don't know, and who don't know you; they have already seen a hundred and eleven aspiring artistes that week...all they really want to do is run to the pub. The only thing to do is...something different, original, unique or to make them sit up and take notice. My most joyous audition was for the very first company opening the new Northcott Theatre in Exeter in 1967.

By this time I had done a lot of theatre jobs and music hall turns, so doing two pieces and a song was no hassle. I wore a cute black dress and with lots of flair performed Shakespeare's 'First Fairy' and Shaw's 'Candida', followed by a very polished rendition of the song 'Meet the Family' from *The Crooked Mile*. We were in a West End Theatre, and when I had finished, the two directors out front, Tony Church, and Robin Phillips, leaped from their seats and came running down the aisle and on to the stage.   I've never known anything like it. They practically handed me a contract there and then. I did fit the roles of the three parts I auditioned for perfectly, not like the numerous occasions when I have been either too short, too tall, too fat, too thin, too young, too old and once, and this is my favourite turn-down of all, too good! ("overqualified," they said).

West End Take Over
For the fourth time in my early career, Sheila Reid suggested me for a part, which she was relinquishing in a West End Musical. Sheila and I have never worked together, but we still connect socially. There are certain similarities in our appearance...height mainly! Sheila's credits, however, not only added up to many more than mine, but were both impressive and enviable, especially in theatre work. Although she remained 'unknown' for many years Sheila, like me, had certainly been to the edge and looked over. Then, quite late on in her career, she drove over the edge in her mobility scooter in *Benidorm*, and 'Madge' became a 'household name'.

This audition was to take over the part of 'Flo Bates', which Sheila had created in *Half a Sixpence*. Having tipped me off about the recasting, she even suggested I put a dark rinse on my hair (which I did) as hers was darker than mine and "they have no imagination". The audition went well and I was re-called.

The second time there were only three of us, and after some deliberation it was down to two. We both performed again, then were asked to wait together in one of the dressing rooms. We were held in suspense for some time, during which I discovered that the other actress wasn't bothered too much about getting this job as she was already doing late night cabaret... and...was getting married at the weekend. After what seemed like centuries, the company manager, who clearly knew the other actress well, entered the room, flung open his arms and embraced her, saying:

"Darling, it's yours."

Then, with a dismissive glance over to me, he said:

"Oh, you can go now."

This man turned up again as my company manager on the year-long tour of *Oliver!*, which I did soon afterwards. He didn't remember me, and I said nothing about it, but I shall never forget him...or the actress who got the job. Yes, you've guessed it, she was blonde!

Bad Timing

Anthony Bowles, a musical director and wit, loved and admired by hundreds of actors, including me when I joined his 'actors' choir', was also a great friend of Andrew Lloyd Webber and was MD for many of his shows. Ant, as he was known to everybody, let Andrew know very early on that his least favourite song in the world was *The Impossible Dream*. So one day, for a joke, Andrew put the song down as an audition piece, and many artistes performed it that morning. Finally a rather large actor launched into the song, with gusto, and tap, tap, tap…

"Excuse me", said Ant, stopping him after a few bars.

"Yes, Mr. Bowles,"

"You are singing *The Impossible Dream* in 4/4 time."

"Er - yes, Mr. Bowles".

"*The Impossible Dream* is written in 3/4 time. Thus you are making an insufferable experience one third longer."

Casting Sessions

What used to be called 'Cattle Calls', where a hundred or more might turn up for the same part, could take two days to get through. Mercifully, due to the changing pressures of time and money, we 'unknowns' who toil in the lower regions of 'the business' are now called at specific times, usually one every five minutes, and are mostly seen within the hour.

One actress I know, in this category, went to a private house for a 'casting' and was asked to wait in the interviewer's office where she noticed five box files on a shelf individually marked…

ONE LINE ACTORS
ONE SCENE ACTORS
GOOD ACTORS
LEADING ACTORS
STARS

Alas, she didn't even get the ONE LINE part she was up for.

We generally turn up to find a room full of

people, all looking like ourselves, and are given a breakdown of the story with a short piece of dialogue to memorise. We are also asked to fill in two or three forms which will include health issues, some quite intrusive or irrelevant. There's one question I love. 'Is your partner pregnant?' One day, for a laugh, I spoke this out loud, followed by:

"I hope not, he's 73!"

When committed to the casting session, I always throw myself into the situation, especially to get laughs, although I do find myself being put up for commercials I'm not really right for. Once, at a party, I asked a friendly casting director, who had brought me in several times for commercials I didn't get, why he persisted with me.

"That's easy, Christine," he said. "The clients always love you."

About a year later I did get a job through him. Hurrah!

*****

Note to self: auditions can be more about pleasing the casting director than actually getting the job.

*****

Mostly I am 'unknown' to the film company or advertising agency, and certainly to the clients, and this led to a disastrous result on one occasion (see my Malaga story in: 'Desperate Replacement'). Looking through my record of commercial interviews since 1973, I have been for 380 castings, and got sixty jobs. Roughly, one in six, so not bad, actually. Most people reckon one in ten to be a good average.

Some artistes really try to 'dress the part'. On one occasion, with advanced warning that the character was a Magician's Assistant, one actress turned up in the full kit: black fishnet tights, sparkly leotard, long gloves, etc, prepared to do the full 'presentational' bit, but all we had to do was lie flat on our back on a long table and keep absolutely still, while the Magician tried to levitate us. Poor cow.

Recently my brief said that the elderly couple would be wearing 'onesies'. The man I auditioned with had brought his own *Scooby Doo* onesie. I would never be that brave, but we went down well and he thought we stood a good chance. The result was that I was re-called, but he wasn't. Yes, re-called...this would be no more than four or five seconds on the screen, but I suppose they needed to match the couples. I went in twice with two different men, which is usually a good sign, and I was put on a 'pencil'. This means you are likely to be cast, but they need to finalise details of the shoot. After ten days I rang my agent to see what was happening; he didn't know, but soon discovered that they had lifted the pencil a week before, but had neglected to tell him. Typical, I'm afraid, with a commercial, they never let you know when you haven't got the job.

Looks are everything in this business, especially for the 'unknown actor'. While I accept this as being part of the job, I notice that both men and women in other walks of life can be harshly criticised or pleasantly judged for their physical appearance. In sport, politics, even royalty, being 'drop dead gorgeous' is a definite plus!

The very worst part of an actor's life is when you are waiting to hear whether you 'got the job' and you're counting down the hours, even minutes, which all make it less and less likely. Then the phone rings! You see your agent's name on the display. This must be it, because they never let you know the bad news.

"Hi-ya," you say, brightly.

"Oh, hi Christine. I've got another casting for you on Wednesday."

Scene 10

Taking Notes

Paradise Lost: (aged 27)

I was thrilled to bits when an established agent sent me off to The Connaught Theatre, Worthing (at last, a seaside job) to play two super parts, with some very well-known actors of the day. The parts were 'Ida' in *Pools Paradise* (the sequel to *See How They Run*) and 'Doreen' in *Waiting in the Wings*, by Nöel Coward. Both these parts were young housemaids, characters I had no problem with whatsoever.

So, I threw myself into the role of 'Ida' with great enthusiasm - it was a lovely part - and all seemed to be going swimmingly. The fact that I received no 'notes' from the director, Guy Vaesen, encouraged me to believe that I was doing everything right. Even at the dress rehearsal 'note' session he ignored me, so no warning bells were ringing.

We opened the play and Act One went tremendously well and I got some huge laughs. In the interval, back in the dressing room, which I was sharing with Caroline Blakiston and Pamela Greenall, he (one's director) burst into the room, hugged both the others and showered them with praise.

"Caro, darling, you were wonderful. Pam, darling, marvellous."

Then he turned to me with an icy smirk and

said: "As for you…I don't know how the audience is going to stand you for the rest of the play."

Struck dumb, and close to tears, I fled from the room. The stage was empty and quiet, so I sat on the sofa in order to gather my thoughts and to work out what on earth he meant, and what to do about it. Perhaps he felt I had peaked too early and had left myself nowhere to go. Yes, that must be it, I thought, so I made a positive effort to begin Act Two in a lower key and build up to the final denouement in Act Three. 'Ida' got an especially good reception at the curtain call, which was some consolation, but worse was to come. Later, in the bar, Vaesen beckoned me over to where he was standing with the theatre's Artistic Director, who spoke first.

"We are in two minds whether to keep you on for the next play," he said. "And we think you should change your accent completely for tomorrow night's performance."

A big ask, but I did manage to change my accent for 'Ida', much to the amazement of the rest of the cast, who had all suspected there was trouble brewing, but no-one had the nerve to tip me off. I was kept on, probably because the next play had a different director, and enjoyed it enormously, but you can see that 'life upon the wicked stage' is not all a bed of roses, and I never forgave the bastard.

Beggar's Belief: (aged 32)

The opposite happened to me during the first season in the newly built Northcott Theatre in Exeter, following my most successful audition. In my third play, *The Beggar's Opera*, I was cast as 'Mrs Peachum' and had several solo songs. I loved the company and all the parts I had been offered, including this one, but at the final 'notes' session, before the opening night, Robin Phillips (one's director) did the exact opposite to Guy Vaesen. He gave no notes to anybody BUT me. The rest of the cast sat there gobsmacked as all these hurtful remarks came flying my way. I could hardly expect anyone to leap to my defence (we were all more than a little in awe of Robin, a spectacularly handsome young actor with a most promising directorial future) so I just had to take it on the chin. Once again, I had to go away and cope with this barrage of criticism and try to work out some sort of solution. After the Guy Vaesen experience, I decided not to give in to this bullying, so I ignored it and made no changes *at all*!

Robin certainly had mood swings - we had witnessed this on several occasions - so at the end of the show his sullen autocracy had given way to cheerful self-congratulation. As he addressed the cast after the show he proudly boasted that he had mentally ticked off each 'correction' I had made to my performance in response to his notes. Huh. The power that some directors hold (or think they do) over actors astonishes me at times; we have to remember, though, that *they* cast *us*, and we all want to work again.

But I had really enjoyed the season and had seriously bonded with some adorable actors. In addition to 'Mrs Peachum', I had played 'Fenella Fullbucket' in *Big Noise at Fort Issimo*, and 'Joan Stradling' in *The play of William Cooper and Edmund Dew-Nevett*. When my contract ended I was offered an extension, to play 'First Fairy' in *A Midsummer Night's Dream*, which they saw in my audition, and 'Mrs Leverett' in *Rookery Nook*. This second part was the one I had played at *RADA* with hilarious results and I was tempted to stay on, but...I turned it down. It had nothing to do with my relationship with Robin, who was directing both plays, as that was now on an even keel. But being asked to recreate a role you loved in a production you thought was perfect, feels a bit like 'climbing back into a wet bathing costume'. Perhaps I should not have rejected the roles, but explained that, for personal reasons, I had to be back in London for a while.

*****

Note to self: Never say: "No." Try, "I'd love to, but..."

*****

My Word!

John Sharp, a wonderful character actor, once said something very profound to me; he said:

"All actors are treated like shit."

Well, perhaps not all the time, but I bet there isn't a single actor in the world who couldn't come up with an applicable anecdote to this end. There seems to be an underlying, shall we say, resentment of actors by almost everybody.

"They get PAID to do something they LOVE."

You can hear them saying it. Well, we don't always LOVE every job we do, believe me, and we certainly don't always get PAID.

Genuine actors possess the entertainment gene. Their one desire is to affect an audience, to make them laugh or cry or think or learn or…something… to make them feel different afterwards, from the way they felt before. That's all. In order to have this effect on people, actors have to use their imagination and their emotions. They need to study others' emotions and reactions to everyday life, in order to recreate the way people behave in joy, stress, comic situations and in tragic ones. Their own emotions are raw and laid open, and for these bullies to interfere with this process, is damaging in the extreme. These sadistic directors, taking advantage of their powerful positions, can inflict untold damage on unsuspecting actors. They do exist, believe me, and I don't even have to name them because there are numerous sufferers out there who will know exactly who I'm talking about.

I would advise any actor who is being intimidated by 'directorial notes' to react as follows. Be seen to write the note down. Smile and say: "Yes, of course." Then, if you don't agree with the note, ignore it. The director will probably say: "There you are, I told you it would work." Or, if they say: "You didn't do that note," you take out your notebook, re-read the note, and say: "You're quite right," then write it down again, and still don't do it. Be brave, after all, what can a director do? You are the one performing and, frankly, you should know best.

*****

Note to self: go for it! After all, what's the worst that can happen`?

*****

Christine Ozanne

Scene 11

Old Time 'Musical'

A Big Fish
In the 1960s, 'old time music hall', as a form of pub entertainment was very popular in and around London, probably due to the success of *The Players' Theatre* underneath the arches of Charing Cross station. The most renowned of these was set up in The Green Man pub at the top of Shooters Hill in southeast London. Four people had originally started these 'concerts' in an attempt to raise money to rebuild the Greenwich Theatre, and the one which exists today is the very result of that fundraising effort. It was a long-term project because I, for one, worked there regularly over a period of at least five years as a much-needed filler between office, theatre and television work. The format was to present 'music hall' items, with about four performers, plus chairman and pianist, on Thursday, Friday and Saturday evenings every week. Each programme would play for two weeks and the Artistes would be given £1.00 per performance. It took so long to get there on the 53 bus you had to take sandwiches.

The audiences became very familiar with all the actors and their 'turns'. I was asked over and over again to sing *Why Am I always The Bridesmaid?*

110

Hmmm. I saw hundreds of people work there over the five years, many of whom went on to be famous. One of my favourite memories was of Ronnie Corbett singing a duet with his wife. She towered over him as they stood there together, then he turned to her, his head more or less level with her naval, and sang:

"If I could plant a tiny seed of love in the garden of your heart."

In 1965 my career was in the doldrums and consisted of the occasional 'special week', the Greenwich music hall, and casual work with fellow 'out of work' actors in a dusty, overcrowded office near Charing Cross Station. Then in the autumn of that year, when hopes of a fulfilling career were fading, I was encouraged by Kim Grant, a fellow music hall artiste, to audition for a year-long tour of *Oliver!* He told me they were looking for 'characters' for the chorus with understudying thrown in. Now, in music hall you are definitely a big fish in a small pond, which I relished, but I always, suspected that should the situation be reversed, ie - becoming a chorus girl in a large cast musical, this could lead to a year of utter misery. Yet while I was reluctant to subject myself to this possible torture, it was twice as much money as the current office work. So £22.00 a week for a year had to be considered.

This was undoubtedly a major crossroads, which needed careful negotiation. I could stop at the red light and stay in London, doing temporary work, taking the occasional acting job hoping for higher recognition, OR I could throw caution to the wind, give up my cheap flat-share and risk the hazard of a year on tour. Once again my spirit of adventure won the day and when the green light said 'GO', I went.

As it turned out, in addition to the financial uplift, I have much for which to thank Kim Grant.

A Chorus Line-up

Unlike most girls, I had never visualised myself 'walking down the aisle', or had any ambition to marry or have a baby. In fact, I could never imagine meeting anyone who might wish to share those things with me. To remain single was very unusual...quite rare, in fact, in my family, but there was never any pressure from my parents to 'settle down' to this popular way of life. They had freely supported my chosen profession, and since entering 'the business' I had only ever wanted to work continuously in all its disciplines.

By the time I was 29-years-old I had completely given up on the possibility of ever finding a soul-mate. I had seen most of my fellow *RADA* students marry and start families, but I felt no envy because all I ever wanted to do was get acting jobs where I felt completely at home.

Optimistically, I saw my life ahead as a working actress, sharing flats with one or two others in the same situation, but I could see no further than that. As with most actors, I nurtured a belief that one day I might achieve a breakthrough in my career and do some more prominent work, but the necessary 'break' required for this was little more than a dream. I maintained this belief until quite recently when it became crystal clear that 'fame' in old age is seriously unlikely. I am a realist.

I knew full well that my contribution in *Oliver!* would lead me nowhere as an actress, but as it turned out, being taken on in 'the chorus' of this musical did change my life in one very particular way. We were still in rehearsal before opening at the Manchester Opera House, when I spotted a new crew member who had been sent to join 'the company' as a technical assistant stage manager. He was sitting alone in the pub looking a bit lost, being thrown into a group of actors who already knew each other. I remember his mop of hair, his dark rimmed glasses, his beard and his very lived-in duffle coat. His name was Patrick Tucker and, after a hiatus in my crowded digs, I moved into Mrs McEwan's welcoming abode in Chorlton-cum-Hardy, where Patrick was already ensconced with a few other members of the company.

After the show and supper each evening, we would have some wonderful conversations - our jovial landlady joining in - and I realised that I was coming across opinions and attitudes I had never before encountered. Patrick was an intriguing influence and this was very attractive to me. What I hadn't quite realised was that he was seeing something in me that was lacking in his life, and on Valentine's Day 1966, as I was alone in the kitchen waiting for him to come down for breakfast, he arrived and presented me with a handmade card. It was thick, plain pink paper on which he had drawn his face, with the glasses and curly hair, and for the beard he had cut off bits of his own and stuck them to the card, with an appropriate 'Valentine' message. It was wonderful. Our romance blossomed and we have travelled together ever since.

My life had undoubtedly taken a different direction. I was introduced to so many new ideas and ways of thinking, but most importantly, at the age of 29, I had my first serious 'boyfriend'! After so many years here was a man who saw me in a different light. He seemed to be more attracted to my personality, humour and attitude to life than my physical attributes, and although he often compliments me on my appearance, both 'looks' and 'fashion' in anybody, including himself, is very much a secondary issue.

Before the end of the year I was to give up smoking (after eight years) pass my driving test (first time) 'replace' my 'right' political bias with more liberal thinking, 'replace' my Christian beliefs with atheism and - most revolutionary of all - 'replace' my skirt with my first pair of trousers!

It is impossible, without exercising extreme discipline, to be brief when talking about my beloved, except to say that Patrick shared my lack of interest in marrying and having children, but I must play the editor here. This memoir, after all, is an exploration of my career, and where it has taken me, but to live with the same person for 50 years is bound to have an influence of major proportions.

Theatrically speaking, these were humble beginnings...I was in 'the chorus' and Patrick (and Cameron Mackintosh) were both ASMs. Sadly, Patrick was taken off the tour for the most part to work on other shows for the same management, and only came back when *Oliver!* moved on to another theatre. He was in charge of the motors that made the scenery revolve which, for years in the West End, had been pushed round by stage hands hidden inside the set.

So, needing another 'soulmate' I became a great friend of the actor playing 'Mr Sowerberry', Barry Howard (later to play 'Barry' in *Hi-de-Hi*); and to this day Patrick and I still use words and phrases coined by him. For instance, because of my appearance and my own self denigration (short, fat and ugly) he came up with SHFUG to describe me or anyone else with similar proportions. It makes me laugh even now, and I never thought of it as an insult; more as a compliment actually. Barry was a past master at throwing out disparaging remarks and getting huge laughs in return. My favourite was when he was at a party and, carrying his bowl of chilli con carne back into the kitchen, confronted the hostess.

"Did you make this yourself?" he said.

"Yes," she said, proudly.

"Umm," he said, raising an eyebrow and turning to leave. "Remind me to give you the recipe sometime."

Genius.

Stealing the Show

My experience of touring for a year in *Oliver!* was not so much full of mishaps as misfits. A large company of musical artistes should have been a pleasant enough group, and I made one or two firm friends, but there was a good deal of friction with people who just didn't 'gel'. Roughly halfway through the tour an extraordinary thing happened. One of the actors reported a theft of cash from his coat pocket which was hanging in the dressing room. When it happened again, the management decided to alert the police who put a 'trap' in place.

One man and one woman were given some money, which had been sprayed with detectable powder, and asked to leave it in their dressing room at all times. They happened to choose me and Barry, and it was his dressing room that came under fire. During the final chorus number before the interval, when almost all the cast were on stage, the thief got to work. When Barry checked his pockets back in the dressing room, alarm bells were rung. The police were called and the company were asked to remain in the theatre and in their costumes. Everyone, including backstage staff, were summoned to the inspection room, one by one, to put their hands under a UV light in order to detect any of the powder. All 'costume gloves' were taken by the police for further inspection and we had to play the next show without them.

Consider Yourself was the first big chorus number involving 'ladies and gentlemen' and as I was standing in the wings beforehand, I overheard the following fragrant exchange.

"How can I be a fucking lady, with no fucking gloves?"

"Oh, piss off, Jackie."

"Don't you fucking swear at me!"

They tracked down the thief, but it was rather a sad case, connected with drink, and nobody was sacked. Apparently, during the chorus number, one male character had to leave stage left, and a few minutes later, enter stage right. In this short time he passed the men's dressing room, did the deed, then made it back for the end of the song. Shortly afterwards, this elderly actor retired, due to ill health.

Interlude

A friend recently confessed that, although he loves taking over in musicals, he will not - ever again - be in one right from its creation. The pain of coping with all the alterations - "until we get it right" - is just too much to bear. I know what he means. Some years ago I went to see a friend in a preview of a new West End musical which had already done several weeks on a pre-London tour. She was playing one of the six wives of Henry VIII, and the following happened when I went back stage afterwards to commiserate...erm... congratulate her.

She was already hysterical after weeks of battering rehearsals and rescheduling, and could hardly speak without welling up. Suddenly, there was a Tannoy announcement.

"Ladies and gentlemen, there will be a full company call at ten o'clock tomorrow morning as there is a new choreographer arriving to restage all the numbers."

Chaos ensued. Women weeping and wailing; *I* started to blub, and my friend was beside herself. I left her dressing room, and as I made my way down the corridor, cries of despair issued forth from every doorway. As I left the building, a stage door Johnny, spotting a weeping woman, came over and put his arm round my shoulder.

"Oh, don't cry, love," he said. "I thought you were wonderful."

*****

Note to self: so, fame is possible, without even doing the job.

*****

Childhood memories

with Mum and Dad

and brother Gordon, Bridlington, 1939

Howzat!

Leicester Drama Society

My debut (far left) in *Noah*, 1955

(left) as 'The Baroness' in *Anastasia* with
Rita Barsby as 'The Empress', 1956

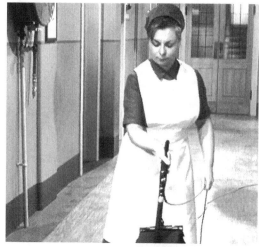

My film
debut,
'Fat Maid'
in *Carry on
Nurse,* 1958

with
Christopher
Dunham and
Jenny
McNae,
Music Hall,
Greenwich,
1964

The '
'Historic
Handshake',
1964

Pool's Paradise, Worthing

(l-r) Me, Brook Williams, Ken Wynn, Pamela
Greenall, Bill Wiesener, Tim Barrett, 1963

'Northcott', Exeter. 'Fenella
Fullbucket' (right) 1968 'Joan
Stradling' (below), 1969

with Ronnie Barker in *1899: The Phantom Raspberry Blower of Old London Town* by Spike Milligan, *LWT*, 1970

Once a bride!

Roy Kinnear, Avis Bunnage, Winifred Sabine, me, James Hazeldine in *Everybody Say Cheese, BBC*, 1971

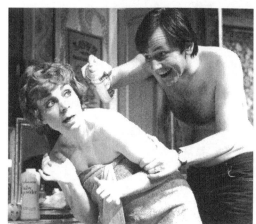

My first juvenille lead, aged 43!

with Tim Meats in *Bedroom Farce*, Salisbury, 1979

Favourite parts

as 'Mary Featherstone' with Christopher Emmett in *How the Other Half Loves*, Hornchurch, 1972

as 'Miss Prism' (right) with Joan Peart in *The Importance of Being Earnest,* Hornchurch 1973.

Original cast of *Dirty Linen* by Tom Stoppard (l-r), Luan Peters, Richard O'Callaghan, Malcolm Ingram, Edward de Souza, Peter Bowles and me, 1976

as 'Ida' with the author Philip King in *See How They Run,* Cheltenham, 1978

as 'Capulet' (left) with Ambrosine Phillpotts in *Ring Round the Moon*, Windsor, 1979 (below) with Mary Kerridge in *This Happy Breed*, Windsor, 1982

'Lady Bracknell', Salisbury, 1980

The height of my 'fame'

(l-r) Dickie Arnold, Christopher Ryan, me, Michael Elles, and Big Mick and (right) with Joan Blackham in *A Small Problem*, *BBC*, 1986

Flying in South Africa, 1994

BT poster campaign, 1983

2nd Intermission

The 'West End' Replacement

Replacement No.5: (aged 32)
A follow up to my tour of *Oliver!* came in 1968 when one of its ASMs became the company manager for a musical play called *Close the Coalhouse Door.* It was coming into the West End, and he had suggested me as a 'replacement' for 'the singing pit-woman'. The creator of the role was a local performer living in Newcastle-upon-Tyne. She was brought in for the three-week run in her home town, but when it was promoted to a run at the Fortune Theatre, she was not eligible to work in the West End. That was the rule in those days. I was suddenly called upon to join the cast during its last pre-London week and, with practically no rehearsal at all, went on for the last two performances in Nottingham.

The part I played required me to sing a solo, during a scene change, and understudy the grandmother, a role created by Brenda Peters. Should I ever have to 'go on' as 'Grandma', the singing pit-woman's song would simply be cut so, basically, I was understudying and standing around as a neighbour in the miner's house. Then, one Saturday afternoon as I approached the stage door, just in time for the 'half hour call', I saw the company manager, my friend from *Oliver!,* standing like a nervous kitten, tapping his watch ready to whisk me off to the wardrobe mistress.

"You're ON!" he screeched.

So insignificant had been my participation in this production that several members of the cast, who barely knew me, almost 'dried' when I uttered my first line as 'Grandma'. They hadn't even noticed that Brenda wasn't there. I know this sounds improbable, but things were fairly casual in those days. The men, for instance, never wore any make-up and, probably having donned their character's garb beforehand, stayed in the pub almost until curtain up (I do not exaggerate). The look on the faces of Bryan Pringle and John Woodvine, at the sound of a strange new voice , attempting a Geordie accent for the first time, was incredulous. A moment to treasure. Following a 27-week run at the Fortune Theatre and a two month country-wide tour, we ended up back in Newcastle.

Replacement No.6: (aged 36)

To avoid any accusation of nepotism, Patrick and I adopted a policy that we would never work together unless I was absolutely right for the part. Patrick was now an established director and in 1972 he was asked to direct Nöel Coward's *Blithe Spirit* at the Richmond Theatre in Surrey. The part of 'Edith', the maid, is a role, which I was born to play, if ever there was one. Then disaster struck. Patrick arrived home from an early production meeting saying he had been told that the theatre manager had received a letter from an actress thanking him for offering her the part of 'Edith' and, although the manager couldn't remember the conversation, he felt that the offer should stand. How clever, I thought, what a neat way to get a job, just write and thank them for offering it to you. Then an amazing thing happened. During rehearsals, the poor girl got shingles. She didn't want to let Patrick down, of course, but he told her not to worry.

"Your health is much more important," he said.

She graciously retired from the cast, and I gratefully accepted the part.

Scene 12

I Venture Abroad

Better Late Than Never

I was 30-years-old before I left the shores of England, unless you count the Isle of Wight ferry, when I made my maiden voyage over the channel to France. Would there be any British born person 'under-thirty' today who had never been abroad? It's almost unthinkable, but apart from anything else I couldn't afford more than a long weekend in Weymouth, and I know of only five occasions when my parents made it abroad.

Around 1916, my mother was taken to St Peter Port, Guernsey, her father's birthplace, as a holiday treat, and she thought she was going to die on the over-night ferry. It was an horrendous journey, clearly, and for the rest of her life she would avoid anything more adventurous than a boat on the lake, and even that could be a matter for negotiation. When I was 12-years-old my mother's benevolent uncle flew her to Guernsey for a much needed holiday. She loved it, but leaving me as the only female in the house for two weeks was a learning curve...too early. Dad still had to go to work, and helped me out a bit with meals and washing up, but my brother clearly expected me to do all the housework. I was never more relieved to see my mother walk back through the door. Her uncle also took her to Ireland for a two-week holiday some years later, and that was the sum of her travels abroad.

My father's foreign trips were both shorter and less elaborate. I still have a postcard he sent to my mother during a day trip to Dieppe, well before I was born. I also remember an anecdote he told following a short trip he made to Belgium with a couple of colleagues. As they stood on the steps of an imposing building, surveying a beautiful but unfamiliar town, Dad turned to the others.

"Well," he said. "We're the foreigners, now."

To which one of them replied.

"Who are you calling a foreigner?"

Remembering my father's wartime map on the wall at home, I now have a 'map of the world' on my own wall, with tiny pins attached in all the places I have visited either on holiday or for work. It includes crossing the Atlantic to New York on the QE2, and an eight-day journey on the Trans-Siberian railway... plus the world's highest passenger train line in the Peruvian Andes. Then large areas of North America and Canada, the Antipodes, the Orient, the Middle East, North and South Africa, the Mediterranean and numerous European countries.

Behind the Iron Curtain

My parents were still alive when I first ventured abroad, which by today's standards was a pretty modest affair. The year was 1966, the month November, and the destination Budapest. I had met Patrick on the *Oliver!* tour which had ended just the week before our hastily pre-booked train journey on The Golden Arrow and overnight ferry to Paris. Patrick was already well-travelled for those days, having studied for a degree at Boston University and taken several jobs in North America from Victoria in Vancouver Island to Victoria, Texas.

As I stepped from the train in Paris it really did feel foreign. We spent the day sightseeing, then boarded the Orient Express for another overnight journey to Salzburg. This may sound incredibly romantic, but don't be fooled by what you see in Agatha Christie movies. It wasn't like that in 1966. In fact, I don't even remember a restaurant car, and the best we could do for the overnight was a couchette. But it was exciting for me to sleep (or try to) on a night train.

Salzburg was truly magical. I couldn't believe how 'different' it felt. The buildings, especially the churches, the food and the homely local cafes with their gingham table cloths were new to me. When we felt we could push the boat out, we had a tiny carafe of wine.

We had seen *The Sound of Music* about six times during the *Oliver!* tour, and I'm almost ashamed to say that I relished having the 'house by the lake' pointed out to me and, surely the hills WERE alive with the sound of...you know what!

Our next destination was Budapest and the journey took in some wonderful scenery, but as we approached the border into Hungary, the train came to a halt and armed guards began to enter each compartment to inspect our passports. This was, after all, the 'iron curtain', and from the train window we could see Colditz-like watchtowers and even more armed guards. The sound of our compartment door being flung open was alarming enough, but when the guard looked back and forth between Patrick and his (beardless) passport photograph things did not look good. The guard pointed at Patrick's face and said something in 'foreign', then made shaving motions, pointing towards the washroom. Patrick was defiant. He had not shaved since he was a student in America, some three years before, and was certainly not going to do so now. Happily, the guard finally conceded, and we continued on our way, but I confess to being nervous about this incident for quite some time. (To this day I have never seen Patrick without a beard).

We stayed in Budapest for seven days. I think we covered all the regular places of interest, plus the wonderful children's railway. Up in the hills there was a line which, apart from the engine driver, was run entirely by school children on a rota basis. In the evenings it was a revelation to visit the theatres. We couldn't resist buying tickets for *Copperfield David*. Because we must have looked very…foreign…the beard!…we were placed in a box, very much on show with the audience looking at us almost as much as the play. All the men at that time wore long trench coats and trilby hats and were, of course, all clean-shaven. This was about ten years after the revolution and many of the bare, grey walls were still littered with bullet holes. These were the facades concealing the shops and restaurants, making them quite hard to track down. If I had thought Salzburg felt foreign, it was nothing compared to Budapest. A good many of our early adventures abroad were to places still unspoiled by the growth of tourism.

Time to begin the journey back to England. First stop Vienna and, being mad about *The Third Man*, I couldn't wait to ride on The Big Wheel. Closed. Well, it was November. Planning to do whatever a city is famous for, we managed to get tickets for *The Magic*

Flute at the State Opera House. Our seats were in a box and we couldn't see the stage...at all. There was a slight gap in the front row and if we crept forward, almost kneeling, and peeped over the balcony edge, we could just see half the stage.

Could this have been the moment that put me off opera for the rest of my life? I have never enjoyed it. I've been to Glyndebourne and the Sydney Opera House. I've seen Chinese opera (no thank you) and heard plenty of extracts from many famous works, but although the music is marvellous, the grand arias completely turn me off. I love musicals and oratorios, but...no, it must be the vibrato. Could it be the childhood memory of the church organ?

Interlude
When she was in her 90s I asked Patrick's mother, who had just watched the *BBC*'s *Pride and Prejudice*, whether she had drooled (like the rest of us) over the smouldering Colin Firth?

"Not really," she said. "He's not my type."

*****

Note to self: nothing and no-one is universally loved.

*****

Travelling by train up the Rhine Valley came next and we vowed we would return one day and really look at those wonderful castles, and we did just that...42 years later. In 2008 we spent Christmas touring, actually staying at hotels which were those famous castles. The over-night ferry from Ostende to

Dover awaited us and we were all but home. Then the wind got up...this was going to be a moment of discovery. Were we good sailors or...were we going to be throwing up all night? The answer came within minutes of leaving the harbour. I was a good sailor, and Patrick was going to be...

I left him to his misery and quietly sidled off to buy sandwiches. Oh, not in order to indulge myself on voyage, but because I suspected, and it turned out to be correct, that Patrick would be starving once we boarded the London train. After what seemed like hours, I returned to the wretch. He was green, but managed to ask if the lights we could see in the distance was Dover. I went off to make enquiries and, to my horror, I discovered that it was still the coast of France. Should I deliver this grave news? Would it actually help the situation? Apparently, the Captain had been instructed to hug the French coast in order to make the shortest possible crossing over the channel. I told him the truth. I had to...he'd have found out sooner or later, anyway. We made it to Dover, and he devoured the sandwiches before the train pulled out of the station. Once back home and recovered from this extraordinary holiday, we did the sums. Two weeks, three cities, eleven B & Bs...trains, trams, buses, boats, theatres, food and drink. Total cost for the two us...£67.00. Well, it was 1966.

Scene 13

Make 'em Laugh

The Wacky World of the Sitcom: (aged 23-79)

It was clear from my *RADA* success that I was destined to settle in the world of comedy. Miraculously, at the end of 1959 after my typing skills had come into their own at Scripts Ltd, I landed my first sitcom job. It was an established ITV series called *Tell It To The Marines* in which Anna Quayle and I played Wrens. With Anna being at least a foot taller than me we made for a comical duo. Anna was a total original and a comedienne I had admired from watching her at *RADA* when I was a new student. Both of us won *The Gilbert prize for Comedy and Farce*, but two years apart.

One particular incident is worth recording, simply because it couldn't happen in today's high-tech world. In one episode we were dressed in long, old-fashioned dressing gowns, with our hair in curlers covered by heavy nets tied under the chin. We looked suitably hilarious. We had finished one scene and had a ten-minute break before the next one, so decided to sit in the studio and watch what was going on.

The scene being recorded involved two actors who were sitting at a table in front of a window, the scenery suggesting that they were at least two floors up in the building. Suddenly, Anna turned to me and whispered that she was just popping back to the dressing room for something, and off she went. I turned to watch the monitor and to my horror saw Anna carefully tip-toeing between the window and the scenery, appearing to be walking 'on air' past an upstairs room. However horrified they must have been in the control room, they had no option but to leave it in. And there she was on transmission for all the world to see.

Some years later, when I turned up in her West End theatre dressing room, she simply sank to her knees in my presence, still mortified and remembering her humiliation as if it had happened yesterday. Ah! early television technicalities...never again, please.

Unbelievably, I have appeared in at least 20 of these popular TV sitcoms, two of them as 'a regular', but fate would have it that none of them took off. I don't even appear in one episode of an audience favourite...so no nice repeat fees, but some of the following anecdotes do explain my failure to become a 'popular' sitcom artiste.

For the next ten years I worked mainly in rep and television dramas, then in 1968 I appeared in an early Granada sitcom called *Nearest and Dearest* and experienced stardom at its worst. Jimmy Jewell, best known for his radio double act with Ben Warris (Jewell and Warris) and Hilda Baker, a popular Lancashire comedienne, were in the leading roles.

I cannot for the life of me remember what part I played in this unholy show, nor how I slotted into the story, but I got the measure of where I stood in the pecking order when, coming back early from lunch one day, I settled comfortably into a welcoming armchair. I was almost dozing off, when I became aware of a door slamming and heavy footsteps pounding purposefully in my direction. Stopping right in front of me and glaring down with an accusatory smirk was Hilda Baker, and at her heel, with an equally menacing glare...the Chihuahua! Hilda spoke.

"Excuse me, luv, that's my chur!"

"Sorry," I said. "I - I - I didn't realise..."

I moved away at some speed, whereby the mutt, which had been waiting like a coiled spring, leapt into the soft, warm place I had just vacated, and curled up in preparation for its afternoon siesta. Madam squeezed herself in beside it, and peace reigned once more.

Jimmy Jewell and Hilda Baker were playing rival siblings who had inherited a pickle factory. Their 'comic' loathing for each other was reflected more seriously in real life, and war was declared every morning round about 11 o'clock. Frankly, they were welcome to each other.

Back again to Granada TV in 1969 for my third sitcom, *The Dustbin Men*, directed by Les Chatfield. A male dominated cast (naturally) among them Bryan Pringle, who I had just finished working with on stage in the West End. He was very funny, as they all were, and made me laugh a lot. I remember having a much better time in this show than my first experience of Manchester! I played a Welsh cousin, along with Helen Fraser, and in those days you were expected to be able to do regional accents without actually being a native.

There was a magical day in 1970 when the phone rang and my agent's voice was saying:

"Ronnie Barker would like to meet you."

He was looking for a 'little woman' to play his

wife in a sketch called *How to Get Married*. The first thing he did at the meeting was to stand close in front of me and look down. "Fine, he said. "Wonderful."

I got the job, which was to play Ronnie's fiancé in a filmed insert called *How To Get Married*...an episode of the *Hark at Barker* series, a David Paradine (David Frost) Production for *London Weekend Television*. Ronnie was very much a team player and unselfish in his willingness to give his fellow actors their share of screen time. He stayed loyal to his cast in this series, which included Josephine Tewson (who shares my passion for cricket) and who partnered Ronnie in further sitcoms, and with David Jason as 'Dithers' the gardener. David's accomplishment in character parts was well established by the time he appeared with Ronnie as old 'Blanko' in *Porridge*.

Six months later I was contacted again by *LWT* for a series of separate short stories called *Six Dates With Barker*. The episode in which I played three different roles was called *1899: The Phantom Raspberry Blower of Old London Town*, written by Spike Milligan...the raspberries blown by David Jason (mercifully, off screen). This story was re-written and extended to spread through a whole series of *The Two Ronnies*. It was completely re-filmed (without me) but it's not generally known that it was originally made as a half-hour 'short' some years earlier. At the end of many dramas in those days, as the cast list appeared on the screen, an announcer would interrupt by saying: "Joe Bloggs is a National Theatre player." For a gag, as the credits rolled on *Raspberry Blower*, Ronnie's voice was heard announcing that:

"Christine Ozanne is a National Hunt Jockey."

Three years later the *BBC* booked me to re-film

the *How to Get Married* sketch to be included in an episode of *The Two Ronnies*. Originally filmed in black and white, it needed to be in colour for the more up-to-date show. This was great fun to do, especially as it was now set in the grounds of Blenheim Palace, and we all stayed at The Bear in Woodstock. Ronnie Barker, alias Gerald Wiley, one of the writers on the series, said that if you fancied a change of scenery with a glamorous location, you only had to write, 'He is punting on the river with Magdalen College Tower in the background', and you'd be guaranteed an Oxford location shoot with all the trimmings that go with it.

Also in the early 1970s, I was introduced to John Ammonds, the producer of the *Morecambe and Wise* classics, and he put me into several episodes of *The Dick Emery Show*. These were more a series of comedy sketches rather than sitcoms. We would meet on a Tuesday and rehearse all week before the recording on Sunday. In one particular sketch, where I played Dick's wife, travelling in a railway carriage on our way to Ascot, we were a really 'naff' couple sitting among a bunch of 'toffs'. The wife goes to sleep for most of the journey while the husband rabbits on and bores the pants off everybody. She then wakes up and announces that she has dreamt the names of all the winners. I made the big mistake of getting laughs at the read-through. When it finished there was a whispered conference between the writer, the producer and Mr Emery, after which I was told to go home and wait for the call to come back in and rehearse the show. Two days later. I returned to find that the sketch now had the husband going to sleep and dreaming the winners. The real joke being that I still got laughs as the boring wife. Oh well, whatever works.

Tiny parts followed in two ghastly sitcoms - *Girls About Town* and *The Mating Machine* then, in 1985, Ronnie Barker thought of me again for a part in *Open All Hours*. I was cast as the local post-mistress, the girlfriend of 'Granville' (David Jason), complete with her bicycle, and our 'exterior' scene together was filmed on location in Yorkshire. To get their reaction, this extract was then shown to an audience during the studio recording of the main bulk of the show. I was in the audience at the time and watched the whole episode, including my scene, then saw my name in the cast list at the end. After it was transmitted, my brother rang to say he had seen my name - but hadn't seen ME. This was the moment, experienced by many actors, when I discovered I had been cut out of the episode. Sad for me as I had hoped the character might become a semi-regular one.

Interestingly enough, many years before, I had been cast in a *Comedy Playhouse* pilot sitcom called *It's Only Me - Whoever I Am*, starring David Jason as 'Quentin' with me as his girlfriend 'Brenda'. Just as in *Open All Hours* it had been written by Roy Clarke and directed by Sydney Lotterby. The pilot was transmitted in 1974 but, sadly, it didn't take off and a series was never commissioned.

I first met David in 1969 when he played 'The Scarecrow' in Patrick's production of *The Wizard of Oz* at Bromley rep, where, coincidentally, he had started his theatrical career as an electrician. He was among the 'unknown' actors for quite a while, and struggled with establishing himself in early sitcoms until he finally got his foot in the door, big time, with *Only Fools and Horses*. We still meet on social occasions and reminisce over those old sitcom days and laugh a lot when remembering Syd Lotterby and how much we both owed to the great Ronnie Barker.

Roy Clarke later wrote a sitcom called *Rosie* and had me in mind for the girlfriend, based on 'Brenda'. The director called me in but, since he didn't know me...at all...preferred someone else. I would meet up with Sydney many times in the *BBC* canteen at the North Acton rehearsal studios. In 1987 while producing a new sitcom called *Divided We Stand* he brought me in to meet Mike Stevens, who cast me as a 'regular' in this new show. We went on location to do some pre-filming, but were then hit by an electricians strike, and the whole series was postponed...to be remounted when the leading actors were again available!

Some months later this sitcom was remounted, but I heard nothing...no letter, no phone call...nothing. Then I learnt on the grapevine that, once again, a new director had been appointed and had cast my part with an actress better known to him.

*****

Note to self: get to know more directors.

*****

Sydney now owed me a great favour, or at least an explanation, and when he saw me across a crowded *BBC* canteen he came over, put a hand on my shoulder, leaned in and said:

"We must talk." Then he disappeared.

I only met Syd one more time, on the platform at Turnham Green tube station, but by then he had retired. He clearly remembered me, but he appeared to have forgotten what it was "we must talk" *about*. But for the wonderful bulk of work he gave us,

Sydney Lotterby can be forgiven anything.

In 1971 in *LWT*'s *Doctor at Large* I played a working class mum who had brought her young son to the surgery. I had one very funny line, which got a huge laugh on the night (from the studio audience) but there was a technical problem and we had to re-take the scene...TWICE! When the audience has become familiar with a 'joke', it feels phoney having to laugh again...and again. An actor relies heavily upon the 'warm-up man' (it was always a man in those days) to explain the situation to the audience and trust them to repeat their original reaction as spontaneously as possible. I'm pleased to say that I got the same big reaction twice more. David Askey directed this episode, and five years later I did an episode of *Doctor on the Go* with the same leading actors, but a different director, Bryan Izzard. I was to work with both directors again, but neither of them remembered me the second time around!

In 1981 John Inman came back into my working life when I was cast as a regular character in *Take A Letter Mr Jones*. This show was set up for John who, of course, had made his name as 'Mr. Humphries', but I had previously worked with the 'unknown' John Inman. We never lost touch and socialised as neighbours during his elevation to sitcom stardom. Over those many years John never changed from the kind, generous, industrious and immensely talented performer he always was. I know that he would pre-plan something just to make me laugh, and would carry it out with the same meticulous detail as he would for any celebrity occasion...oh, I really miss those beautifully, well thought out gags. My greatest thrill was when he travelled down to Hornchurch to see me in what I always think of as my best role,

'Mary Featherstone' in *How the Other Half Loves*. To hear John's familiar laughter from the audience in response to something I'd just done on stage, was a tremendous compliment. I'm sure he had something to do with my being cast as 'Daisy' in *Take a Letter Mr Jones*.

Interlude
Only a few months before John took on 'Mr Humphries', which undoubtedly brought him fame. He had played the very similar camp part of 'Emory' in *Boys in the Band*, which Patrick directed him in at Richmond Theatre. Well, these ideas have to start somewhere.

In *'Mr Jones'*, the 'boss' was played by Rula Lenska and John was her Secretary. There were three very contrasting women in the office; one really tall; one really sexy; and one really... well, neither of these things. That, of course, was 'Daisy', with a crush on 'Mr Jones'. My chum, Miram Margolyes, played a crazy Italian au pair, and entertained us hugely, off screen, with her particular brand of humour! This show had promise, especially as a vehicle for John, but either he, or the public, decided that one series was enough. It did turn up as a DVD, so I have a record of an enjoyable time, although the director, Brian Izzard, could be really unpleasant. At one point, I wanted to know whether my hands could be seen. Was it a medium shot or was it just a close up of my face? So I asked him what was the 'size of shot' in this scene.

"You do your job, dear, and I'll do mine. Right?" he retorted.

I can hear some of you actors saying:

"If that's the worst remark you've ever heard from a director, you're very lucky." Well no, it certainly isn't the worst. Guy Vaesen and my misery at Worthing springs rapidly to mind.

*****

Note to self: never ask about the size of shot... only ask the cameraman where the 'cut off point' is.

*****

Ideal for small parts

In 1981, when things were drifting along...unpromisingly...I was summoned to the *BBC* to meet none other than David Askey, who was the producer/director of a new sitcom called *A Small Problem*. This was to depict discrimination against anyone under five feet. Askey was having trouble finding a short, middle-aged actress, with a good track record in studio audience sitcoms but who was not a 'name'. As I walked into the room he came towards me with a big grin on his face...that of someone who might just have won the lottery. He was very excited about finding me, but, before he could make an offer, wanted me to take all six episodes home to read through and be sure I wanted to do it.

I had no doubt I wanted to do it. You bet. A regular part in a sitcom...what a break! It was a very funny script and we laughed our way through the next two months. There was one nightmarish moment during a studio recording when an actor 'lost his lines' and we had to perform the same scene several times over. The same trick as before (in *Doctor at Large*) the brilliant warm-up man coming to the rescue once again, but a really tough call this time.

It was (I believe) the first sitcom to go out on *BBC2* and the morning after the first transmission the lines were jammed by the public ringing in to a daily phone-in programme. *They hated it*. The overwhelming opinion was that it insulted people with disabilities, especially those 'vertically challenged', and needless to say...it died a death.

Quite recently I was brought in to meet Ricky Gervais and 'the team' including the leading actor, Warwick Davis, for a small part (no pun intended) in *Life's Too Short*. This was to be a series about 'small' people, and I found the dialogue in my scene extremely distasteful. I was sitting directly opposite Mr Gervais and after we had videoed the scene I looked at him with a bit of a twinkle and said:

"This is outrageous."

"Oh, there's much worse than that," he said.

Then he broke into one of his wide-mouthed guffaws and, of course, we all joined in. What I really wanted to say was: "Listen mate, I did a sitcom about small people for the *BBC* 25 years ago, and it BOMBED." Anyway, when that particular episode was transmitted, both that character and the ghastly dialogue had gone.

I have mentioned that once or twice my character has been re-cast. These were times when the whole production was postponed for some reason. One such series was called *Outside Chance* starring Brian Conley, who was a charming guy, and I was playing his 'Aunty Dot'. Brian, at one point, had to lean over and kiss me...very nice...except that his next line included the phrase: "It's like kissing Yasser Arafat", which indicated that my character had a certain amount of facial hair. Red rag to a bull for 'The Ozanne', who is never further than an arm's length away from a pair of tweezers. When the show was remounted, a new director was in place with his own casting preferences...here we go again! Well, some-one else was welcome to that part.

All-in-all, I've had my ups and downs with sitcoms, but one series I was in, entitled *Sir Yellow*, starring Jimmy Edwards (another early radio favourite) did give me a record-breaking credit. A recent survey listed the 50 worst sitcoms ever made. *Sir Yellow* came TOP (or should that be bottom?) Well anyway, the worst of the worst! Mind you, I watched a new sitcom recently that was absolutely terrible. I mean, really bad...so bad, in fact, I was surprised I wasn't in it.

If there is anyone out there who's thinking of recreating *The Producers*...in 'real life', that is, to produce a show, 'guaranteed to fail'...you could try putting me in it; that should do the trick!

3rd Intermission

The Famous 'Replacement'

Replacement No.7: (aged 38)

Following yet another regular casting session, I landed a heavily-featured role in a wonderful commercial for *Crawfords' Cheddars*. It ran for 30 seconds and I was in 22 separate shots. The day went well…very well…almost too well, in fact. The director appeared to know exactly what he wanted and how each set-up would go with no faffing about. A heavy schedule for me being on call every minute and going into over-time, but it was clear that this shoot had been meticulously planned and executed.

When the advert came out I was thrilled with it. It was shown a great deal and my mother would rush into the room whenever she heard the familiar jingle. I got quite used to the situation (experienced by all recognisable actors) where someone spots you…say, on the tube…then covers their mouth over and whispers to their friend, who then looks straight at you and you pretend not to notice. Being in a few popular commercials in the 1970s and '80s were the only occasions when this ever happened to me, but it was quite exhilarating at the time. I was even recognised by our guide in the catacombs in Rome.

"It's our family's favourite commercial," he said.

Some while later, at a casting session, an actress chum came up to me and said: "I was surprised to see you in that Cheddars commercial, Christine."

"Why?" I said.

"Well," she said. "Because I auditioned for the part and got it. I made exactly the same commercial a couple of months ago, so when I saw you in it, I realised they had replaced me and made it all over again."

What a cruel world? I felt really sorry for her, but could only confirm that I knew nothing about the previous filming, although I had wondered how they could hope to do what should have been a two–day shoot in twelve hours.

Interlude

I had been in several plays at The Theatre Royal, Windsor, and was invited to an anniversary performance and reception at the theatre one Sunday evening. The audience consisted of very many famous faces. In fact, I was the only person there I'd never heard of (sorry...old gag). Among them was Elaine Stritch. Now, I was a great fan of hers since seeing the first performance of the show *Company* on its opening night in London.

About 15 years before the Windsor event, I had been in a modest little Christmas show at the Theatre Royal, Stratford East, called *The Pied Piper*. In the cast was the American actor, John Bay. A sweet, friendly man who had later married, yes, Elaine Stritch. He was there with her that night. I saw him in the Windsor foyer, and hoped that, if I caught his eye, he might introduce me to his wife, although I thought she might be quite daunting to meet. I stood just outside his immediate circle, hardly daring to believe he would recognise me, but we suddenly made eye contact and without hesitation he yelped: "Christine!", then turning to his wife, grabbed her arm and said:

"Darling, this is Christine from the Cheddars commercial."

She swung round and exclaimed:

"Oh my God, I think you're wonderful!"

And all I could say was: "Oh no, that's my line. That's just what I was going to say to you."

Replacement No.8: (aged 38)

In the 1970s, Jacqueline Clarke and I shared an agent. He was a very good representative for comedy actors, and had several talented comediennes on his books. Jacqui was one such, and was well-known for situation comedies in particular, as well as being a regular on the *BBC*'s children's programme, *Crackerjack*.

Jacqui was booked to make the Long Playing Record of *Crackerjack* at the *BBC* studios in Langham Place. A few days before this event, our agent discovered that Jacqui was double-booked to record a TV sitcom on that same Sunday, and the proverbial doodoo hit the fan. Knowing that I could do comedy and sing, he rang me and tentatively asked if I was doing anything at the weekend. I wasn't. But now, I was. I had two days, including one rehearsal to learn two quite tricky songs and familiarise myself with several sketches. I think I gained some brownie points for the whole endeavour and, if nothing else, I did get my picture on the back of the record sleeve.

Replacement No.9: (aged 42)

I had worked with George Layton in an episode of *Doctor on the Go*, and when I met up with him again he'd had a nose job. This intrigued me, because I'd had a 'thing' about my nose ever since the angled mirror incident in my teens, when I gazed at my profile in dismay. So he gave me the name of his plastic surgeon, who took photographs of me, then drew what my 'replacement' nose would be like, and hopefully how my profile would look afterwards. I went ahead with this amazingly painless operation, and was delighted with the result.

I tell this story because, shortly afterwards in December 1978, I had a phone call from my agent, asking if I would be interested in doing a Christmas show in Basildon. It was a musical play by David Wood, called *Flibberty and the Penguin* and I was offered the part of 'Mrs Silly Cuckoo'. It was a jolly good part so I decided to accept, although at the first rehearsal it was clear that I was...yet again... 'replacing' Jacqueline Clark, because her name remained on the posters outside the theatre all through the run. As it happened George Layton was also in the cast, and the real irony was that both of us, with our new noses, were playing birds and had to wear huge beaks on our faces. My costume came with an enormous amount of padding around the waist, which 'replaced', thanks to WeightWatchers, the svelt-like figure I had acquired by the loss of sixteen pounds in weight. Frankly, with a large beak and enormous padding, it could have been anybody under there...even Jacqui Clark!

*****

Note to self: in the end, who cares?

*****

Scene 14

Oriental Studies

Full of Eastern Promise

When Patrick was first invited to Korea in 1983 to direct *The Merchant of Venice* (in Korean) we decided to do a bit of travelling once the show was on. After several weeks rehearsals I was to join him for the first night performance, but this was my first long distance trip alone. I stood in a side street in Soho early one morning, with my modest luggage, waiting for a coach to take me to Gatwick to board a Cathay Pacific jumbo to Hong Kong. There was a re-fuelling stopover in Bahrain, and it seemed to me a very long flight. A fellow traveller, who was holi-daying in Hong Kong and couldn't wait to get to her hotel for a kip, asked where I was staying and was gobsmacked to learn that I was just changing planes and flying on to Seoul; not only that, but there was another stopover in Taipei. It took 23 hours to get there, and I was not only exhausted when I arrived, but rather desperate for sleep, although it was still in the middle of the day and Patrick (who thank good-ness managed to take time off to meet me, otherwise I'd have been sunk) took me straight to the rehearsal room.

Korean traditions and customs are unusual, to say

the least, and they base a lot of them on hierarchy according to age. As I entered the room I was immediately welcomed with great warmth and asked:

"How old are you?"

I was 47, and just at that in-between age when you really don't want to 'come clean', so I'm sure you can imagine my reaction. Patrick came to my rescue saying that they need to know, and that he would explain why later. It's all to do with 'respect'. The older you are, the more you are 'put first' as it were. For example when you are with a group say, having a meal, no-one can leave until the oldest person present decides to go. This proved to be very embarrassing for Patrick when he first arrived since no-one told him of this formality, and at a meal that went on for ever, and well past his bedtime (in desperation) he rose, apologetically, and began his 'goodnights'. Much relieved, the entire group rose as one and left with him, as they had been waiting for 'grandfather' (him) to make the first move. He had suffered extra hours of unintelligible small talk through not understanding Korean protocol. The local firewater, by the way, is called Soju, and every Friday they would have a 'Soju' party!

Theatrically, the Koreans keep up this 'respect for the elderly' tradition by making sure that the oldest member of the cast takes the last 'call' at the walkdown. So, in Patrick's next production of *A Midsummer Night's Dream*, 'Philostrate', who has five lines, took the final curtain.

Long Ago and Far Away
One day, with some time to myself, I ventured out into the suburbs of Seoul and found a small University campus. It was more like a village really, where I

found a 'café', and managed to buy a cup of 'something' to drink, and as I sat among a sea of Korean students, sipping an unfamiliar liquid, I suddenly heard the strains of *They Try To Tell Us We're Too Young*. I was transported back 30 years to my school assembly hall during a very conventional and innocent teenage 'social' event. It seemed incongruous to say the least, since there was no hint that Korea had been touched by the outside world's pop culture, and I wondered what on earth these youngsters would make of it. I mean, Jimmy Young?!

We fitted in a one-day trip to the Sarak mountains, which separate North and South Korea. We encountered a huge number of newlyweds having their photographs taken in front of... well, any kind of view or famous monument...and the brides would all be wearing little court shoes with thin heels (on those mountains?) which came to be known in our household as Korean 'honeymoon' shoes. It was almost comical to see them tottering up these steep steps which took them to the summit of the mountain, with the bashful groom trying to help as best he could. I was grateful that I had bought my first pair of 'trainers' for this trip. I'll go so far as to say they changed my life.

Sounds Familiar
We soon realised that words like 'lipey' - their English for 'live fish' - meant that at a restaurant you would view a tank full of fish swimming around and choose one. It would turn up on your plate ready to eat raw a few minutes later. The Koreans do have trouble with our 'f' and 'l' sounds, so they drink morning 'coppey', and eat midday 'runch'...and when Patrick asked his producer why his beloved did

not join them for supper, the host replied: "Because she is the wipe, and she stays in the kitchen - like all other wipes."

Meanwhile back at the theatre, *The Merchant of Venice* was in full flow, and Patrick had persuaded them that, when a boat went across the stage, a traditional gondolier's song should be sung. This, he told them was 'O Sole Mio', which in Korean means, 'What a wonderful thing a sunny day', but to me the tune meant, 'Just one cornetto', as sung by the gondolier in the TV commercial. The actor sang with gusto, and I was the only one laughing out loud in a 2,000-seat theatre. Magic.

Far Eastern Reaches

Once the show was up and running we went forth into the unknown, taking a train through most of the country to Pusan on the southernmost tip of Korea. We boarded an overnight ferry to Shimonoseki then on to Fukuoka, just north of Nagasaki on the south-west coast of Japan. Our first excitement was standing on the edge of the steaming volcano called Mount Aso, (pronounced 'ah, so'). To get there, we took an ordinary public bus and sat at the back followed by some local children travelling to school. One small girl suddenly caught sight of Patrick and, as if she had seen some sort of monster, raised her eyebrows and drew back her mouth exposing her bottom teeth. I expect it was the beard...well, I'd like to think that's all it was! Then began our Bullet Train experience, first taking in Hiroshima with the museum depicting the atom bomb horror, which I certainly remembered. An indescribably moving experience, followed by the tranquil temple at Miyajima with its famous giant torii gate, then more of the high speed train (phew...) to Tokyo.

Priding myself on top-notch map-reading skills, it was shattering to come across a city where I couldn't even work out which direction I was facing. The streets run at all angles, and the signs are naturally in Japanese with no English subtitles anywhere. Maybe it is different now, but at one stage we had to rely on an elderly gentleman guiding us to a venue. He took one look at our map and set off. We walked for a full 20 minutes and he never once looked back to see if we were following. Then he stopped, turned, pointed to a building and disappeared.

The transport system in Tokyo is wonderful and the instructions on the buses are dead easy to follow. You board the bus and take a numbered ticket. There is a display of numbers, which move along at each fare stage. So when you get off, you just check the current number and pay according to how far you have gone. Inside the bus there is a moving picture display of buildings and places of interest along the route, so you can look out of the window and double check what you see with the moving map. It's just brilliant.

Before moving on to adorable Hong Kong, we called in on Taipei for a day and discovered the 'best museum in the world'. No, really. One level is devoted to the development of civilization, with a thick line painted on the walls, about five feet above the floor, and continuing round several rooms. Above the line is the chronological development of China, and below is how the rest of the world fits in. China, it turns out was way ahead for centuries, then for several more centuries it all but stopped and the rest of the world shot ahead. I absolutely loved this - it made everything so clear. Reluctant to leave, we had to take a cab to get us to the airport on time, and the driver went berserk, put his foot down, went through red lights, ignored our manic protestations, but somehow got us there in one piece. I wonder if *he* is still alive at all?

Staying at the Hong Kong Hotel in Kowloon, with the Star Ferry being a favourite way to get to the Island, with its spectacular views and delicious local food in Aberdeen's floating restaurant, was just the touch of luxury we needed before the long flight back to London.

The Greatest Train Journey
The longest one-way journey we have ever undertaken was in 1986 when Patrick was asked to direct his second production, this time of *A Midsummer Night's Dream* in Seoul (also in Korean). As this was a return visit to Korea, we had to work out another exotic trip. Once the play was on we knew that the first stage of our journey would be spent in Japan where Patrick had been invited to open the new Shakespeare Globe Centre in Tokyo.

Looking at a map of the Far East we pinpointed the main places we would like to visit. These were Hong Kong, Shanghai, Xian, Beijing and travel home via the *Trans-Siberian Railway*. Easy-peasy. All we had to do was track down a London travel agent specialising in China and Bob's your uncle...hah!

Well, we found *China Travel Services (CTS)* in Shaftesbury Avenue who seemed delighted to help us, so we left them with the job of arranging our movements from place to place on the dates we needed to travel. Because Patrick was leaving for Seoul six weeks before I was due to fly out for the first night of '*The Dream*', I was left entirely alone to check on the progress of the arrangements...AND...deal with *Intourist*, the one and only travel agent (in those days) for all journeys and accommodation in Russia. Aaarrrhhh! This was a tough ask at the best of times, but, on my own? There was also the small matter of visas!

Before Patrick left, we had been told that his departure was too far in advance for a Chinese visa to be issued. The only thing to do was to send a fax to the appropriate visa office in Tokyo and pick it up there ourselves. A Chinese visa for me was a matter of formality, but I was horrified to discover that our entire trip could depend on an eight week old fax sitting in an office somewhere in Tokyo. *China Travel* said that we would need visas for Mongolia, although we would only be travelling through on a train, and that these visas could only be bought in Beijing. Dealing with *Intourist* was a laborious, time-consuming business with much investigative questioning, but I finally collected the Russian travel documents and visas for us both.

Two days before my departure I turned up at *China Travel* to pay for, and collect all the documents, tickets, maps, etc for our journey through China. We were to start in Hong Kong, go by train to Canton (now Guangzhou) fly to Hangzhou, take a train to Shanghai, then fly to Xian (see the amazing Terracotta Warriors) and take the overnight train to Beijing and stay for five nights before embarking on the great train journey home.

He was such a nice man, the one in *China Travel*. He greeted me with a wide grin, a slight bow and presented me with a slim envelope, which contained two A4 size sheets of paper. No tickets, no Chinese airline documents, no maps - nothing else at all. I was to turn up in Korea and present Patrick with two pages of writing, one in English and the other in Chinese, to cover our somewhat perilous progress through a totally strange land. What was actually written on the A4 page was a list of 'contacts', people we had to track down at each stage on our route, who would hand over our tickets for the next leg of the journey. Just two pieces of paper! It was a nightmare scenario.

I arrived in Seoul in time to see Patrick's wonderful production of *The Dream*, which had a speciality about it that I have never seen before or since. The design was such that the scenery changed from normal (human) size to having gigantic props for the fairy scenes, which made them appear to be very tiny, and so invisible to human eyes. It was a joy to behold, and I took some lovely pictures to savour the experience. After a few days in Seoul, we flew to Tokyo where we were hosted by no fewer than two professors, one male, one female, both connected with the Tokyo Globe Centre, and purporting to be Shakespeare 'experts'. They seemed to be competing with each other as to who could 'wine and dine' us more lavishly. During the opening ceremony, we had one excruciating experience while watching a 'Noh' (classical Japanese musical drama) demonstration of a *Hamlet* soliloquy. The actor started at the back wall and progressed forward so slowly that you simply couldn't see his movement, but you knew he was getting closer. His words were delivered with equal slowness as in: 'I...lur...b...O...pee...lyah...', which we realised - eventually - was the beginning of the 'I love Ophelia' speech.

We were seated at the front and noticed that our host and a photographer were standing in a strategic position at the side of the stage, so that they could observe and record our 'appreciation' of the actor. Unfortunately, we got the giggles so badly that any effort to disguise our inner mirth was almost bound to fail. I put my best plan into action, which always worked on stage during a 'corpse'. You press your elbows into your ribs and squeeze until all the breath is exhaled, then, as you breath in, it should be impossible to laugh. But for once it was not working for me, so I clenched my fists so hard that my nails practically drew blood.

*****

Note to self: severe pain is the only thing that works on occasions like this.

*****

We made one seriously exotic visit to the home of a famous Japanese silent movie star. We simply had to sit crossed-legged on the cushioned floor, but each person's meal came in individual lacquered boxes with small compartments, and the food was arranged to represent beautiful, delicate paintings. We hated to disturb them, but when we did, it was delicious.

Our main job in Tokyo, was to track down the office for Patrick's essential China visa. With a little help from the natives, we finally arrived at the appropriate place and waited patiently in a short queue. Nervously I asked for Patrick's visa, only to be faced with an extremely cool response from the clerk whose look of doubt, after searching her records, put the fear of God into us. She said that no fax has been received from London, so there would be no visa. This was the most vital element of our progress back to London - by our planned route - we asked her again and again, but still got: "No fax."

In despair, I fell back on the old *RADA* 'begging - pleading - tears' routine. Very reluctantly, she produced three enormous ring-binder files of faxes going back years I should imagine.

"You rook trew yoursells," she said.

Patrick and I stood side by side and began a laborious search. After about fifteen minutes, and with despair creeping in, I suddenly turned a page and...there it was! Patrick Tucker. Visa Application! Drama over, and with great relief, we paid up and got the visa with a big smile from them.

" You very rucky!" she beamed.

Phew! Talk about touch and go, but our perils were only just beginning.

We arrived in Hong Kong on a Sunday with one purpose in mind; to find our contact and collect the tickets for the next leg of the journey which was a train to Guangzhou (formerly Canton). However, we drew a blank on Sunday and had to find the man and do the whole transaction on Monday morning, getting our tickets and on to the train just in time. We settled into our reserved seats and somehow I tried to relax and recover my equilibrium when Patrick chirps up.

"Oh, look darling, a Chinese chicken!"

I rushed to the window, to do a double take on the birds, which, of course, look like any other bloody chickens. He always finds a way to make me laugh.

Our luggage consisted of two big cases, two small cases and a fan. This 3ft long Korean souvenir, which has been mounted above our bed now for 30 years, was wrapped tightly in a cardboard container, but was nevertheless quite cumbersome. So that was our count at every stop-over...two big, two small and a fan.

Disembarking in Guangzhou, we were totally surrounded by hundreds of Chinese citizens and even I felt tall. We clearly stood out in the crowd, height, colour and the only beard in sight, but we just waited for some sort of thinning out of the masses. Then, ahead of us at the barrier, a man stood waving a piece of paper above his head. He had spotted us, thank goodness, so no need for yet another search, and greeted us with smiles and quite good English. It was miraculous.

He handed over our *China Airline* tickets and bundled us (and himself) into a taxi. We drove through the busy streets, passing men on bicycles, carrying sofas on their heads, and many other strange goings-on. Our contact waved us farewell and we boarded a plane, which could almost have been held together with elastic bands. We were the only Caucasians on board, as far as I could see; clearly, tourism had not yet reached that part of China and would remain the case until we reached Beijing.

This flight took us to Hangzhou. The city's beautiful West Lake is its best attraction and is a *UNESCO World Heritage* site. The lake is littered with pretty, white-fenced walkways, and since this was a public holiday, they were tightly packed with local people. I was grateful that Patrick had bought himself a white jacket in a side street market, so I couldn't lose him in the sea of black tunics. We weren't too bothered about getting a little more attention than usual, until we discovered that this coat was the uniform of the local lavatory attendants...and I thought it was just the beard.

The one spectacular local interest were the dozens of stone Buddhas at the Lingyin Temple, but these were a distance away from the town. Deciding to take a local bus to the site, we got there easily enough, and the Buddhas were certainly worth the visit. At one point, though, needing to find a 'bathroom'. I followed directions with lots of miming on both sides. Did I say 'bathroom'? I tell you, after you have straddled a dry, open ditch in China and survived the stench, you can stomach almost anything.

Our decision to get back to town coincided with closing time. We failed to get on the public buses, due to the mad scramble of the locals. They don't do 'queuing' in China, it's every man for himself. The tourist buses were also leaving, but the privileged passengers gave us a frosty "No", when we asked for a lift back into town. Bastards. For once even my *RADA* training failed to get a result, and their reaction was so fierce, I wondered which Drama School they'd been to. So noticing where the public buses stopped we carefully positioned ourselves so when the mad scramble began we were swept up by it and crammed into the bus. We were so tightly packed we could barely move our arms, but with his extra height Patrick did manage to buy the tickets by passing money down the bus as the shorter passengers raised their hands aloft. After a pause, two tickets appeared to be coming back again, hand to hand, the same way. We were finally sicked out of the bus somewhere near our hotel, exhausted, but triumphant.

The hotel had been booked for two nights, and we had been told that it would be better for us to buy our own train tickets to Shanghai. So we turned up at the main railway station with two big, two small and a fan, only to be faced with about twenty barriers occupied by very long lines of Chinese people queuing for tickets, hundreds of them. Patrick stayed with the luggage while I desperately tried to work out where on earth I should start, when I suddenly remembered the other A4 page! The one in Chinese. I showed it to a man who, at first looked slightly puzzled (worrying) then he turned and pointed to a sign at the far end of the concourse. When I got closer I could read 'Tourist Ticket Office' Aaahh! English. Luxury train! Spectacular scenery! Same Chinese chickens, though.

Shanghai

Our hotel here was wonderful but, sadly, it was for one night only. Nöel Coward and the like had stayed there and we had a suite, no less, which had retained that classic 1930s period decor with its lovely mellow, blue and gold furniture - glorious. But we had to track down yet another contact to get us to our next destination - Xian.

It was mid-afternoon and we needed to find the *YMCA* building where our contact would be, and our flight to Xian left at 15.35 the next day. We grabbed a taxi and I showed the Chinese A4 page to the driver, who looked at it for ages before setting off into no-man's-land. 'Cutting it fine' or what? Panicking slightly, fighting our way through these overcrowded streets, we drew up outside the *YMCA* building.

Now quite late in the afternoon, we raced to the reception desk and again, showed them the A4. A pleasant young woman wrote down the number 908 and pointed to an alcove across the lobby. The slowest lift in the world finally arrived at the ninth floor and we found ourselves almost in the dark groping our way along a corridor. We could just make out the numbers on the doors and there, at last, was 908. The door was slightly ajar and we entered to the sight of an unmade bed, a low table with some dirty mugs on it and beyond, another half open door. We entered this second room and stood facing a man sitting behind a desk. We gave our names and he calmly opened his desk drawer and produced some papers, which he handed over with a half smile, but not a word. They were the flight tickets and hotel reservations for Xian. I got the strong feeling that he had just been waiting for us to collect them before packing up for the day. Honestly, the scrapes we got into. We thanked him and left the room. We made our own way back to the hotel in order to soak up the atmosphere of this vast metropolis, but found the streets so crowded that we had to queue up to pass a lamppost.

Interlude

Young Liverpudlian woman, back from her first trip abroad to a popular holiday resort.

"Well, it was lovely, but it was so crowded. If they could do something about that, I think a lot more people'd go there."

Xian

We were put into the luxurious Swedish-built hotel *The Golden Flower* and, because the now famous 'warriors' had only quite recently been discovered, foreign visitors were fairly new. I was saddened by the sight of the local people standing several deep outside the hotel railings, just for a glimpse of the outside world and the strange 'big' people with long noses within it. The buffet breakfast alone suggested that the Americans were going to be regular guests. In retrospect, I was grateful for the few days of luxury before the Beijing beds and train bunks that were to come.

The sheer privilege of walking on a platform just above the army of warriors and horses heads already on display in Xian in 1986 will remain an outstanding memory. Among the ancient, man-made phenomena I have seen; the Pyramids, The Treasury at Petra, the Great Wall of China, the Terracotta Warriors stand apart simply because of the vast number of figures and the fact that they were all individually featured and must have looked fantastic in their original colours. I bought a 10-inch high replica of a warrior from a young boy at the bus window, who beamed broadly at me and the money, as I added it to my swelling luggage.

Beijing

I notice in my diary for 1986 that I boarded the overnight train to Peking (that's going back a bit) but for clarity I'll stick to Beijing. From Xian we shared a four-berth compartment with two local men... enough said. Arriving in Beijing we stood outside the most imposing station building wondering how to find our hotel, when we were approached by two adorable children, aged around 11 or 12, who were on some sort of community 'help the poor lost tourist' service, and gave us perfectly accurate instructions. I found myself thinking of them during the Tiananmen Square crisis in 1989, and hoped they would still be too young to be involved. We arrived just before 8am on Sunday the 4th of May and were due to leave at 7.40am on Wednesday the 7th. The train journey across Mongolia and Russia had already been booked and paid for, but there was the one last travel detail to deal with, the dreaded Mongolian visas.

As it turned out, there were a number of 'tourists'

who would be travelling on the same train, who also
needed to acquire a Mongolian Visa, and we all
pitched up at the relevant office on the Monday
morning before doing the sights of the City. I remember queuing for over an hour while they dealt with
each person slowly and methodically. Finally it was
our turn, but not a word had reached the waiting
queue that they were being fussy about the currency
needed to pay for the visas. Shock horror! Only US
Dollars would do. What? We offered Yen? "No!"
Sterling? "No!" But we had no US Dollars. I went
down on my knees again, begging, tears. "We must
have these visas, our whole journey home depends on
it." *RADA* would have been proud, except that this
time it didn't work.

We asked where we could get US Dollars quickly.
"Any Friendship store."
We said we would go and come back within the
hour.
"We are closing, you will have to come back
tomorrow."
"What? But we are booked on a coach trip to The
Great Wall."
"You must come tomorrow between 9 and 10 am
or you will not get visas."
So, that was it, then, on our last day...no Great
Wall? Wait a minute, that's why we're here, that's
what we've come to see.

In the end it turned out to be a blessing in
disguise, because after collecting our visas the next
morning, we found a taxi man to take us to 'the
Wall'. For $20 he spent the whole day with us on a
round trip to 'the Wall' including bits not on the
normal tourist route, and other famous places,
including The Winter Palace and the lake where a

marble boat still rests by the shore; apparently the Empress, like my mother, would get sea-sick, even on a lake! So she'd sit on the unmoving boat and pretend she was sailing, waving at any passing fowl...(Chinese ducks, this time?).

You cannot be but overwhelmed by The Great Wall of China. I thought it would be the sheer length of it - some 2,000 miles long (you can stand at certain points and see it stretching out into the distant horizon) - but it is the size and shape when you stand on it that all but takes you breath away. Actually, it is two walls running parallel, about eight feet apart, and are separated by the steps or path running in between. Each step must be about 15 inches high and is jolly difficult to climb when you're a titch like me. There are long stretches of slopes with some steep gradients, and the steps going down leave you with thigh strain for days afterwards, and that's only a taster for about half an hour.

Interlude

I used to think Stonehenge was a miracle of ancient manpower and ingenuity until I saw the pyramids and, one of the greatest achievements of all time, Egypt's Abu Simbel. Not just the original temple constructed in 1250 BC, with its perfect alignment with the sunrise, but then, in 1968, the entire complex was dis-assembled and rebuilt on higher ground nearby to escape being flooded by the newly built Aswan High Dam, with exactly the same perfect alignment to catch the sunrise on the face of Ramses II twice a year. But China's Great Wall really is something else.

Back in Beijing, at the very early hotel breakfast on the Wednesday morning we heard a typical British outburst from the husband of a retired couple.

"They don't know how to do breakfast here, do they? Can't even boil an egg."

I quietly wondered what his attempt at a spring roll would be like?

Out of China

It was a long train, which set out from Beijing, to carry us through Mongolia and into Russia. Just two coaches were allotted to the 'tourists'. These were considerably more plush than those occupied by the non-tourists. We had bunks for one thing, and a small table in front of the window with a cute little lamp and two tea mugs…with lids. Life was good. As far as I could tell, the locals simply had wooden benches for the entire journey of several days and nights. We were very fortunate to have two young American girls as companions in our compartment (the 'retired' couple were next door) and soon after we fell into conversation with the girls it transpired that one of them had only met one Korean person in her life on a job in Japan, and he turned out to be Patrick's assistant director from *The Merchant of Venice* in Seoul two years before. The other girl said her only contact in the theatre was her best friend in California, and she turned out to be Patrick's stage manager for *Cymbeline* at the Berkeley Shakespeare Festival, several years before. It appears that the more you travel, the more seeming 'coincidences' you encounter. Or is it just, the longer you live, the more strange stuff you come across?

The beds were reasonable as, indeed, was the food at this stage. The restaurant car waiter was a Mongolian 'Buster Keaton'. I was transfixed. The lugubrious, motionless face, the flat hat and the bent right arm balancing a silver tray, with a white cloth draped over the other one was riveting. He moved slowly through the carriage taking one order at a time, then going off only to reappear with that meal, before taking the next order. Yes, you could have starved to death, but what the hell, we had the time. The menu consisted of a 16-page booklet, but almost everything was 'off'. More like, it was never 'on', because whatever salad you ordered, and there were four pages of them to choose from, exactly the same thing would arrive - every time - just seven slices of cucumber arranged to overlap each other across the plate.

We were to see The Great Wall again from the train window and some spectacular Chinese land-scapes before entering the Gobi Desert, heading for the Mongolian capital, Ulan Bator. Here we only had about ten minutes to step out on to the platform to stretch our legs and view the city from some distance away. The desert scenery was, as you would expect, a lot of sand, with the occasional camel train, trian-gular shaped brightly coloured huts (homes?) and horseback riders, at regular intervals, saluting the train with their small flags. We saw one galloping at a great pace, holding up a small flag with one hand. He was obviously late getting to his assigned place to salute us.

Entering Russia

It was approaching midnight when we reached the Mongolian/Russian border, and the routine was that each coach had to be detached from its wheels and individually hauled up by cranes, then lowered onto new wheels because the track gauge in the two countries differed. This would take about two hours during which time we tourists would be allowed off the train to change our money, etc. The train came to a halt and some officials came aboard. The carriage door opened and two uniformed officers stood there.

"Passport...passport," one screeched, alarmingly.

The girls showed theirs first, then took them back. Patrick and I handed over ours, which were not handed back. The two officers studied our documents, shook their heads, mumbled something in 'foreign', then one of them pointed (unnecessarily sternly, I felt) at us both.

"You...you...off!" he said, flinging his arm towards the corridor.

This armed officer, who had his jacket rather casually slung over his shoulders, looking like Robert Shaw in one of his 'nasty' parts, led us into the station building. Glancing back at the train we could see the faces of our horrified companions pressed against the steamy windows, and I whispered to Patrick.

"Do you think it's because we've been in Korea?"

Quite calmly he assured me:

" No. I expect *Intourist* have fucked up".

We were then taken into an interrogation room where there was an empty table in front of a two-seater couch, which we were asked to sit on, with one armless wooden chair opposite us. There was a single light bulb hanging over the table, and there was another, more senior officer, sitting some distance away on another couch.

Robert Shaw took hold of the back of the wooden chair, swivelled it round, and with an elaborate leg gesture, sat astride it facing us. Boss man then spoke to him in 'foreign', which he interpreted to us in thick-accented English. This is how the next 20 minutes was spent. The questioning was on the lines of "where have you come from?", "where are you going?" and "what do you know of Chernobyl?"

Wow, this was getting serious. The Chernobyl incident had happened a week or so before, and we had read about it in *The China Daily*. This paper is printed in English and was full of world news (including the English county cricket scores, you'll be relieved to know) so we knew that it was a huge disaster and many people had died.

"We heard that there had been an accident, yes," said Patrick.

At this point a lot of 'jabbering' went on between the two of them. Then, with a firm Harvey Smith gesture he leaned forward slowly and said:

"Two, just two people die. You tell others on train, just two!"

"Yes, of course, just two," we said.

But why had they chosen us to deliver the 'good news' to the others on the train?

"What were you doing in Korea?" says RS.

Uh-oh, I'm thinking, here we go. At which point Patrick leant back on the couch, crossed his legs and quite matter-of-factly said:

"Well, I was invited there to direct Shakespeare, actually."

Short pause.

"Aaaahh!! Shackers-pier!" says boss man.

Quite suddenly the atmosphere completely changed. We were treated like compatriots, had our passports returned to us and were politely escorted back to the train, much to the relief of our fellow passengers, who could now leave the train and change their monies.

Patrick was right, of course. *Intourist* had dated our visas for the day we were due to arrive in Moscow, not the date we arrived at the Russian border.

*****

Note to self: if you're ever in a similar pickle, mention Uncle Bill...it works wonders.

*****

Although it was May and we began this journey in the heat of Hong Kong, it was now very cold...so cold that we were about to see one of the most spectacular things imaginable. As we approached Lake Baikal, the deepest and largest freshwater lake in the world, the train got as close to the water as the Devon main line at Dawlish does to the sea. This lake was so big that it produced waves like the sea at high tide, only here, the temperature is so low that as they roll over they freeze and just hang in mid air like in a painting. It is, literally, unbelievable. This goes on for several miles and takes your breath away.

We disembarked at Irkutsk where we stayed for two nights before joining the trans-Siberian train which comes in from Vladivostok. We checked in at the hotel and Patrick immediately asked the receptionist for a list of theatre shows.

"Oh, you will not understand."

"It doesn't matter."

"But you will not enjoy."

She will not be persuaded that we WANT to see a play.

"There is organ recital, or circus?"

"No, a play, the sort that the local people would

go to see."

"But, you would not understand!"

They clearly did not want tourists to see their 'everyday' theatre, they wanted us to see their 'specialities'. In spite of the fact that you can see circuses in most places, and hear church organs everywhere!

Finally he was allowed to see a list, which he perused, then pointed to the title of what looked as if it could have been a Ray Cooney farce.

"How does this translate into English?" asked Patrick.

"That means...erm... how do you say...it's a musical called I Love My Wife."

"That's it," said Patrick. "How do we get there?"

"Main street, turn left at Marx and right at Engels." (statues, of course).

And there it was, a really big, old fashioned theatre.

The production was hilarious (to us) although the audience laughed and appeared to appreciate it enormously. The set was crammed with 'stuff', including a grand piano, centre stage with a gigantic vase of gladioli plonked on top, thus reducing the 'playing area' for the actors to, well, next to nothing. They mostly had to come downstage and act the whole play in front of the piano. For the first song, an actor sat at the keyboard to accompany himself, then, after a couple of lines, he stood up and faced out front to sing the rest, while the piano accompaniment continued as if being played by the invisible man! This was the pattern for the songs throughout the play, but when it came to a duet, an actor and actress chased each other round the piano, briefly taking turns to sit on the stool for a few seconds pretending to accompany the other. Desperate stuff this, as they tried to keep in step with the pianist playing in the pit. We were getting hysterical, although it was clear that the regular audience found it most enjoyable - not to be 'laughed at'. Finally, it proved too much to bear, so when the first interval came, we politely left and went for supper. Our policy, when viewing foreign theatre, is to see enough of a show needed to take in the style and range of the acting, design and direction, then quietly leave.

Joining the Big Train for Moscow, with the same companions, we discovered that there was even less food to be had than on the Chinese train from Beijing. Pullet's eggs, boiling fowl, and stacks of thick sliced white bread, no butter - but the same cucumber salad! We noticed that the train would make some unscheduled stops, and that the local people would be standing by, as the conductor was selling the train food, for more than a few kopeks no doubt. One of the American girls had cleverly purchased a very large jar of the most delicious marmalade in Irkutsk, and it pretty much saved our lives over the next few days… yummy on the white bread.

Each carriage on the Russian train had three things permanently situated at one end of the corridor. A Commissar…ours was a squat, rotund female with metal teeth, a Samovar for a constant hot water supply, and a small set of steps. One trick Patrick had discovered, since these trains were not washed en route, was to grab the steps and jump out at each stop, with some paper to clean the window of our compartment in order to enjoy the view more fully. 'Metal teeth' protested, but he continued, ignoring the ridicule this provoked from the other tourists ('retired couple' were still with us). He smiled smugly when they all wanted to crowd into our space to see the famous Obelisk signalling the boundary between Asia and Europe, as by now, all their windows were too dirty to see through. We knew it was coming up, so had the camera ready. One second to get it. Snap! Perfect.

Siberia meant three days of continuous silver birch trees. How boring, you might think? For some unaccountable reason, the very fact of this 'sameness' day after day was irresistible. Puts the geographical size of things into perspective, I must say. The Urals came and went more of less unnoticed, then the outskirts of the big, famous, familiar but slightly scary capital began to reveal its endlessly fascinating sprawl.

Moscow
All I could think about was a bath...and there it was. Not the most luxurious in the world, but within minutes I was immersed in the deep hot water. Patrick, of course, had gone off to seek out the possibility of a theatre. Ten minutes into my wallow, he came back and leant over the bath.

"I've got good news and bad news," he said.

"The good news is that *Uncle Vanya* is playing in the theatre next door! The bad news is...it starts in ten minutes."

I contemplated divorce, but was forced to rule that out on the grounds that we weren't actually married. Needless to say, as always, we were in our seats by curtain up.

ACT I Sc 1: The Garden:
Oh, no! There's the hammock, the swing, the guitar, the samovar, an old woman serving tea, the others

175

drinking it, her collecting the cups, carrying trays here, there and everywhere, feeding the chickens... endless business.

ACT I Sc 2:
Indoors: change of set (that was quick). More riveting business. Young woman spent entire scene inspecting Uncle V's clothes. Notices a button missing, removes his jacket, takes it over to her sewing basket, searches through her various jars of buttons till she finds a good replacement, takes out her kit, threads a needle, sews on the button with elaborate gestures, takes the jacket back to Uncle V and helps him on with it. Then rushes to the window for more feeding of the chickens. All this business was going on throughout the dialogue...Stanislavski would have been proud. Then...hurrah! Interval! Now we can go for supper, we're starving.

With one whole day to see the sights, I think we covered most of the specialities. The Kremlin with its beautiful onion domes, St Basil's Cathedral, Red Square with the famous Gum Department Store, and the University. We decided not to spend hours queuing to see Lenin in his tomb, apparently half his nose had fallen off by then, anyway.

Leaving Russia
Now for the last leg of our train marathon...Moscow to the Hook of Holland, via Warsaw and Berlin. Interesting views and no problems...until...the Dutch border. All off! No more train! The whole of main line Holland was on strike and we had to make our own way through the country as best we could, using different local trains, doing a tour of the more obscure Dutch branch lines. We had a booked ferry

to catch from The Hook of Holland to Harwich, which we would now be bound to miss. Another slight problem, in addition to our two big, two small and a fan, was that we seemed to have picked up a lonely and terrified babushka, (no English, of course) sicked on to us by her family who had begged us to take care of her all the way to England. What a nightmare.

With a little help from the local railway staff and a series of different trains we made it, with granny, and saw her safely onto English soil, but several hours later than planned. She suddenly whooped with joy seeing a familiar face, and rushed off to be surrounded by her family, who were all too distracted to remember to say thanks. But by then we were past caring and after one more train journey to Liverpool Street and a taxi to our final resting place we arrived at our home in Maida Vale. Phew! Well, we survived, and in exchange for those two sheets of A4 paper, we had a whole trunk full of brilliant memories, plus...the FAN. Two days later I noticed an identical one on sale in *John Lewis*!

But, hold on, there's more to come

My third and final trip to Korea in 1988 was in order to see *Les Misérables*, which turned out to be the first ever non-Trevor Nunn production of the show, directed by Patrick in the 4,000 seat Sejong Cultural Centre in Seoul. This lead to the exchange of letters between Patrick and the Cameron Mackintosh overseas department claiming that this must be an illegal production and that he (P) was stealing 'Trev's' ideas. He replied that he was perfectly capable of directing the show with his own thoughts and ideas, and that the Korean producer claimed to have received permission to mount the show from the French writers themselves. I remember one solicitor's letter cost £60.00! A lot of money in 1988.

Patrick flew out to start rehearsals in February, and in early March I had a call to say that Tom Conti wanted to see me for the part of 'Lady Saltburn' in *Present Laughter*, which he was directing at the Theatre Royal, Windsor. I was summoned to his sumptuous home in Hampstead and after a nice chat over coffee, he offered me the job. 'Lady Saltburn', up until now, had always been played by a tall, imposing actress, but Tom clearly had other ideas, not only about Lady S, but many of the other characters, including his own, 'Gary Essendine'. Looking through the *Spotlight Directory* for 'short' actresses, he came upon 'one' at four foot eleven.

I was thrilled because the dates fitted in nicely with my trip to Seoul, and our subsequent plans to visit Bangkok and Nepal. So, off I went again on my own to the Far East at the end of the month. *'The Mis'* was terrific, with a brilliant set consisting of two watch-towers, which revolved 360°, depicting many scenes. My favourite one being when a bridge is anchored between the two towers for Javert to fall to his death. I managed to take some pictures at the dress rehearsal, which told the story of the production.

Nepal

In mid-April we flew to Bangkok and did the sights for a couple of days, and then on to Nepal for a week. I had booked in to the Kathmandu Guest House, but our taxi couldn't actually get to the building. We had to unload and walk through narrow passageways before discovering that the 'guest' house was a traveller's lodge. Backpackers galore, meagre facilities and no running water...on the day we arrived! This last disaster was rectified eventually, but what a start? It was ghastly, so we took ourselves off to the Annapurna Hotel to take advantage of their five star sophistication, restaurant and washroom.

Back outside the hotel there was just one remaining taxi at the rank, and the driver was standing leaning on it, looking rather sad. When we gave our destination (the Kathmandu Guest House) he sighed and asked us if we would like to go to Bhaktapur. Seeing our puzzlement he explained that this small town, about 40 minutes drive away, was his home town, and that tonight - and this only happens once a year on April 13th - we could see the 'Bisket' Festival. He was clearly dying to go himself, but had to work, so he offered us the round trip for $20. Anything to put off the dreaded 'guest house'...we jumped at it.

What happened next was an utterly unique experience. This medieval town was in complete darkness, except for candles and lamps at all the windows in every building, giving enough light for the crowds (all the townsfolk and two tourists) to watch the procession of the chariot. This resembled a large hearse, covered in decorations and jangling bells, which was pulled uphill from the place where it has rested for a year. Up, up, up to the town square by the strongest men, with thick ropes attached to either side. This was done in a jerky, but rhythmic fashion to loud chanting and cheering from all the onlookers.

The whole procedure took well over an hour. We were completely surrounded by these beautiful people, even pressed against the wall at times; the pressure and the heat, and the perfect lighting effect lent an atmosphere that I can still drum up in my mind, and relish.

Needless to say, I have never met anyone before or since who had even heard of this spectacular event, but I'm telling you, if you find yourself in Nepal on April 13th, make for Bhaktapur! I bet it still goes on, and is just the same and just as wonderful.

We simply had to visit the National Theatre of Nepal. *Romeo and Juliet* was their offering. A cavernous hollow space with a flat floor, and rows of those heavy, metal garden seats set out in uneven rows. We sat at the front and waited with baited breath. What the hell were we in for this time? Another disaster (had you guessed already?) but just the sort you relish, so bad, it's almost enjoyable. Just before one character turned up on a horse, we heard off stage tongue-clicking sound effects of 'cli-clo, cli-clo, cli-clo, cli-clo', by a human being, into a microphone. Not even *Spamalot*-style coconut shells. Once again, the 'watching Noh Theatre technique' came in useful.

The real treat was taking a taxi up into the hills where, on a plateau, we could look back down the valley, and forward to the beginnings of the Himalayas. A very welcome diner served the best rice pudding I've ever eaten, including my Mum's. Back in town, we were welcomed into the westernised home of friends of friends, when I was beginning to feel distinctly unwell. I was clearly coming down with amoebic dysentery, having eaten some dodgy meat. When I enquired of my hostess how common this illness was among visitors and residents, and why, she simply replied.

"You lick your lips, don't you?"

Then I remembered the constant wind blowing

over the outdoor lavatories (which were just 'the outdoors').

The flights home were almost intolerable. *Pakistani Airlines (PIA)* known locally as 'Particularly Inefficient Airlines', took us to Karachi, where we changed planes for Islamabad. At 01.45 we departed for Heathrow airport, with a stop-over in Amsterdam. Each plane seemed to be carrying people who had never flown before. I saw one man testing the various buttons on his arm rest and registering surprise (almost shock) when lights and cold air came and went, then he became fascinated by the seat button, pressing it over and over again, from reclining to upright like a child with a new toy. The majority of passengers seemed unable to work the mechanisms of the loo, and these became 'out-of-bounds' shortly after the seat belt signs had been switched off. On the final flight out of Pakistan, I found myself at the rear of the plane surrounded by a group of Muslim men in deep discussion. Finally, they sought my help.

"I wonder," said one, pointing to the windows left and right.

"Would you know, please, which direction is Mecca?"

I'm afraid I couldn't resist some fun at their expense, and gently pointed downwards, through the floor.

Feeling queasy and in view of the loo situation, I was immensely grateful for the number of stopovers, making full use of each airport bathroom. I only mention my incapacity, because we arrived at LHR at eleven in the morning, knowing I was starting rehearsals for *Present Laughter* the very next day. Most of the cast appeared to have suffered from dysentery in the past themselves so there was plenty of sympathy, but I was still not right by the time we opened. Thank goodness I had only one three-minute scene.

Sad Interlude

You will realise, having read my earlier account of Nepal, that the 2015 earthquake has destroyed almost everything I saw and experienced, and later I write about exploring the beauties of Syria, before the conflict destroyed most of that country. We may have lost some spectacular tourist attractions, but it is the suffering of the local people, who have lost almost everything they possessed, that troubles me most. Whether it's wars or earthquakes, the outcome is the same, destruction and loss. There are no winners. All we can do is send help to the needy.

Scene 15

Playing It Straight

Despite my leaning towards comedy, there were several calls upon my ability to play a straight part. Not many, I admit, but there was 'Mrs. Hubble' in *Great Expectations* where the costume was made up from a beautiful lavender blue Liberty print and cost far more than I did. There was 'Barbara Muelech', who became the wife of the German astronomer, Johannes Kepler in *I Measured the Skies*. This was in the *BBC Play for Today* series and director, John Glenister (Philip and Robert's dad) won all our hearts. Happily, John cast me again in an episode of *The Canterbury Tales*.

Some years ago, because of storage problems and a belief that television was transient and only film was permanent, the *BBC* had a policy to wipe the tapes of many of their early dramas, including early episodes of *Dr Who* and, even more, the treasured scripts by Dennis Potter! This has turned out to be a tragic misjudgement. I, personally, was in one or two of those destroyed programmes, and would dearly love to see them again. *Keep the Aspidistra Flying* with Alfred Lynch and Anne Stallybrass, which was directed by Christopher Morahan, who remembered me 40 years later and cast me in *Hay Fever* at Theatre

Clwyd, when he confirmed that he, too, had been searching for a copy, but sadly failed to track it down. I can barely remember what I played, but I think it was more than likely a prostitute.

I do remember that my title in *The Death of Adolf Hitler*, with Frank Finlay in the title role, was 'Second whore - Rape Victim', and that one of my fellow actors, a large, strong man, more used to extra work if you ask me, took my character a bit too seriously. At one point he practically threw me down a flight of stairs, such was his belief in 'being real'.

Then there was the more gentle, but distinctly humble 'Hannah Danby' in *The Sun is God*, house-keeper to J W M Turner; Leo McKern turning in a magnificent performance as the great artist. What perfect casting he was; it was directed by Michael Darlow. In a scene filmed by the Thames at Strand on the Green, the actors were sprayed continuously by the local fire brigade's hoses, since the scene was set in the pouring rain, and there was none that day in Chiswick. I sat in one of those wonderful pubs soaked to the skin, trying to enjoy a hearty lunch. Not the most comfortable day's filming I've ever known, but the finished piece was a joy to watch.

I had turned down a virtual 'walk-on' in the *BBC* serialisation of *Crime and Punishment*, but I got a personal telephone call from the director himself, again, Michael Darlow. When the big man rings you, to insist that you are perfect for the general banquet scenes, which need wonderful character actors to flesh it out, well, you don't say "No." Now, I know I'm no oil painting, but I ended up covered in rags, warts and matted hair, and had Fuller's Earth (artifi-cial dirt) blown straight into my face before every 'take'.

It was on a Friday afternoon, some while later, that my agent rang with a casting for the following Monday. This was for a television adaptation of Mervyn Peake's book *Mr Pye* and the character was called 'Kaka'. Armed with no more information, I went to the local library, found the book, scoured the pages, and there she was. The description was as follows:

'Kaka is a very old woman, she is stone deaf, blind in one eye, and has a cleft pallet'.

The director, it turned out, was Michael Darlow... up to his old tricks again. In the end Patricia Hayes was preferred. I wasn't sorry.

I might just mention that I played Queen Victoria in two television series, *The Love School*; depicting the Pre-Raphaelite painters, with the practically 'unknown' Ben Kingsley as 'Daniel Gabriel Rossetti', and *The Flaxton Boys*, a beautiful children's series set in Yorkshire. By contrast, in a film starring Oliver Reed, I was one of a group of nuns facing a firing squad. The location was at Haddon Hall in Derbyshire, and touring round the area with Patrick years later, we happened upon the Hall and paid it a visit. Inside the building we stopped at a window and I looked down to a walled area below.

"Look," I said excitedly. "There's the courtyard, that's where I was shot."

Then, looking round at the other visitors, I realised my remark had produced a variety of reactions - not least of which was shock horror! I decided to enjoy their confusion, and walked away.

Scene 16

Never Count Your Chickens

I often found myself in children's serials and one such was *The Baker Street Boys*, directed by Michael Kerrigan, in which I played a music hall artiste called 'Madam Pompadour'. All filmed in a deconsecrated church in Lewes; this was, you might say, just up my street, and Michael called me up again some time later. He was setting up a single play, again for children, and asked me to read the script and choose any one of the female parts I liked. The play was called *Fowl Pest* and was about a family living in a small house with a sizeable back garden. Mum's birthday is coming up, so dad and daughter decide to buy her four chickens which could fit nicely into the garden shed. The film would then depict the chickens (played by four actresses) in their 'coop' discussing their living conditions and planning a rebellion.

Given the choice, as I had been, I plumped for 'Beryl', the boss of the chicken coop. Michael wasn't sure.

"I think you would be a perfect 'mum'," he said.

So 'mum' it was.

On the day of the read-through, I had to find my way to a rehearsal venue in Kennington, entirely new to me, and I was going to be late. I found the building, but was panicked by my bad timing. It was an enormous place full of corridors with rooms off, and I looked into several of them trying to spot Michael. In one room I saw some actresses standing together drinking coffee. I recognised Joan Sims and Irene Handl among them, so I backed out and carried on down the corridor. Then a voice called out: "Christine?" It was one of the production team.

"Yes, this is the right room," she said.

Together with Sheila Steafel and Sherrie Hewson, Joan and Irene had been cast as 'the chickens'! Apparently, Michael had always nurtured an ambition to work with these comedy icons, so no wonder he thought I would be a perfect 'mum'.

The director, Peter Cregeen, cast me 'sight unseen' for five episodes of a serial called *The Fortunes of Nigel*, starring a young and beautiful pre-*Brideshead Revisited* Anthony Andrews. There was no full cast read-through, so I learned my lines and was taken to a location somewhere in Bedfordshire. I was playing 'Janet', a Scottish servant, and although the accent was no problem, no one had actually checked that out. After going to wardrobe and make-up, I was called to do my first scene. I found myself in the middle of a field where I met the director for the very first time. To my surprise, he greeted me warmly and gave me my instructions, then without checking my Scottish accent, shouted: "Action!"

After the pre-filming sequences, we were in the *BBC* studios for the rest of the interior scenes, and at the end of the six weeks' schedule, a wrap party was arranged. This meant I could meet up again with all the cast, but there had been a question mark in the back of my mind about why Peter had cast me for this role, which I should explain was a kind of handmaid to the leading lady. I sought him out and posed the question.

"Peter," I said. "I'm intrigued to know why you cast me as 'Janet' without meeting me first, or checking that I could do a Scottish accent?"

"Well," he said. "I know your work."

"Really," I said. "What have you seen me in?"

"I saw you in *Gaslight* at Watford," he said.

This was the first play I did at Watford, playing 'Elizabeth', the Scottish housekeeper, some 13 years before.

"I can't believe you remember me, and my accent, from one performance all those years ago; how come?"

"I was on the book," he said.

The phrase used for sitting in the wings, giving cues and prompting the actors when (heaven forfend) it ever comes to that! That'll learn me; he had seen every one of my performances. I had forgotten both the name and the look of our assistant stage manager.

*****

Note to self: make friends with everyone on the way up, you never know when you may meet them again, and not necessarily on the way down.

*****

Scene 17

Those Little Extras

'Walk on' parts or 'extras' in films and television are usually performed by people with some background in amateur dramatics, although not necessarily and, in one film job, I came up against an interesting situation involving two of these artistes.

The film was called *Stick With Me Kid*, and the scene was in a village hall full of local residents. During a mass meeting of villagers, the speakers at the top table ask for questions from the audience. Four or five actors were strategically placed among the audience and, on cue, would stand up and deliver a line or two. I was surrounded by 'extras' and got talking to the very pleasant woman sitting next to me. These scenes always take ages, so our conversation developed and she was curious to know why I had secured this small part.

"How did *you* get to say a line, because any of us could do that?"

I explained that any speaking part in a scene like this would require an experienced actor, and I had attended a casting session, along with about a dozen others, where my performance was videoed for the director to watch, and make his choice. This woman couldn't believe it and insisted that anyone could stand up and say one line.

One by one each 'actor', including me, stood and said their line, often several times over if the shot wasn't quite right, then, suddenly, everything ground to a halt. Shock, horror, one of our 'actors' was missing. In fact, he simply hadn't turned up and no-one had noticed. How this could be I do not know, but it was absolutely true.

The director was in a real pickle as the line to be delivered by the absent actor was vital to the scene. What happened next was fascinating. The male extras were asked if any of them would be prepared to take on the one line. Sure enough, a hand went up and an elderly gentleman happily volunteered his services. He was shown the script and given a few minutes to digest it, then they lined up the shot and went for a 'take'. He almost got through it, but fluffed at the end.

"Cut! Going again. Re-set. Standby. Running. Take Two...and...Action!"

All familiar phrases to us professionals, but how would the new kid on the block fare, if this should go to six or seven 'takes'? The tension became almost unbearable. This poor man made mistake after mistake and with the best will in the world, had not understood, as my friend in the next seat had not, that there is a good deal more to this acting lark than meets the eye. Eventually he struggled through. When the agony was finally over, my neighbour turned to me with a wry smile and said:

"Umm, I see what you mean."

Scene 18

Those Little Mishaps

Palace Theatre, Watford, 1960 - 1964

I worked at this theatre regularly and long enough to do *Murder at the Vicarage* twice. I began by playing 'Mary' the maid, and ended up as the mem-sahib, 'Mrs Price Ridley'. As the maid, my first entrance was to come on and remove the trolley which the vicar's wife had laden with crockery while clearing the dining table. On the opening night, after the curtain had gone up, the trolley was still in the prop room, and when the stage management was alerted to the debacle, an ASM was ordered to get it round to my side of the stage... pronto! I heard it thundering round the back of the set and it arrived just seconds before my cue. As I entered, with the trolley, I could hear suppressed laughter coming from the audience, because the back wall of the vicarage dining room was still wobbling, and the dinner service was spread all over the furniture - the sideboard, the sofa, the desk, even on the floor, in a frenzied attempt by the leading lady to clear the table with no trolley available.

In my final appearance at the Palace, I was cast as 'The Witch' in *Sleeping Beauty* and one of the 'spectacular features' was the witch flying on a broomstick. I was required to wear a harness, which

could be attached to a wire, enabling me to fly…
cackling…across the stage. Careful not to involve
the broomstick handle, I would put my hand out to
touch a fixed vertical rope and turn myself round,
then I could fly back to base. One of the stage hands
was instructed to wire me up to the harness before
each take-off, but with three shows a day, of course,
the inevitable happened, and at one performance, he
didn't show up. After urgent calls you could hear in
the upper circle, he arrived with seconds to spare,
hooked me up and signalled to the 'pulley man' to
"Go, go, go." I shot into the air, my cackling sounding more like screams for help, and somehow the
momentum wasn't there and I couldn't reach the
fixed rope the other side. The result was that I flew
backwards across the stage, this time my cackle
turning to shrill and somewhat hysterical laughter,
which the audience appeared to enjoy enormously…
so that was alright, then.

Although I still have the programme for this
pantomime, I was too frantic in the weekly rep
system to collect any for the other shows I had
appeared in. When I returned to Watford to do *Once
a Catholic* in the 1980s, and asked the management
if there were any records of those early productions,
an apologetic secretary told me they carried no
archive material at the theatre.

"You could try the Museum," she said.

Everyman Theatre, Cheltenham, 1978
Another play I did more than once, playing different
parts was *See How They Run*. The first of these was
at Chelmsford when, still in my twenties, I played the
aging spinster 'Miss Skillon'. John Inman was directing and playing 'The Reverend Arthur Humphrey', a

192

beautiful performance during which he did a somer-sault over the couch with a glass of milk in his hand. Landing in a perfect sitting position, he crossed his legs and slowly drank the milk. I later discovered how he did it...a trick glass, of course.

Although I enjoyed playing 'Miss Skillon', it was in a production of this play at Cheltenham that I got to play 'Ida' the maid, a perfect part for me. This time the author himself, Philip King, was playing 'The Bishop of Lax'. The theatre's artistic director, Malcolm Farquhar, was playing a lead role and directing the play at the same time. This led to a clash of directorial instructions, since both he and the author had done the play umpteen times and wanted to put every bit of business they had ever seen into this production. A nightmare. 'Ida' has one priceless moment when, after calling the Bishop "Your Highness" several times, he finally loses his patience and says:

"Don't call me 'Your Highness', say 'Your Grace'."

To which 'Ida' replies:

"For what we are about to receive..."

I cannot tell you how many times we went over the different ways these two men thought this line should be delivered, 'no, do it this way', or 'it's funnier if you emphasise that word'. In the end, of course, I just did it my way; trusted my own instincts and got the huge laugh, which the line itself merits.

I had asked the wardrobe department for an appro-priate apron for the first scene when I was serving afternoon tea in the country vicarage. At first they said they couldn't find anything, but just before the dress rehearsal they produced a full length PVC apron with a gigantic Guinness bottle on the front. A bright, shiny coloured thing, as unsuitable as you could imagine. How could I get laughs with a ghastly distraction like that? It was dreadful, so the next morning I went scouring the charity shops, finding a perfect little half pinny, and wore it for the next performance. To this day I feel that my belligerent intervention was responsible for my not working there again, especially since I discovered that the designer had a say in the casting at that theatre.

*****

Note to self: never get on the wrong side of 'Wardrobe'.

*****

The mishap in this production came one evening when the whole cast was on stage for the denouement. Anthony Head, playing 'The Intruder', produced a letter from his inside jacket pocket, which solves the various puzzles of the play. With great aplomb, Tony went to produce the...no letter. Does the usual checking of all pockets, nothing. Malcolm with all his experience - and knowledge of the play - stepped into the breach and went through the contents of the letter transferring it to perfectly logical dialogue, as if the whole thing was somehow meant. We all left the stage ready to burst and I overheard Malcolm saying to Tony:

"That'll teach you to check your personals."

Sadly, a mishap of a different kind took place during the second of the three-week run, when Philip King (after a performance) collapsed and died. The next show was cancelled, and an actor who had recently played the part was sent for and took over the next day.

Playhouse Theatre, Salisbury, 1980

I did one or two 'stints' at the Playhouse Theatre, and enjoyed all of them very much, but I had one of my worst 'drys' ever when playing 'Lady Bracknell'. I make no excuse for what happened, except to say that I was doing three plays on the trot and was going through a spell of hyperventilation at the time (as a result of an asthmatic condition). 'Lady Bracknell' has some of the longest sentences to deliver in theatre history, and I struggled a little with breath control, but I sailed through the first week very successfully, getting all the usual laughs, until the Saturday matinee. In the third act, I am quizzing 'Cecily' on her background and income etc, when I suddenly lose all knowledge of the next line. Not one word would come into my brain...it was like the world had stopped. It is truly the actor's nightmare. Except, this was no dream. No-one on stage could help me, and they were all stunned by this inexplicable silence. The ASM on the prompt book, was not only hidden in a cubby hole situated halfway up the side wall so that he could see the stage and give lighting and sound cues, but he was a young lad with a broad north-country accent. By the time he located the line and attempted to deliver it, I had opened my mouth and spouted what can only be described as complete gobbledegook. Not one word made any sense to me or to anybody else. It was totally horrible. I wanted to die. Somehow normality was restored, but at a cost to my confidence and short-term reputation.

The next week went well, and the incident was more or less forgotten, until the Saturday matinee.

Exactly the same thing happened again. The SAME place, the SAME line…and…the SAME gobbledegook. Now, explain that if you can?

Caught Red Handed

When I'm asked: "What's the worst job you've ever done?", I have no hesitation in replying: "*Red Handed*." This was a TV reality programme where a member of the public is caught red-handed on camera doing something 'a bit naughty'. Sounds fun, doesn't it?

Let me describe the scene. An advertisement has been placed in a women's magazine asking if any female would be prepared to have her boyfriend or husband caught eyeing another female in a compromising situation.

A fashion boutique is hired and a female assistant (an actress) put in place. A woman (a volunteering member of the public) enters the shop with her unsuspecting partner. She settles him down with some magazines directly facing a changing cubicle. The woman chooses some clothes and disappears with them. Meanwhile, another young, pretty girl (an actress) comes into the shop, chooses a garment, then goes into the cubicle opposite the 'boyfriend'. The curtain covering the cubicle is delicately arranged so as to reveal the girl in her skimpy bra and panties. There is a hidden camera on 'the boyfriend', and at the first sign of him being distracted by the pretty girl, his woman comes bursting in saying she has seen what he did, then challenges him about "looking at another woman when her back is turned"… or words to that effect. At which point yet another woman (ME) steps out of her cubicle and accuses him of watching HER changing, too. When the poor man is suitably embarrassed…not to say irate…all is revealed. People (the crew) come from behind walls, where there are other hidden cameras, hand him a large pair of bright red gauntlets and cackle in unison: "*Red Handed*!" I wanted to die, no, I really wanted to die.

When I finally realised what was involved, I felt terrible about doing this job, but once committed you simply have to 'go for it'. Then, a strange thing happened when the third woman turned up with her 'victim'. He was quite a bit older than the two previous men, and when I came out of my cubicle to make my complaint, he recognised me! Or, at least, he seemed to realise I was an actress he had seen on television. Just when you don't want to be recognised, eh?

Playhouse Theatre, Liverpool, 2006

This was the theatre that all we students craved to work at, because every year they offered a one-year contract to a single *RADA* graduate. I didn't expect, for one moment, to receive this coveted prize, but hoped one day to work there. The chance came, some 48 years later, when I was aged 69. 'Florence' the grandma in *Billy Liar* presented no difficulties for me, but the process of the rehearsals certainly did. The director used the first 12 days to research the period (the 1950s) with no hint of looking at the script. I had all but learnt my lines before joining the company, since I was a little out of touch, but the lines were starting to go, and I was getting apprehensive...not to say annoyed at this procedure.

When we finally started to block the play, I arrived at the rehearsal room to find all the 'prop' furniture round the walls of the room, and the floor marked up with tape to represent the different areas. The director then asked the actress playing the mother, to tell us where she would place the furniture. I was horrified by this. Wasn't that the designer's job, in consultation with the director? How deeply unfair, not to say embarrassing, to ask an actor to give their 'character's' opinion. After wasting a whole morning, with most people chipping in with ideas, we ended up with a living room so crowded with furniture, it was an obstacle course getting from the kitchen to the front door.

My character, granny, had a running gag...she talked to the sideboard. In the French's edition of the play, which lays out the ground plan for the set, the sideboard was placed downstage right, against the wall, and my chair centre stage. This meant she had a nice long walk across the stage (allowing time for comedy biz) each time she felt a conversation coming on. But in this production, the sideboard was reduced to a small cupboard placed by the side of granny's armchair. It is supposed to be locked, hiding a lot of files that are not to be seen at any price until later in the play, but granny, in her frustration, has to kick the cupboard! After a few performances, when I did this, the door flew open and all the files fell on the floor. I had no alternative but to bend down and put them back in the cupboard, trying to close the door with a very fragile, insecure handle, but the game was up and the Act Three plot was blown.   Needless to say, the audience was fully aware that this shouldn't have happened, and shared the embarrassment of this debacle, not with laughter, I'm happy to say.

*****

Note to self: fight for your character - get the props right!

*****

Scene 19

All Change At Crewe

The Sunday Train Call

Practically nobody in the theatre owned a car in the 1960s, and it's difficult, even for one who's lived through it, to describe the magnitude of having to move from one town to another on a Sunday, by train. Crewe was legendary as the hub of the railway system. Whether going north to south or east to west you would inevitably change at Crewe. You would only bump into chums by chance, since tele-communications were unheard of, and long distance phone calls were expensive and almost impossible to make without shed-loads of coins.

The Management would, of course, pay the train fare between each date, but this would not include bus or tram fares for any diversion you may wish to make. You would probably have sent the bulk of your luggage on with the scenery truck, but there would still be plenty of hand baggage to lug around, plus life-saving sandwiches and, if you were really flush and had the foresight, a flask of coffee.

One weekly tour I did took us to Brighton, Hull, Wolverhampton, Newcastle-upon-Tyne and Bourne-mouth...in THAT order. Between the last two of these dates I, and two chaps in the company, decided to take the overnight train to Kings Cross so that we could spend Sunday at our London bases. We managed to get a compartment all to ourselves, but found it impossible to sleep. Things got very silly as we decided to sing all the various raunchy songs we knew, teaching each other the alternative words to familiar tunes. We became hysterical when one of them sang their version of *Away in a Manger* and I then had to try and sing it keeping a straight face. This went on all the way to Kings Cross and still, to this day, I cannot manage it without giggling. Oh, you're dying to know how it goes? Well, for the sensitive among you please go to the next story... NOW!

A queer bird, the cuckoo, it sits in the grass
Its wings neatly folded, its beak up its arse
From this queer position it seldom doth flit
For it's hard to sing cuckoo with a beak
...full of shit.

OK? Now you try it!

Beloved Landladies
Once you had accepted a job touring round the country, you had to write ahead to various digs, often finding that the best were already full. Wherever you pitched up would just have to do, and stories of theatrical landladies are legendary.

I had arrived in Liverpool on a Sunday evening to begin a tour, and was greeted by a landlady who plonked a ham salad down in front of me and said:

"You're not Jewish, are you dear?"

I responded with a nervous: "No," without the faintest idea what she meant.

Another actress visiting Liverpool to see a friend in a show, decided to try her old digs near the docks to get a room for the night, but the landlady greeted her with:

"Oh, I'm sorry love, I'm full of seamen."

I think it was in Hull, while touring with Charlie Chester and John Inman in a play called *Done in Oils*...yes, really...that my widowed landlady insisted on pulling up a chair and chatting to me over breakfast every morning. One day, after delivering the Full English she settled herself down, leaned towards me, uncomfortably close I felt, and said:

"D'you know, dear, the day my husband died, he coughed up a lump of phlegm as big as that egg you're eating."

Charming!

It was deepest winter on this tour, and I remember a girl standing in the wings in just a bikini waiting to go on. Shivering, she turned to me and said:

"I'm so cold, I'm wearing two pairs of false eye-lashes."

One winter, in a town with a regular touring theatre, I was fortunate enough to book in with a very popular landlady, and really looking forward to a 'lie in' I asked, tentatively:

"Er, what time do you do breakfast?"

"Is half past eleven alright?" she said.

"Oh, that's very accommodating of you." I said, thinking I could have a good lie-in, and it would 'double' as lunch. Doing a pretty good impersonation of Hilda Baker, she folded her arms across her ample bosom and sniped:

"Oh, I know your lot," she said. "In bed all morning, pictures all afternoon and the minute the curtain comes down...at it like knives!"

Probably the most famous, apocryphal, landlady story is one which comes down to us from heaven knows where, the reporter being (as yet) unrevealed. It concerns a theatrical gentleman who decided his digs could not be tolerated without some additional sustenance, so he bought a bottle of sherry to cheer up his evenings. Then he noticed that there was less liquid in the bottle than expected, and a few days later a little more had gone. He decanted the rest of the sherry into a plain empty container and concealed it in the wardrobe, then decided to pee into the original bottle. Alarmingly, small amounts continued to disappear. Finally, he gently mentioned this to his landlady.

"Oh, yes" she said. "I hope you don't mind, I've been putting it in your trifle."

No, I don't believe it, either.

Digs with a difference in the USA

Sadly, the old fashioned digs with the theatrical landlady are more or less a thing of the past, but Patrick and I more recently experienced some unusual lodgings run by Mr and Mrs Jones in Cedar City, Utah. From the outside the Jones' home, built by them in 2001, closely resembled a Civil War governor's mansion as featured in *Gone With the Wind*. The picket fence, white balustrades, the flagpole and the porch complete with rocking chair; and inside, expensive furniture, period ornaments and objet d'art littered the place. You could barely move for 'stuff', on tables, shelves and even chairs, where one might have liked to sit down. Each bedroom had a different theme; ours was nautical...there was even a real lifebelt with 'San Francisco' stencilled on it, hanging by thick ropes in front of the window, making the closing of the curtains a very tedious manoeuver. Seafaring pictures covered the walls, and collector's items littered the table-tops. *The Book of Mormon* (had you guessed already?) lay comfortably in my bedside drawer (sadly, not the script of 'the show') so I delved into it in order to glean as much information as I could about this mysterious form of Christianity. Not only were our hosts Mormon, but all their (other) guests appeared to be too. When we felt brave enough to make some enquiries, we discovered that they do not drink alcohol, tea or coffee, smoke or do drugs, not even caffeine, so we had to rely on the stash of M & S extra strong tea bags I never travel without. One particular visitor from a nearby state got curious.

"Do you like living in England?" he said.

"Of course," we said.

"But that's where terrorists chop your head off," he said, clearly having just heard about the Woolwich murder on *Fox News*. We were endeavouring to point out the comparison between that and the inordinate number of murders perpetrated by gun owning American citizens, when our landlady chipped in.

"Oh, we love our guns," she said.

"But this is such a beautiful, peaceful state, why would you ever need to use a gun here?" we enquired.

"Oh well, you see if (she probably meant 'when') the terrorists attack Las Vegas with bombs or chemical weapons, then thousands of people will come north into Utah looking for food and shelter, and there won't be enough to go round, so we'll need to protect ourselves," she said, quite seriously.

Almost stuck for words I gasped: "So, you mean you would shoot your fellow Americans?"

"Yeah, you bet, if needs be," she said.

Their Sundays are devoted almost entirely to Bible study with the children, and church-going with the whole family. We were scorned for attempting to buy a copy of the New York Times...at any time never mind on a Sunday (according to them it was danger-ously left-wing).

"But I'm going there tomorrow," I said. "I want to check it out."

"Then you can buy it there tomorrow!" screeched a middle-aged, male supermarket shopper standing behind me at the check out.

("But I want to read it today, you moron") I felt like saying, but settled for:

"Can I get one here, anywhere in town?"

"Hell, no," he said. "You'd have to go to Las Vegas for that rag,"

That would have meant driving south for two and a half hours. I didn't think I would bother.

In Cedar City's only bookshop I spotted a copy of Bridget Jones' Diary under 'Biographies'. It seemed an appropriate epitaph.

4th Intermission

The Posh Replacement

Replacement No.10: (aged 39)

In the early 1970s, while Patrick was working as Assistant Director for the *RSC* in Stratford, I would spend many happy weekends with him enjoying all the fun of the Company's leisure time, so life was good. One blissful Saturday afternoon I was sitting at a table in the actor's canteen when I felt a hand on my shoulder. Without looking up, I recognised the voice of John Riley, one the of theatre musicians.

"Can you read music?" he said.

"Yes," I said.

"Come with me," he said.

John was in a pickle. He had organised a performance of *Façade* at the Shakespeare Institute in a week's time and one of the performers had withdrawn from the venture. John was taking an enormous risk asking me to fill the gap, since he knew nothing of my work, just my personality in and around the Green Room. Bravely, he was willing to go ahead and sent me back to London with the text and 'rhythm' music. This was in the form of dots all on the one straight line, but spaced rhythmically so that the spoken words were delivered exactly to the rhythm of the musical accompaniment. Tricky stuff, I can tell you. Very tricky. I had never done anything like this before. Oh, he gave me a recording of the whole piece performed by (among others) Hermione Gingold, who is just about the hardest act in the world to follow.

Thankfully there was going to be one other reciter, an artiste of great talent and experience who had performed the work several times before. We did have equal amounts to do, and I spent all week at home familiarising myself with these tongue-twisters, written by Edith Sitwell, and the beautiful, more familiar tunes by William Walton. Back in Stratford the following Saturday, we had a run through with the musicians and performed on Sunday evening with no hitches that I can recall.

Replacement No.11: (still aged 39)
On Thursday, the 18th of March, 1976, I was about to leave for Stratford, to join Patrick for the weekend, when the telephone rang. I had been delayed slightly by a visitor and was likely to miss my train, but the actress in me (it could be my agent…) had to find out who was calling. It WAS my agent.

"How do you feel about fringe theatre?" she said.

"I'm not keen," I said. "I've never done it and don't enjoy watching it much, either."

"Well," she said. "It's a new play by Tom Stoppard."

"I'll do it!" I shrieked.

Without realising it, this was practically an offer. Normally, even for fringe theatre there are interviews involved, but in this case the production was already in rehearsal.

"They want you to read it before you commit yourself," she said. "They're sending the script round in a taxi so that you can look at it on your way to the rehearsal room."

What?

The play was *Dirty Linen* and the actress, cast as politician 'Mrs Ebury', had walked out mid-rehearsal because she found the whole thing too right wing. Wait a minute, this was Tom Stoppard! I just thought the whole thing was hilarious. Of course I would do it.

I managed to get a message to Patrick that my weekend was cancelled, and arrived slightly flustered at a City Farm in Kentish Town. Ed Berman, an American who was just about to receive British citizenship, ran both the farm and The Almost Free fringe theatre in Soho's Rupert Street. He also happened to be a friend of Tom Stoppard and had commissioned him to write a play about this new citizenship application.

A sweet girl met me at the door and, realising the situation, sat me down with a cup of tea and told me to relax. Suddenly I looked up and noticed a piece of the wall open like a secret panel, where a man emerged and straightened up. It was Tom Stoppard. He came straight over to me and kissed me on both cheeks.

"Thank you so much for helping us out," he said.

He took me back through the hole in the wall where the cast were rehearsing. They stopped as I entered, and I was relieved to see some friendly faces. Edward de Souza and Benjamin Whitrow, both from *RADA* days, and sitting next to Ed Berman was Jack Emery. Suddenly everything slotted into place. Jack had been the script consultant at The Northcott Theatre, Exeter when I was in its first company in 1968 and he had remembered me when this sudden debacle occurred in Kentish Town.

The next few weeks were the most wonderful fun. There were ten in the cast and we all shared one big changing room at The Almost Free. The main play *Dirty Linen* involves a select committee of MPs meeting to discuss a political sex scandal, when the Division Bell takes them off to vote. The second play, *New-found-land*, takes place in the same room, which has been vacated by the committee, and two men, played by Richard Goolden and Stephen Moore, discuss the merits of an American who has applied for British Citizenship.

So popular was this production that they were queueing round the block, with some happy to sit cross-legged on the floor, almost on the stage. I spotted Clive James doing exactly that at one performance and we almost tripped over him. *Dirty Linen* transferred to The Arts Theatre, in Great Newport Street, and I stayed with it for the first year of its run. The play had a cast of eight men and two women and the theatre had only three dressing rooms. The 'leading lady' needed a room to herself, so I mucked in and shared with two of the chaps. I loved this because it was like the old 'mixed school' feeling all over again and we reckoned it was the first bisexual dressing room in the West End. So I spent a year staring at myself in the mirror, not enjoying the view, especially my profile, and thoughts of a possible nose job were beginning to enter my mind. After about ten months of this I announced:

"I'm thinking of having a nose job."

Ben Whitrow was standing by.

"Oh darling, don't be silly," he said. "Your face is your fortune."

I was 40 years-old.

"Well, I don't see the money in the bank," I said.

I went home and revealed the same thought to Patrick.

"Why not?" he said.

*****

Note to self: I can always trust Patrick to say the right thing.

*****

The effect, when the bridge of my nose was reduced, was that it opened up my eyes so that you could see both of them from a much wider angle. I felt so much happier about my looks.

Interlude

Princess Margaret came to the show one evening and a reception was arranged for her to meet the cast. I knew that she had very recently attended the opening of the Lyttelton Theatre at the National, so when it came to my turn, I asked her about it.

"They put me in the front row of the circle," she said. "And I couldn't see the stage floor because the balcony edge was too high."

Then she looked straight at me and said:

"They never cater for we small folk, do they?"

I suppose a reminder of one's lack of height from a sympathetic Royal is, well...quite reassuring.

Permission to Speak

During the run of *Dirty Linen,* John Riley, the musician from Stratford, contacted me again.

"There is going to be a huge fundraising show on the main stage at Stratford," he said. "And all the current company are doing scenes from *The Boy Friend*, but Trevor (Nunn) wants a curtain raiser and thought *Façade* would be perfect."

John went on to say that Tony Church, Judi Dench and Michael Williams were on board, but he would like to balance it with another woman. No-one in the company was willing to take it on, so could I come up and do some of the same pieces?

It was happening on a Monday night, so I had to ask the management for permission to take the night off. This was no problem, since some of the cast were having time off to do tellies and films. So I accepted *Façade* again.

Of the cast I would be appearing with, I knew Michael Williams from earlier times at *RADA*, and had played Tony Church's wife in *The Beggar's Opera* in Exeter, but I didn't know Judi Dench at all, and was thrilled at the prospect of our appearing together. It was not to be, however, as Judi would be playing 'Madam Du Bonnet' in *The Boy Friend* later in the evening, and who could blame her for relinquishing the earlier piece to Eliza Ward?

I was dressed in something flamboyant from the *RSC* wardrobe and felt a million dollars. I have to say it was a magical evening, and Trevor came round to all the dressing rooms afterwards full of praise and thanks, although I could tell he didn't have the faintest idea who *I* was.

Scene 20

Brave New World

Does this title ring a bell? How about *Band of Brothers, Present Laughter, To the Manor Born, The Darling Buds of May, This Happy Breed, Murder Most Foul, We Happy Few, All Our Yesterdays, Perchance to Dream, Salad Days*. Familiar titles? Yes, of course, and all taken from the Works of Shakespeare. Please don't be put off by the mention of Shakespeare; this is not the 'serious' section of the book, there isn't one, but there are some rum anecdotes coming up, so stick with it.

A Whole World Opens Up
Apart from a few soliloquies learnt by heart as a child, playing 'Hermia' in *A Midsummer Night's Dream* as a student, and 'The Nurse' in *Romeo and Juliet* at Crewe, my knowledge of Shakespeare was severely limited until Patrick was taken on by *The Royal Shakespeare Company* in 1971 (me aged 35) and I began to make regular visits to Stratford. I watched a lot of plays there, of course, but it wasn't until Patrick took off to America on a teaching programme for the *RSC* that his deeper study of Shakespeare's text began. After he came across a facsimile of The First Folio in The Strand Book Shop

in New York, he noticed the differences between that and the text used by the *RSC*. Making new contacts in America, he set up workshops where he could develop his discoveries. In other words, he noticed that all edited versions of Shakespeare varied, not only from the First Folio, but from each other.

I sat in on many of these workshops, and gradually the information began to sink in and I made a collection of all my favourite monologues, Elizabethan letters and anecdotes, and after a while I had enough ammunition to teach these new practices in my own way.

On many occasions I would relate what I called my 'fun bits' to actor friends with an enthusiastic response. I was also able to demonstrate the clues in the text, getting actors to understand that it was Shakespeare helping them in many different ways. He guides you towards attitudes, gestures, moves, thoughts and relationships, without you having to understand where you fit in, where you're going...or even what the play is about.

Patrick wasn't home when I answered the phone one day and found myself speaking to Sam Wanamaker calling from America. He had heard about Patrick's direction of *Cymbeline* at the open air theatre in Berkeley, California, and was intending to invite him to join the Theatre Committee of the group that was trying to rebuild Shakespeare's Globe in Southwark. Plays would be performed there in the open air and in daylight, the very conditions in which Patrick had just been working.

Once established on the Committee at the Globe, our work on Shakespeare's First Folio text became known more widely. Not always with approval since there was an element of resistance, even at the Globe in those early days, to any use of the Folio, or even mention of it. Patrick was regarded as some sort of crackpot for the earnestness he applied to the Folio text. It is interesting to note that, although the company doesn't work from it even now, a facsimile of the Folio text is printed for each current Shakespeare production at the Globe, and these are now on sale in the shop!

The point is that Shakespeare only intended the text to be read by actors in order for them to perform the plays. They had no director or academic to unlock the text for them, so they had to rely entirely on the author's instructions within their own lines...I say their own lines, because that is all the Elizabethan actor had to work from. They had no rehearsal either, and did a different play every day. That is madness, of course, and can't possibly be done.

My contribution to the Shakespeare industry is not huge, but exists because I teach both professional actors and students in the original practices of those heroic Elizabethan actors. Although the First Folio was printed seven years after Shakespeare died, it was overseen by two of his actor friends, John Heminge and Henry Condell, who pay tribute to 'their friend' in the book with the assurance that the text is indeed the work of William Shakespeare.

In My Own Words
During 1990/91, I was engaged by *The English Speaking Union* to visit a number of schools around England adjudicating competitions in Shakespeare monologues. I was partnered, in most of these, by Patrick Spottiswoode, currently Director of Globe Education, and once we had finished our summing-up and awarded prizes we had a few minutes to

elaborate on our own teaching specialities. On one occasion, in the Minerva Theatre, Chichester, after I had talked about the Folio and the two actors who put it together, one of the teachers approached me, excitedly, telling me that she was descended from John Heminge, but had never heard anyone mention him before. After a brief chat, she invited me to come and develop my lecture with the senior girls at her school. Thus began my association with Roedean, the girls' equivalent of Eton.

I had often passed this imposing building which overlooked the sea near Brighton. Once I had discovered it was Roedean I looked upon it with awe and wonder; part of another world in story books which talked of high jinks in the lower fifth, tuck shops and pillow fights in the dorm. A public school I would never have any reason to visit...until now.

The English Department welcomed me with open arms. One of their guests on my first visit to Roedean was Sean McKenna, a delightful man who, immediately after my lecture, announced that he would be talking to *LAMDA* about me and my theories. He headed up the *LAMDA* examinations, and all of that led to my working both for him, adjudicating the Licentiate exams and holding masterclasses with the main academic students. Isn't life strange?

The Generation Gap
This was truly revealed when, in 1996, (aged 60) I was invited to Stoneyhurst College to lead a workshop for a group of 14-year-olds in a Lancashire classroom. My subject was rather boringly advertised as 'Shakespeare - The First Folio'. I stood in front of this bunch of bored looking school children, gripped with a feeling of naked terror and a deep desire to be

somewhere else. Anywhere! Suddenly inspired, I took up pen and paper and asked them to tell me anything that they had in their lives that an Elizabethan 14-year-old would not have had. Brilliant idea this. The suggestions came thick and fast and I wrote each one down until I had a list of thirty items. As you can imagine, many of them were connected with communication technology, and household objects powered by electricity; plus credit cards, foreign holidays, family cars, trainers and so forth. I looked at these items and realised, to my astonishment, there wasn't a single thing on that list that I had when I was aged 14. Not one!

Pursuing this line of teaching Shakespeare in colleges and drama schools, Patrick and I ran a specific Workshop at Cambridge University, taking five actors performing scenes from *Measure, For Measure*...their set piece. We did this for six consecutive years in the 1990s, and made great advances in our own discoveries, and our Masterclasses at *LAMDA* became a regular feature. Our most exciting engagement was with the *RSC* when they were setting up the ambitious 'Histories' season, because we were working with top line professionals. The clues in the First Folio help the actors, and this works best when they have the talent to put them into practice.

How the Clues Appear in the Text

Shakespeare 'scored' his text, much like a composer scores his music. A musician will notice clues such as time and key signatures, sharps and flats, accidentals, crochets, quavers, minims, rests, bars and so on. When he plays the music, he will hear the tune and the rhythm, which will enable him to interpret the score in his own way. Likewise, an actor reading the

First Folio, will notice many visual clues, and when speaking the text, will hear sounds and rhythms, which will also aid his approach and interpretation.

The Folio text contains hundreds of colons and semicolons, which, if observed as part of a sentence, keep the thought going until the full stop (or period). There are thousands of random words given a capital letter, which help with a character's delivery and attitude, as well as an aide mémoire. There are also many half-lines followed by a space, which indicate a 'pause for business'. All these unusual elements help the actor, not just to speak the verse, but to theatricalise the clues.

It is worth pointing out that modern editors, when compiling their own 'Collected Works of Shakespeare', remove many capitals from the Folio text, and a great many colons and semicolons, replacing them with full stops. By 'correcting' the punctuation, they destroy the careful structure of natural speech. It may appear more like 'good literature', but it was never written as such. They close up nearly all the half-lines and 'regularize' the verse. Editors, of course, do not look at the text through actors' eyes. Shakespeare only meant actors to read his work, theatricalise it and perform it for an audience.

Shakespeare also gives his actors specific instructions through the lines...and remember these plays were performed in daylight. Take for example the 'Chief Watch' (*Romeo & Juliet* V-3) when he enters the tomb with a 'Boy':

Chief Watch: "Lead boy, which way?"

Boy: "This is the place, there where the Torch doth burne."

Chief Watch: "The ground is bloody. (*Then instructing the Boy*). Search about the Churchyard.

(*Then calling to others off stage*) Go some of you, who ere you find attach."

The torch indicates that it is dark, and for him to know the ground is bloody, he must feel the stickiness underfoot, bend down, touch the moisture, sniff it, maybe even taste it, before saying his line.

The scene continues with 'hidden' instructions for each actor, using theatrical common sense, and by the end of the scene the 13 characters are perfectly placed as in a tableau. The two opposing families, together over the bodies, are mourning their dead children.

Satisfying results

In North America the two of us have peddled the whole gamut of our Shakespeare wares from Vancouver to Orlando...San Francisco to Boston. Most recently we were appointed the 'Eccles Scholars' at the Southern Utah University. The benefactors, Mr and Mrs Eccles having long since died, had left an enormous legacy for visiting experts on classical subjects, and we were there for one week doing our Shakespeare 'rum-tee-tum' in Cedar City. All went very well, the students were most receptive, ultra-polite and eager to embrace this subject.

On the last day, at a special lunch in our honour, all the faculty, including the Dean, the Provost, the President and the Director of the Theatre Company, were seated round the table. In front of each place was a copy of our jointly written book *The Actor's Survival Handbook*, and after the meal they formed a queue and waited patiently as we both signed each of their copies. I suddenly thought, Christine Smith from Leicester...what are you doing here? Then we flew off to New York, took a train out of Grand

Central Station to New Haven, Connecticut and gave a two-day workshop for the students at Yale. Well, it sounds good, doesn't it?

*****

Note to self: Would a higher education have brought me to this pinnacle? No. Only the route I took could have done that.

*****

Patrick and I are now convinced that all the help actors need is there in the text, and the more the editors muck about with the text, the more they remove or alter the original instructions to the actors. We have proved this over and over again. If you encourage actors to do the Folio text, they will give better performances, because the instructions are all there…in the lines! And, instead of audiences coming away from a play owning up to not understanding the language and being 'bored' for three hours, they will appreciate and, hopefully, enjoy the effort they have made to go and see a Shakespeare play.

Here endeth the lesson.

Scene 21

An Original Idea

Saving the Rose

By 1989 I could hold my own in any open forum on the performing of Shakespeare. At a friend's birthday party which Patrick couldn't attend, I found myself talking at some length about my 'fun bits' to a wrapt audience of fellow actors. By the end of the evening one of them, Gillian McCutcheon,decided to open her house on Sunday mornings for Patrick to 'workshop' her actor friends (for a small fee) in his First Folio techniques.

At first, we just worked on monologues in order to introduce the 'clues' and identify them in each speech. The next thing was to get two or three actors to play out little scenes, but only giving them their individual character's lines, with a few words (their cue) leading into each speech. This is called a 'cue script'. By only knowing their own lines, and the few words spoken before them (but not who says those words!). It means that they need to listen even harder and concentrate on the dialogue, in order to 'pick up their cue' and speak as soon as they hear it. By the way, Shakespeare never gives the same 'cue' twice, unless he wants two people to speak at the same time! Using the music analogy you could say that the flute player, for example, has just his own notes (for the flute) and does not see the whole orchestral score.

They soon got the hang of it, and the fun was detecting clues in other people's speeches as well as their own. After a while we held some public demonstrations of cue script scenes and in 1990 we were asked to put on a show at the Haymarket Theatre, as a fundraiser for the 'Save the Rose Theatre' campaign. Fifty actors were eager to endorse the cause, and most of them attended a meeting at the National Theatre, set up by actor, Peter Woodward. Ralph Fiennes, Sam West, Susannah York, James Fox, Prunella Scales, Barry Rutter, Greg Hicks, Jean Boht, Art Malik and Gary Wilmot, were among those involved in the final showcase.

After Patrick explained the rudiments of working from a cue script, he asked them all to write their name and address on an envelope, and the number of lines they were prepared to learn (from one to 40) then we went home and worked out how to cast 16 scenes from different plays, according to the actors' requirements.

All *they* had to do was learn their lines, not read the play or the scene they were in, and not find out who they might be acting with. Then most of them came to us for a 'verse nursing session', and the great and the good would sit on our sofa, largely confessing extreme nervousness at the prospect of what they had let themselves in for, but the 'game' was on.

In front of a packed house on a Sunday evening, Patrick was introduced to the audience by Dame Peggy Ashcroft. We delivered 20 unrehearsed cue-scripted scenes, with some triumph I have to say, and as prompter, I wasn't over-used. Behind the scenes, all these famous actors were trying to guess who they might be acting with, but duty bound not to reveal their own character, so they would discover the casting only in front of the audience. There were some hilarious consequences, especially when Serena Gordon, after her 'Juliet' soliloquy, looked round to see Jack Shepherd coming on in drag as 'The Nurse'. There were many revelations both from the very brave actors and, of course, Shakespeare's brilliant text. The result that night was probably quite close to the experience of the original Elizabethan actors 400 years before. I believe we raised about £23,000.

Correcting the Errors

A few months later, during a hilarious performance of the central bulk of *The Comedy of Errors* at the Mermaid Theatre, in front of a full house of professional actors, we made one delicious discovery. Because we had a limited number of cue script-trained actors, we were never going to find two who looked alike for the two sets of twins. I know Patrick has always favoured the best artiste, rather than the one who looks right, so we cast two great comedy actors as the Dromios; Hugh Walters, five foot eight and Richard Cordery, six foot four. We put them in identical costumes and left it to the other characters to react accordingly. The point being that the audience then knew exactly which Dromio was which and did not have to spend time working it out. Later, we realised that the original company would have done exactly the same thing; the 'comics' play the clowns regardless of their appearance. Would they have had two clowns who looked alike?

After the show, an actor who had just played one of the Antipholus twins in Regents Park, bounded up to us saying...

"Our director (Judi Dench, no less) chastised me

one evening when she noticed I was wearing my own very small earring which I had forgotten to remove, but now I realise that too much was made of the twins being identical. I'm sure your way works best. The audience should be able to recognise the different actors, then the mistaken identity by the other characters on stage is much funnier."

Along with actor, Graham Pountney, Patrick and I discussed the possibility of founding 'a company', now that we had a loyal band of actors willing to strut this stuff upon the stage. It was while we were sitting in a tea shop on the Isle of Wight, wondering what to call it, that I wrote the word 'original' on a paper napkin. It had occurred to me simply because of the double meaning of how they did it originally, and the originality of our presentations, thus the *Original Shakespeare Company* was born.

Prompt Copy

Patrick and I organised, mounted and presented 27 full length plays in Germany, Jordan, Australia, Canada, the UK and three years running at Shakespeare's Globe in London. Apart from one occasion in Canada, we never repeated a performance with the same cast, but tried to recreate the conditions of the original Elizabethan actors. The gap of 400 years makes it impossible for anybody to place themselves back in time, as there is far too much knowledge in our heads which cannot be ignored. We know so much more than they did, and this knowledge is constantly with us, so by taking away the full script, the director, and the rehearsals, we go some way towards achieving the 'original' practices.

I rarely took part as an actor in any of our productions, but I cast myself as the prompter, and sat on stage with the full script throughout the performance. During the opening scene of Laurence Olivier's *Henry V* film, a man sits on stage at 'The Globe' with the prompt book on his knee. Unfortunately, they don't show him prompting anyone, which makes me think they missed a trick there, but it clearly demonstrates the belief that he was a necessary part of the performance.

Having worked on The Globe stage, it is obvious that the prompter would need to be among the actors because you couldn't possibly hear a prompt from backstage. It isn't just prompts that are needed, the prompter acts more like the conductor of an orchestra. I would literally have to bring people on sometimes with hand signals, but more often I would need to gesture to them to go off. The actors would keep an eye open for visual instructions when it was not quite clear what to do, as well as glancing over at me for reassurance that they were saying the right line. I could often tell from their faces that they might need a prompt, and if an actor ever said a wrong word, I would be prepared for them to 'dry' a line or so later. I would have my finger on the words being uttered all the time, and be ready to throw a word out loud and clear at the slightest hesitation from an actor. Merely prompting a forgotten word is the easy bit. The most difficult thing to do is to get the actors back on track if someone skips a speech, since that could throw everything into chaos, so I found it best to give them the line they should be saying, loud and clear, and that seemed to work as well as anything.

When I was called upon to play a role, through necessity in Jordan, I grew to admire our regular actors hugely. If you have never tried working from a cue script you might, quite understandably, believe

it to be impossible, but this does not explain the number of our actors coming back for more...and then
even more. "It's like a fix," they would say...some-
thing to do with adrenalin, I shouldn't wonder.
Anyway, it's better than popping pills.

Patrick has been one of the Artistic Directorate at
the Globe from the earliest days, even before Sam
Wanamaker received permission to develop the
building, so we know the whole background story. To
be allowed to mount three productions there was a
great privilege, but these were always intended as
demonstrations, not for our productions to be
analysed as contenders for modern theatre awards or
accolades. A small example might be from our
production of *Cymbeline*, in a scene where 'Imogen'
meets 'Clotten' for the first time. Looking at their
parts, *she* thought she was in a tragedy and *he* thought
he was in a comedy. Sticking strictly to what their
own lines were telling them to do, the scene worked
wonderfully well, because neither of them knew
where the scene was going or what the outcome
might be. If we had rehearsed the play for weeks,
with all the moves 'set in stone' so to speak, it would
have been harder for the actors to show 'genuine'
surprise. This way, they just did what the lines told
them to do, and suddenly you begin to understand the
real genius of Shakespeare. Instead of going on stage
with your mind stuffed full of director's ideas, with
complicated business and meticulous moves; this way
you are as free as a bird. Nothing is set in concrete,
and there are no rules...you can just fly with it, and
respond naturally to what is going on, just as in real
life. Remember, actors are very brave children.

Talking to the veteran actor Frank Thornton
('Captain Peacock' in *Are You Being Served*) I learnt

that he had worked from cue scripts in his early rep days. In one play his cue was: "...up your mother's skirt?" followed by his own line: "With pleasure!"

Exit.

His curiosity knew no bounds. Eventually he heard the full line: "...and could you call at the dry cleaners and pick up your mother's skirt?

Busy or what?

Looking back through my old diaries, to check up on all the organisation, training workshops, costume fittings, verse nursing sessions and travel arrangements involved in mounting these 'extravaganzas', I find myself open-mouthed at how much I did every day, every week! Not only was it 'never a dull moment', but how the hell did I fit it all in?

One of the saddest things I ever saw, sitting next to a young woman on the tube, was when I caught sight of her open diary showing every day of the week. It was completely empty except for Friday where she had written 'Miss McKenzie's retirement party'. I don't know whether I felt more sympathy for Miss McKenzie, or the young woman, who clearly led an uneventful life, but I do know that I didn't envy either of them.

*****

Note to self: A busy diary may be exhausting, but as Oscar Wilde put it: "One should always have something sensational to read in the train."

*****

Having said all this about busy diaries, I am in

danger of making my life appear to be one endless round of enthralling adventures and jobs of all kinds, I should point out that my diaries also show that my life was not always one exciting thing after another. There were, in my early and mid-career, weeks, months, even years with no acting work at all. The jobs I went for and didn't get would leave me dejected and (Patrick will bear me out here) crying into my fried egg. There seemed times when all the effort to get work went unnoticed, and the brick wall of casting directors was insurmountable. As the work dried up, so did the agent's ability to capitalise on any good past credits I may have had.

In the 1980s only the development of my interest in Shakespeare, and passing the information taken from Patrick's workshops on to other actors and drama school students, kept me going. The founding of the *Original Shakespeare Company (OSC)* saw my renewed energy and enthusiasm for performing and offered the perfect showcase for my various skills. It's a wise actor who expects disappointment, for it will come, and learns to handle it in a way that makes sense to him. There will be times when you know you are perfect for the part, then they give it to somebody else. But one day that somebody else will be you, and in the joy of the moment I wonder how much you will care about how the other contenders are feeling?

Scene 22

Germany Calling

Patrick's connection with The Globe had come to the attention of a German producer working at the already built Globe theatre in Neuss, near Dusseldorf. This was an all metal construction and was not open to the elements, but in shape it did resemble a circular playhouse. They wanted two different plays to be performed on consecutive nights, and the phone conversation went like this.

"Vot is in your repertoire?"

"What do you want?"

"No, you do not understand, vot is in your repertoire?"

"You name the plays, we'll do them."

"No, no, vot plays can you put on?"

Not understanding that we could do any play in the canon, we gave in to his request and Patrick started to list some favourite plays.

"*A Midsummer Night's Dream, The Merchant of Venice...*"

"I will have those." the producer said, and put the phone down. Perfect apparently.

Performing them back to back was fraught with danger. We cast the plays from our regular group of actors, pretty well trained in the techniques of cue script acting. We held three half-day workshops, and fixed costumes, props and the minimum of scenery, mainly curtains and benches. Each actor would be playing two, three, or even four different parts, and this was before our verse nursing sessions had been introduced, where each actor would come to us privately and we would make sure they had observed all the clues in the text. So although we were skating on very thin ice, we had to trust these experienced actors, with all their talent and ingenuity, to deliver the goods, which, of course, they did…in spades!

We booked a luxury coach to take us all the way. Included was a ferry from Sheerness, and we arranged to pick up the actors at strategic points en route, so my map-drawing skills were being called upon once more. The sea voyage was a hoot, there was a pool and a cinema, for our relaxation, but we soon realised that some of the actors had never met each other before, let alone acted with them, so the trip was a useful 'getting to know each other' time.

The *OSC* policy was to provide the basic costumes and props, but we gave the actors full permission to adapt them, or even make their own - an excellent decision as it turned out.

It was June, 1993 and we travelled to Neuss on a Friday, played *A Midsummer Night's Dream* on Saturday, *The Merchant of Venice* on Sunday and returned to London on Monday, without any rehearsal of the two plays, and with the actors only seeing their own lines.

We cast Richard Cordery as 'Shylock' in *'The Merchant'*, with a very small part in *The Dream*, but we hadn't reckoned on his prodigious capacity for line learning, when he expressed his desire to play the substantial role of 'Puck'. This could be the tallest 'Puck' ever, so we anticipated something special, and upon arrival at the theatre, he surveyed the building looking for places where he could make as many different entrances as possible. Running across the balcony, his foot made contact with something heavy, which put paid to his best laid plans.

"Patrick," he said. "I'm afraid Puck won't be running tonight."

"Well, just walk then."

His leg continued to stiffen:

"Patrick, Puck won't be walking either."

"In that case, just stand still and say your lines. After all, nobody knows what you were planning to do, anyway."

After his first scene, instead of exiting, he just said to the audience: "I am invisible," then drew his hand over his face, like a curtain coming down and stayed where he was. The Germans were fascinated.

"A very interesting interpretation," was their conclusion at the end.

Next morning, one of the actors went into town and found a long black walking stick with a beautiful silver handle. A handsome addition to Shylock's image as he limped around the stage. Another interesting interpretation? Nicholas Day, also a senior member of the company playing 'Bottom', was equally inventive. For 'Piramus' he had made himself a toga, which was just a bit too short, causing him to tug at the hem from time to time to protect his modesty. Then he had ripped the long gold fringe from a lampshade and made it into a beard which swung from side to side as he walked. He managed to conceal this vision until he appeared on stage where most of the cast were already playing the scene. They began to giggle. I, as prompter, could barely contain myself and so the 'play within the play' slowly progressed.

We were still endeavouring to stifle our laughs, when it came to the moment where 'Piramus' stabs himself to death with a dagger. Nick had made his own prop out of an extendable car aerial, which gave the appearance of the dagger being plunged deeper and deeper into his chest as he says: "Die, die, die, die, die." And as if that were not funny enough, Nick had concealed in his palm an inch-wide red ribbon, wrapped tightly round a heavy button, which he released on the first 'die'. It shot out in a big curve and looked for all the world like a huge spurt of blood.

That was it. The place erupted, the audience was delighted, the actors were helpless, I was hysterical, and on top of all that, Nick had 'corpsed himself', so although it may have looked like 'Piramus' in his death throws, we all knew it was Nick shaking with laughter. He claims that this was one of the best moments of his career. He had been given the freedom to create something hilarious, and it was entirely HIS invention. We knew we were on to something by letting the actors fly and, with these comical interpretations, Richard and Nick had blazed the trail for others to follow.

Ladies or Gentlemen?

We returned to Germany once again when the *OSC* was invited to present some scenes from *Two Gentlemen of Verona* in Detmold. We prepared our actors in the usual way and when the day dawned, one of our stalwarts and master of props and furnishings, went outside to begin loading the equipment on to the coach. After a while I met Lewis in the dining room, pouring himself a coffee.

"Everything ok, Lewis?" I asked.

"Yes, we're loaded up," he said.

Then, slowly stirring his coffee and looking straight at me with an expression of incredulity mingled with a hint of amusement, added:

"Wait till you see the driver."

This was a long distance coach driver, hired to take a bunch of excitable actors to Folkestone then, after the ferry to France, drive us through Holland, Belgium and part Germany, in one day.

Standing before me was a person in high heeled shoes, fishnet tights, black pencil skirt and black v-neck top, curly ginger hair, crooked nicotine-stained teeth, bright crimson lipstick, and a necklace with a gold centre piece forming the word '$J~u~d~y$'. When Judy spoke, it was the voice of a deep, masculine, broad Glaswegian navvy.

We collected our actors en route, but it wasn't until we arrived in Folkestone and made our way to the nearest public convenience that we could be sure whether we had a man or woman driving us. Judy made straight for the Ladies. Phew! We gradually learnt that she was, indeed, making the transition from male to female, but was at present about half way through the process. Apart from, rather alarmingly, losing her way in Belgium and circumnavigating Brussels twice (a city completely off the scheduled route) she was a good egg, helping to set up the stage, and constantly hoovering up our mess along with her own cigarette ash. A treasured moment came when Judy grabbed a hammer and, banging nails into the stage, announced: "Och, you just need us girls to sort things out."

For the return journey, Judy was clearly quite relaxed with the actors, and selected to wear a bright orange roll neck sweater, and as we approached London, one actor enquired: "Should we give Judy a tip?"

Heinz Spaghetti, 1971

KitKat, 1974 (old nose)

Shell, 1985 (new nose)

Peugeot - "Gary's Cat" 2012

"Yes," *Radio Times*, 1974

David Jason and Christine Ozanne
Comedy Playhouse (BBC 1, 8.30).

TV Times Magazine, 1981

Open a packed file on comedy with Daisy (Christine Ozanne)
and Graham (John Inman) in *Take a Letter Mr Jones* at 7.35.

as 'Daisy' in *Take a Letter Mr Jones*, Southern Television Series, 1981

Presenting Shakespeare

The Bear Gardens, 1994

Mermaid Theatre, 1991

Nicholas Day
and Richard Cordery

with Patrick

Ross-on-Wye, 1997

Jonathan Roby, David Jarvis and me

King John at The Globe, 1998

Sonia Ritter and Callum Coates

Judith Paris and Philip Bird

The Middle East

Jordan, 2000

Me (left) 'Lady Capulet' with Emma Bown 'Juliet' and Carolyn Jones 'The Nurse', The Artemis Steps, Jerash

Syria, 2000

Belinda Murray surprises me at the Crac de Chevalier

Among the 'original' ruins of Palmyra

'Original' Friendships
LDS

with Doreen Browne and Freda Dexter

RADA

'The Coven': Flick, Jill B, me, Jan, Maggie and Jill S

OSC

Susie Lindeman and Greta Scacchi

The Great Escape

Egypt,
1974,
riding by
The Great
Pyramid

China,
1986,
striding
out on
The
Great
Wall

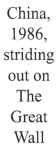

Mystery play c.1947

'Women's
Meeting'
drama
group

Curtain call: Mum (third from left)

Mystery snapshot, 1953

Summer
in
Leicester

with Mum's first cousin, Lewis

Mystery solved, 2009

Christmas
in
Guernsey

with my second cousin, Margaret

Bag lady

This glamorous profession

Old bag

Casualty, BBC 1, 2001
(and below right)

The Harry Hill Movie, 2013

Old hag

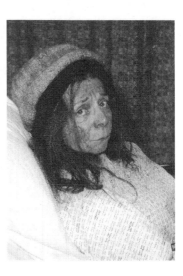

Upstart Crow, BBC 2, 2016

It's the story of my life!

Scene 23

Commercials - Don't You Love 'em?

1969 - 2013 (age 33 - 77)

Very, very few people are famous; that is to say, people who are so well-known that everybody in the world has heard of them. There are only a handful of 'them' and we know who they are. The next lot are those who most people could put a name to, and the right name at that. When it comes to actors, they fall into several categories...those who can be identified by their own name or, at least, by the name of the characters they play...and those whose face is recognised, but "the name escapes me". Know what I mean?

I barely came into this last category, except for the few occasions when I was heavily featured in some popular commercials in the 1970s and '80s. After cutting my teeth with four or five low key 'ads', I landed a part in one that hit the jackpot. The director was the little known Alan Parker, when he was also 'on the way up', as it were. It was for *Heinz Spaghetti* and featured mum, dad, and young son just home from a cub's camping trip. The two memorable things in this thirty-second 'ad' was the dad singing: "Ging gang gooly, gooly, gooly, gooly, watcha, ging gang goo, ging gang goo", then there was the little glance

I gave him at the very end. This 'ad' came second in the 'Best Commercial of the Year' awards, pipped by the brilliant *Hamlet Cigars* campaign, and turned up on a continuous loop in the commercials section in the *Museum of the Moving Image* (*MOMI*). Several times during the casting sessions that followed I was asked if I could do 'that look' for them.

After five more commercials including one for *Rowntrees Texan* bar, which saw me doing a 'Ho-de-ho' in a large barn almost continuously for two days, I was cast by another up and coming film director, Ridley Scott. *McIntosh's Toffo* was the product, and it was set in a little Victorian sweet shop featuring a small, select choir, of which I was one, and a paper-boy. The young lad chosen for this role was called Nicholas Lyndhurst (yes, 'Rodney' in *Only Fools and Horses*) who, if memory serves, would be totally recognised were it to be shown today. He hasn't changed one jot.

'*Paxo Stuffing*' came next. This was a thirty second long commercial, but 'all one shot', which we achieved by the 42nd 'take'. I distinctly remember the rather weary voice behind the clapperboard saying: "*Paxo* stuffing - take forty two." CLAP. The scene was a small kitchen table with two people either side (in profile on the screen) with a freshly cooked turkey in the centre and a dish of *Paxo* stuffing in front of it. There had to be steam coming up from both these items, and that was the problem. Everything had to be perfect and held for a full 30 seconds. It took all day and the strain was immense. After two more 'ads' for *Webster's Children's Encyclopaedia*, and *Woolworth's Toiletries*, I landed the '*Crawfords Cheddars*' commercial in which I was heavily featured, and which is chronicled in 'The

Famous Replacement'.

The next 'ad' I made was for J. Walter Thompson and was one of the very popular *KitKat* series, in which I was an assistant in a shoe shop. My young lady customer is unsure what to buy, so the floor is littered with shoes and boxes. She finally decides and leaves, happy enough, but I am left to tidy up. Somewhat exasperated, I "have a break" and "have a *KitKat*." She then returns, having changed her mind and goes off with a different pair. We laugh together. There is a running narration (my voice) relaying the saga to a friend. I was asked to improvise the script, as I talked to a colleague, listing all the shoes I had shown her. So for a joke, I included a very camp line, lifted from a John Inman pantomime gag, describing his outrageous footwear - "peep-toe, sling-back, triple-decker wedges" - and they kept it in.

Two commercials later I was cast as a barmaid in a *Guinness* 'ad'. The morning went very well as I pulled two pints and handed them to two men, who proceeded to ask me what was on the lunch menu. I then had to recite a list of items very quickly in one breath. It was all great fun, but the camera was behind me so that it could get the reactions from the men. Then we had the lunch break.

After lunch the camera had been replaced behind the men and the whole 'take' would be a close-up of me pulling the pints and reciting the menu. Of course, I knew the list of items well since I had repeated them many times before lunch BUT (and this happens to a lot to actors) I couldn't get through the list without stumbling somewhere along the line. "Cut." says the director, at least half a dozen times. I begin to sweat and find it very hard to appear in control. An horrendous feeling; the more I tried, the worse it seemed to get. The director, Cliff Owen, a kind, understanding man, who had worked with me before in one 'ad' and two films, *Ooh, You Are Awful* and *The Bawdy Adventures of Tom Jones*, quietly suggested that we take a thirty minute break to relax and have a cup of tea. The producer, Terry Taylor, another extremely friendly man, who had directed me in the *KitKat* commercial, wandered over for a little 'calming' chat, at the end of which he said.

"Just think of all the overtime you're earning".

We 'set up' again and I'm delighted to report that we 'got it in one'.

There was another 'shot' we had to do towards the end of the day, which was a 'close up' of me pouring the *Guinness* into a tall pint glass. Sounds simple enough, doesn't it? I had to pick up the glass with my left hand and pour from a bottle with my right, but the glass had to be held at a specific angle in order to see the word '*Guinness*' glinting in exactly the right light. It took ages with many 'takes', but I felt less responsible for the errors this time. Ooo...the things actors have to do! That was nothing compared with what some actors go through on stage and screen. There are things you really can't fake even in the magical world of film. Boy, they earn their bucks.

The history of commercials is quite fascinating. I have appeared in about sixty 'ads' and have been prominently featured in 80% of them over the past 55 years, so I have learnt one or two things about them. Commercial advertising began on radio in America, when they realised that they had a lot of captive housewives at home with domestic appliances such as the newly introduced washing machine. This gave rise to competitive washing powder companies advertising their products during family drama programmes which became known as 'soap operas' then just 'soaps'. The first Commercial shown on television in the UK was for toothpaste, but the 'soap opera' reference caught on, and even now we call some costume dramas 'soaps'. *Downton Abbey* is frequently referred to as "a soap in posh frocks".

In the 'good old days', actors would be paid a fee for the day's work followed by repeat fees. The way this worked was that they would be paid a percentage of their daily rate for every ten showings in each of the 12 areas of the British Isles, and this could be a considerable amount. It would be assumed, therefore, that artistes heavily featured in commercials might be 'stinking' rich but spread those fees over a year, which could be lean in other work, and the affluence is quite short lived. Remember, I am only talking about 'unknown' actors - not stars! They come under a completely different fee category. I am trying in this book to present the picture of how the hundreds, if not thousands, of ordinary actors live and survive.

Nobody Does It Like Us
Another thing which puzzles people is...why are British actors used so much in foreign commercials? I have certainly done many 'ads' abroad, in Holland, Germany, Hungary, Spain and South Africa and my conclusion is that our training enables us to be quick. We get on with it. We don't need motivation and time to 'get into the part', which is the 'method' approach, and we seem to have the stamina for 'take' after 'take'.

There were ten more commercials after the *Guinness* debacle before an exceedingly uncomfortable experience in Madrid. It was very cold weather and the 'ad' required us to appear to be sweltering in skimpy summer clothes. After each 'take' we would rush to the wardrobe and grab our winter woollies. The crew were remarkably inconsiderate in this department, as were the caterers. A lovely actor, Roger Kemp, was with me and we became soul mates for the duration. We were asked to queue up at a van (standing in the cold) and after waiting for some time, were handed a dry, white baguette (no butter) containing a cold strip of thick, what I call 'pantomime bacon', and that was it. Not even a hot drink. Furious, freezing and frustrated, we shuffled off to find somewhere warm to sit, when we chanced to walk past the production trailer. Through the window we saw the producer, director, first assistant and the lighting/ camera man seated round a table, tucking into a steaming hot dinner. Then I remembered John Sharp's profound statement about how actors are treated!

My very next venture in the advertising world took me abroad again, to Holland this time. Margarine was the product but, in order to see winter 'breath', my character was placed in an enormous deep freeze used for storing animal carcases. Sub-zero temperatures for goodness knows how long. I do remember being asked if I could "hold on" just a few minutes longer. It was agony, and I guess it would not be allowed these days with all the 'elf and safety' that goes on. This was (according to my carefully kept records) my 28th commercial. My 29th was a real humdinger, so hold on to your hats.

'Accidents' Will Happen
The same director as the *Cheddars* commercial cast me in one for *Shell*. A middle-aged couple out for a spin in their open-top Morris Minor, travelling down a country lane, accidentally turn off the road and find

themselves inside a motor racing track. They pull up at the Pit Stop, where a bunch of mechanics crank up the car, change the wheels, wipe the man's glasses, give him a quick drink then lower the car and off they go. The husband signals to go left and sees racing cars speeding past his eyes going from left to right. The wife, quite calmly, says: "Hang on Jack, it's a one-way street." The whole thing looked, and was, very funny.

Let me take you back to the night before the filming (which was at Silverstone motor racing track). We two actors and the production team were put up in a five star hotel in Banbury, and dinner came with all the trimmings. The actor playing my husband clearly relished the opportunity to consume everything on the menu…remember? He began with two beers and nibbles before we were even seated, then a rich pâté starter with a second helping of toast, a large rare steak with mountains of veg. He was on the red wine by now, with a sticky pudding and custard followed by the cheeseboard with a port, and coffee and brandy to round it off. I promise you, it's true. I was there, looking on.

Very early morning calls are the norm in filming and we all felt a bit fragile at the start of the day. My actor friend looked wretched. He had clearly had a terrible night and was distinctly hung-over. We were driven over to the location and in contrast to the night before, he was very quiet. The Morris Minor acquired for the filming was very old, the perfect period for the part, but it had not been maintained anywhere near decently and, frankly, was a disgrace. The gears got stuck and were extremely difficult to shift. The actor had to get out of the car at the end of every sequence to let a mechanic take it back to the starting point. My 'husband' was to drive the car past a crowd of cheering fans in the stand, before pulling into the Pit Stop, and 200 extras had been bussed up from London. He had already told me that, although he kept his licence going, his wife did all the driving. Hmm?

After many rehearsals, which took most of the morning, the director decided to have a few of the crowd milling about in front of the stand. He liked the look of this, because it made our car seem all the more unexpected and out of place. Then he decided that one 'extra' should run across the road as our car approached, and a woman was either chosen or volunteered to do this, which looked fine for a couple of 'takes'.

As in all exterior filming, a lot depends on the weather in order to get continuity of sunshine or rain or cloud formation, and such was the case this day. Sunlight was the problem as it disappeared from time to time, and as we were setting up for the third 'take' I heard the director's voice on the crewman's earphones:

"We'll be losing the sun very soon; go, go, GO!"

Then the cue was repeated for us. "Go, go, GO!" which threw the actor into a slight panic and he set off at a slightly higher speed than before.

The next 'cue' was for the woman to start running across the road, but it came a fraction too late and my vision of her was that of a rabbit caught in the headlights. She stopped, as if frozen, in front of the car, and there was no way of avoiding her, even with the best driver in the world and a car with an immaculate braking system. The woman was hit and thrown right over the car, landing on the hard ground behind. The actor leapt from the car and stood banging his fist on the bonnet:

"It wasn't my fault," he repeated over and over again.

After a terrible stillness, things gradually began to happen. Once an ambulance had been summoned, people went to the woman's aid and did what they could to comfort her before it arrived. The atmosphere was dreadfully tense. Her injuries, it transpired, were all external breakages and have left her physically impaired.

The 'driver' and I were taken to a temporary refuge and sat for an hour alongside the director, but barely a word was spoken. I felt that the wisest thing for me was to do and say nothing. When things were more settled, and it was clear they wanted to try and finish the commercial that day, we were asked if we felt okay enough to carry on. We both agreed to, and it was 'in the can' as they say before the light was lost. The woman was left with a distinct limp, and after a long drawn-out legal procedure, where we actors were summoned to give evidence, I'm pleased to say it was settled out-of-court, and she received considerable compensation. This *Shell* commercial also appeared on a continuous loop at *The Museum of the Moving Image*, so I appeared on two of the nine screen displays.

Doubling Up

After popping over to Ireland for a *Brennans* bread commercial, I landed the strangest of jobs. *Complan* was the product; a health drink for the elderly (I think) and my scene lasted just ten seconds, one third of the whole 'ad'. Seated at a table, my character seemed to wilt as if the air was being let out of a balloon. Then she flopped down like a rag doll and disappeared under the table. This action was then reversed and I was inflated again and appeared back at the table with a broad smile on my face and a mug on *Complan* in my hand.

In order to achieve the 'rag doll' effect, they had to make an inflatable rubber model of my body which would be filled with air, then emptied like a pricked balloon, only to be pumped up again to the sitting position. They started off by making a plaster cast of my top half which involved sitting absolutely still for at least half an hour while they covered me all over with white stuff, with two straws up my nose to breath through. This lowered my temperature some-what as the plaster needed to harden. Then they removed it in two sections, front and back, then stuck it together and poured the rubber into it and left it to set. Something like that, anyway. The result was a remarkable likeness which, when made-up and dressed, produced a slightly spooky effect. Lining me up to match the position of the model so that you couldn't see the join, took forever, and meant absolute stillness yet again.

Then disaster struck. *Complan* was made in the same factory as a baby product which had recently caused illness and panic, so all their products had to be withdrawn, and my commercial was shelved. Well, that was that, I thought, all that energy and discom-fort for just a day's fee. Then, a year later, it was re-issued and transmitted, and I made enough in repeats to pay for a new kitchen!

*****

Note to self: Believe it only when you see it.

*****

That's Me All Over
Ten commercials later - including *Twiglets*, *Scottish Widows*, *Pot Noodle* and *Campbell's Soup* came the *BT* poster campaign. This was interesting because of the initial casting session. I was in the room for less than two minutes, during which time the photographer, Malcolm Venville lined me up and suggested some facial attitudes. He then took exactly seven photographs of me, said: "thank you very much" and I left. There were about 50 actresses being seen that day, so I believed I had very little chance of being chosen. But I *was* chosen and, once again, this proved to be a very lucrative job.

When I arrived for the photo shoot, Malcolm had mounted six of the pictures he had taken of me onto a board, so all I had to do was a highly polished version of what I had created at the audition. This was exactly how the 'ad' would appear on the London Underground trains and stations. This meant that my creative work had been done at the audition and the job itself was merely to repeat those expressions...for several hours.

The idea was to catch the eye of young people (mostly Americans) and persuade them to 'phone home'. The character was clearly a loving mother, highly animated - smiling, laughing, tearful, surprised etc, and was based on the Norman Rockwell painting of American characters on the telephone entitled *The Gossips: 1948*.

Sometimes my face appeared several feet high on placards and billboards, and chums would recognise me, although the general public were completely oblivious, even when I sat directly underneath it on a tube train. Ahhh...

Money Talks

One of the most common phrases I hear from non-showbiz people is:

"You got paid all that for one day's work?"

Well let me tell you, that could be £1,000 in total, including the day's fee, say £300, and a buyout of £700 (minus agent's commission, of course). The 'ad' could then be shown for a year with NO repeat fees. It still sounds a lot to you? Think of it this way, that will be a minute part of the total budget for the whole commercial, and it could also be the only money you will earn in weeks, or more likely, months.

Some people, outside the business, have asked me how much I earn as an actress. I suppose they hear about the astronomical fees earned by the 'stars', and their curiosity knows no bounds. So: for the record - in 1993, the year of the *BT* poster campaign, I earned £23,656...and eleven pence. That was by far the highest amount I have ever earned in one year.

Cape Town Caprice

In 1994 I landed a job which would take me out to Cape Town to make a commercial for a Swiss Insurance company with an Austrian film crew and a fellow British actor. You may be wondering why they would take the extra step of coming to London to find a middle-aged couple? As I have already explained ...we're quick and tireless. I checked with *Equity* that it was now permitted to work in South Africa, and they gave the go-ahead and their blessing.

Why Cape Town? Sun! It was January, and the setting for the story was a house and garden being prepared by a couple before going off on holiday. Beautiful weather was required and South Africa could guarantee it. A local crew was brought in to augment the Austrian one, and we were driven out to a strip of wasteland, passing many ghettos on the way. This was my first sight of any evidence of apartheid, although it was technically over. My make-up girl, Sarah, was from England, but had lived in Cape Town since early childhood when her parents emigrated from Yorkshire. She became my source of information when I made enquiries about the current situation and her story was fascinating. Before Nelson Mandela's release, and the acceleration of events, she claimed to know nothing of the outside world's view of South Africa. She and her family were completely happy with their idyllic lifestyle - black servants etc., because they were told that every-body was happy living separately. Even on her few visits to England to connect with relatives, she had ignored any sound or sight of disapproval. In fact, she couldn't honestly recollect there being any, but things were now very different and she had clearly 'seen the light'.

The one hilarious feature of playing the wife in this commercial was that, as I was mowing the lawn, the character I was playing pressed the wrong lever and the machine took off at great speed, propelling her across the garden horizontally, four feet in the air. This meant having to be strapped into a body brace, then covered in the costume and hooked up to a wire. Still holding the handles of the lawnmower, I appeared to be flying. I had asked Sarah if she could take a series of photographs of me from climbing into the brace to being airborne. They told the story brilliantly, and I have the final picture framed on my wall at home.

During the filming I was aware of a black security guard on duty just looking on, intrigued by the proceedings. At a tea break I sidled over to him to have a word. He was slight of build, quite short and a little nervous at my approach. I respected that, and kept some space between us. His story was a grim one of overcrowding and poverty, but he was so grateful for this job which had raised the living standards for his family. When I asked him what was the best thing about the new changes, he simply said:

"Being able to talk to you."

He added that he felt he was being watched, even now as we talked, so I wished him all the best and went back to work. I had misgivings about his future prospects and, I'm afraid, pangs of guilt as I tucked into the speciality crayfish at the harbour-side restaurant that evening.

My hotel room offered the most spectacular view of Table Mountain, and as the last day was work-free before the evening flight back to London, I decided to take myself off to the funicular railway and see it close up. What a thrilling view this place affords. Even Robben Island defies its reputation as a prison and looks indecently romantic, nestling in the sparkling ocean. I took the gentle Alpine trail through bushes and sweet smelling flowers, with chipmunks and brightly coloured birds for company. Boy, am I getting poetical, or what?

Back in town I was spotted by one of the crew who would later be taking me to the airport. He had enough time for a drive along the wonderful sunset coast past a range of weirdly shaped mountains, then on to the place where you can stand and see two great oceans actually meet. The Indian and Atlantic appear to splash into each other at the Cape of Good Hope. Now, that IS a phenomenon.

*****

Note to self: Always accept a sightseeing opportunity.

*****

Interlude
Because I had the most wonderful run of commercials, it might appear that I was in constant work and earning astronomical sums of money. Well, I have already confessed to my highest annual earnings and remember that each commercial takes only one or two days, at the most to make. Altogether I have been up for 333 commercials in 46 years and in the first twenty-three years I got 47 of them; in the next twenty-three years I only got 13. As I got older and graduated from the 'mumsy' roles to the 'grannies', the competition increased and the opportunities declined.

Ad with a Difference
After a further six commercials I did a 'promotion' for *Who Wants to be a Millionaire?* This is regarded as a trailer for a new television show and pays a modest fee for the day's work, and that's it...NO repeats. During the filming, Chris Tarrant came over several times to chat with the actor playing the 'quizmaster', but completely ignored me, playing 'the contestant'. Perhaps he thought I really was one.

Cats! Don't You Love 'em?
Shortly after this I was sent off to Hungary. There was a big campaign going on to promote a certain pet food and I was cast as a sweet old lady with a special cat

that could play the piano!! If you know anything about the film business, you will be aware that you cannot train cats to do anything. No-thing. The crew actually tied lengths of cotton to the cat's legs, plonked it on the keyboard and tried to work it like a marionette!! Catastrophe!!! It was never going to work...I mean, can you imagine?

The temperature in Budapest was over 100 degrees, and I was being followed everywhere by a minion with an electric fan. I took my knickers off which helped a bit, but PHEW! We spent hours on this bloody scene trying to get anything from the cat...I wanted to die. I never discovered what the end result was and I didn't want to know.

A young English actor, staying in my hotel, was also working on this commercial, but on a different day. When I met up with him he looked as shattered as I felt. I told him my storyline and added:

"They got me a cat that couldn't play the piano."

Then he explained that in his storyline he had to walk his dog by a lake, then accidentally fall in till he was out of his depth. The dog was then supposed to jump into the water and rescue his master, except:

"They got ME a dog that couldn't swim!!"

The last commercial I made, in 2013, also involved a cat 'Gary's cat' in fact, and for the briefest of appearances in this *Peugeot* 'ad', I was recognised, not just by friends, but local shop keepers, and even my doctor's receptionist.

Scene 24

Shakespeare In The Commonwealth

Toronto, 1994

After one of our demonstrations at the Globe site, Patrick was interviewed for a Canadian radio station. He answered a few questions about his methods of working with cue scripts and no rehearsals etc, one of many run-of-the-mill interviews, which fades quickly and is soon forgotten. Some weeks later Don Shipley, a Canadian producer in charge of gathering unusual companies for the *Du Maurier World Theatre Festival*, was driving home from Toronto to Stratford, Ontario, when he happened to hear Patrick's interview on his car radio. This guy is insane, he thought. He's just what I'm looking for.

Michael Bouchier sat on our sofa, one of the many who've come with outrageous offers. He had been sent by Don Shipley to make a proposal to us. The idea being that Patrick and I would go over to Toronto and work with their actors; train them up, and put on two performances of *As You Like It* on consecutive nights. They already had an actor and actress lined up for 'Rosalind' and 'Orlando', but the rest would be cast by us after training sessions and auditions, and for the only time in the *OSC*'s history, we were obliged to keep the same cast for the second performance. This proved to be a learning curve as we were able to observe what changes, if any, the actors might make in order to appear spontaneous second time round.

Apart from all expenses and a Best Western Hotel (lovely) they paid for our wonderful *OSC* prompt desk to be flown over. This had been made for us, by the actor Granville Saxton, for our first trip to Germany. I must say I felt quite tearful when I saw the *OSC* metal trunk sitting in the prop room back stage; what a journey. It was a beautiful piece of furniture, rather like an old fashioned desk with a sloping lid for the prompt book and a flat ledge at the top for the bell, which could be rung to start and end the proceedings. He added other delightful features such as little pegs to hang props and other adornments. A feast for the eyes, as well as being practical.

Those actors who took to our method during training sessions were brilliant, and turned out to be extremely inventive, using just the text and our guidelines for inspiration. For example, when the actor playing 'Jaques' began his famous *Seven Ages of Man* speech, he indicated to the Foresters that he was about to launch into it with:

"All the world's a stage", and they, recognising an upcoming purple passage, all moved downstage sitting in a row to listen to 'today's sermon'. The audience loved it, because it looked like the Foresters were thinking: "Okay, lads, it's the big boring afternoon lecture again." 'Jaques' held the pause long enough to show his slight irritation, then continued with:

"And all the men and women merely players."

The next day we would be stopped in the street time and again. "Just loved the show", "Great ideas",

"Wonderful fun", "Best Shakespeare I've ever seen". Clearly, this could work anywhere in the world, so long as you have bloody good actors and bags of courage and commitment.

Sydney, January, 1996

Patrick was invited to deliver a lecture at a Shakespeare conference on the Bear Gardens stage, before the Globe was built, and among the academics present was Professor Penny Gay of the English Department at the University of Sydney who, after-wards, grabbed Patrick and, raving about his insights into cue script acting, said:

"Would you come to Sydney next year and address my Shakespeare Conference?"

To which Patrick replied:

"I've been waiting all my life for someone to say that."

In order to make the trip financially viable she collaborated with Diana Denley of the Sydney Globe Centre who organised workshops for us to run at *The Actor's Centre* there. She set up training sessions with local professional actors with a view to putting on three performances, of *A Midsummer Night's Dream* at the Fig Tree Theatre, with a change of cast for each performance, and working only from cue scripts and with no rehearsal of the play. Madness!

Diana Denley had presented some Shakespeare scenes at The Globe in London, using Australian actors based in the UK. Among them was Greta Scacchi, renowned for her many leading film roles, who was intrigued by our methods and said she'd like to appear in a cue script production. I couldn't believe it. Greta turned out to be incredibly good at memoris-ing lines and private preparation, no doubt due to her experience in the film industry.

We flew out to Sydney in mid-January 1996, and were kitted out with an apartment at Potts Point, Woolloomooloo, where we stayed for six weeks. There were some very talented and enthusiastic actors in the Sydney area and, encouraged by Greta, we gathered a goodly number at the training sessions. As happens all over the world, there were more women than men, but the play is probably Shakespeare's best for accommodating this imbalance, although we had to give Theseus and Oberon three performances each. Otherwise all went well, until Greta was suddenly called back to England to complete some 'pick up' scenes in Emma, which were filmed at Syon House in Chiswick, a stone's throw from where we live.

When Greta was first asked which part she would like to play in *The Dream*, she said:

"Well, I suppose I should play 'Titania', but I've always wanted to have a shot at 'Helena'."

"Well," said Patrick. "Why don't you play 'Helena' in the first performance and 'Titania' in the second? Then you could go back to Helena again for the third."

No stranger to hard work, Greta agreed. But then to be whisked away to London! In the comfort of the First Class cabin, however, she was able to knuckle down to some line learning. She had taken with her the cue script text as a scroll (all the pages stuck together lengthways, then rolled up round two bits of wood) and this caught the eye of a fellow passenger, one Warren Mitchell...('Alf Garnet' in *Till Death Us Do Part*).

"'Ere, what's that you're doing?" he said.

Greta showed him the 'roll' and explained the reason she was studying it so carefully.

"Gor, blimey," he said. "I could never do that, too much like 'ard work."

And went back to sleep.

Back in Sydney we had set up 'verse nursing' sessions, as the multi-cast actors set about learning several parts. Let me tell you that when you've 'verse-nursed' three 'First Fairies' with their "Over hill, over dale"...and so on...you want to scream, but it was important for me to hear each actor privately so that I could be aware of any 'danger' areas for possible prompts. The Folio spelling is a bit strange at first with lots of extra 'Es', as in 'Pucke' for example. Once at a college on Long Island, a young lad came in with his 'Oberon' speech and we heard:

"My gentle puke come hither."

I don't deny that there have been some heart-stopping moments (especially for me as the prompter) when an actor consistently 'dries', and it happened in the third performance at The Fig Tree. 'Lysander' just lost it in the quarrel scene, and I found myself prompting him on almost every line. Experienced actors have a subtle way of taking a prompt, but in this case the actor kept saying "line" loudly, in a strong Australian accent, and there was nothing I could do except "*Carry on Regardless!*" - remember? We have now developed a guideline for the actors who suddenly 'dry'. Stay in character and say: "Prythee" and I will come straight in with the missing word; this has worked tremendously well. Tactfully asking an audience member how many prompts they thought there had been, they said: "About a dozen," but it hadn't spoilt anything as they thought it was all wonderful and hilariously funny. Actually, there were over 50 for that one actor alone, but because the audience heard the prompter, it was as if it was all part of the play.

Never knowing what the actors might come up with I, sitting at the prompt desk, would often be helpless with laughter at an imaginative piece of business. Susie Lindeman, as 'Hermia', unpacking her little bag before 'resting' in the woods with 'Lysander', brought out a bijou pillow with 'Hermia' sewn onto it, followed by a toilet roll, which she placed carefully by the pillow, before settling down to sleep. Then in the four lovers' quarrel scene, I was treated to the spectacle of the diminutive Susie chasing the much taller Greta up and down the aisles and round the auditorium, perfectly timing their lines to link up again with the lads.

On our last day, when we fully expected to receive the sum of money we had settled for, there was something of a hiatus. Obviously they had not made enough from the box office to cover our fee and agreed expenses, so a lower sum was offered. Patrick pointed out that this mis-budgeting was not our fault, and said:

"Christine and I will now leave the room, and when we come back we will expect an offer of payment that is fair."

When we returned they offered us the exact amount that had been originally agreed upon, and we've used this technique successfully ever since.

*****

Note to self: The word 'fair' works wonders.

*****

During our six weeks we managed to see some of New South Wales, thanks to Greta and her family's hospitality. This included a trip into the Blue Mountains, a visit to the delightful Manley with its two magnificent beaches, a sumptuous fish dinner at the famous Watson's Bay seafood restaurant, watching the firework display in Darling Harbour and, my favourite, Sunday lunch at an exclusive Club on Bondi Beach. We took our 'swimmies' and I ventured into the sea. Big mistake. Did you ever see the size of those waves?

"Did you get 'dumped'?" asked Greta as she saw me flopped out on the sand, pale and exhausted. I certainly did. This is when a wave drags you under and you simply have to go with the flow and hope to wash up on dry land. A really scary moment...how different from the dear old seaside holiday as a three year old in Bridlington. I shall have to re-think my beach visits in future.

Toronto revisited, March, 1996

What a year! Back home from Sydney on March 2nd. Quick catch up with the *OSC* gang in London, then off again to Canada on the 28th to work once more with the troupe at the *Du Maurier Festival*. This time it was to be *The Taming of the Shrew* for three performances, changing the whole cast round each night, except 'Petruchio' and 'Kate'. These two roles had already been cast by the management, in their wisdom, but the rest was up to us. Again, they flew our desk out, and many of the same *As You* actors turned up for another 'fix'. Using the same techniques, it was remarkable how different the three performances were. Even the two leads chose different ways to play their parts, and the variety from the others, one could only describe as astonishing.

For example, on the first night David Ferry played

'Christopher Sly' as a tramp, panhandling outside the theatre before the show, and pushing a loaded shopping trolley up the aisle, onto the stage and into the first scene. The second night he played 'Gremio', the foolish suitor...and thereby hangs a tale. We always allow our actors to dress themselves, only insisting that the chosen costume and props should be based on the text. We had been given access to the wardrobe department of the Shakespeare theatre at Stratford (Ontario) and we were walking through on the day the actors were making their costume choices. Suddenly, we saw Dave preparing his 'Gremio', wearing a woman's skirt and jacket and caught him in the act of choosing a handbag to hang over his arm. He looked himself up and down in the mirror (as women do) and we politely enquired how he saw the role.

"I see him as a cross-dresser," he said.

We couldn't wait to see his performance, since we knew him to be a wonderful actor and, once again, David Ferry did not disappoint. In fact, he was sensational. His 'Gremio' was indeed a cross-dresser, and just before he got to the speech, which gave him the 'clue', he opened his handbag, got out a bottle of nail varnish, and was applying it as he said the line:

"Their love is not so great, Hortensio, but we may blow our nails together," then he blew on his freshly painted ones, to the delight of the audience. Whether Shakespeare saw 'Gremio' as a cross-dresser is a matter for everlasting speculation, but it worked like a dream. In the third performance, Ferry played the manservant 'Grumio' exactly as Chico Marx might have done, Italian accent and all. Heaven knows how he learnt it all in the time given, but all three characters were just hilarious and perfectly believable.

One sensational thing happened during the third

performance, which almost beggars belief. Mark Burgess, playing 'Christopher Sly' had an inspiration from the text and found the courage to carry it out. We insisted that 'Sly' be on the stage all the way through the play, as an observer of 'the play within the play', because he is never given an 'exit'. In the interval, Mark put wheels in motion to set up his 'gag'.

Shortly after the interval there was a happy discussion scene between the young suitors and 'Bianca' during which there was a commotion in the audience. I looked out to see a genuine Toronto pizza delivery boy with a large tray strapped round his neck, walking up the centre aisle, then up the steps and on to the stage. Mark, as 'Sly', beckoned him over, took 20 bucks from his pocket, took the pizza and dismissed the poor lad, his tortured embarrassment turning to a delighted smile on realising that he could 'keep the change'.

Mark then shared the sections of pizza round among the cast, including me at the prompt desk, and we all relaxed, munching away and licking our lips to everyone's delight. Once it had dawned on the audience (and us, for that matter) that 'The Pedant' had been referred to, several times in advance of his arrival, as: "The man from Pisa is coming", the laughter grew and grew and lasted all of five minutes.

The audience, I should explain, consisted of many Americans who had booked in to see all three shows since they were avid fans of (our 'Petruchio') Geraint Wyn Davies, star of the cult television series *Forever Knight*. Even some of the local people were booking in again after the first show. Their comments were largely based on how amazingly different each performance was, and they were able to appreciate the versatility of each actor. Most gratifying, I must say.

Later, Mark told us that the inspiration came purely from that repeated Pisa reference, but the authenticity of the whole gag depended on him being able to ring the local pizzeria during the interval. This was his only opportunity in a one-off performance... and someone else was on the phone right up to the Act Two beginner's call, so he only just made it. Oh, I loved him for his bravery and wit. It was one of the most magical moments in the *OSC*'s history, but the lovely thing is that it came out of the text and was secretly initiated by an actor. Thank you, David Ferry and Mark Burgess, for those two wonderful anecdotes.

As a present to ourselves, once the euphoria had died down, we took a train to Quebec City and booked in to the Fairmont Le Chateau Frontenac. This magnificent building, situated inside the walls of Old Quebec, dominates the landscape for miles around. Built as an ideal stopover for rail passengers in the late 19th century, but looking like a grand palace, it is at the peak of a very steep hill with a sheer drop down to the spectacular St Lawrence river. Oh, the French know how to do it. Memories like these stay with you forever.

*****

Note to self: Holidays are fine, but when working in a country, with the local people, you really get to know it.

*****

Scene 25

Monk-y business

On my last visit to Australia I realised that it would probably be the only opportunity I might have to investigate the death of Martin Redpath. A fellow student who had befriended me from our first term at *RADA*, and whose house I had shared in South London, Martin had emigrated to Australia quite early in his career. Although he subsequently visited England several times, he had died near Canberra a few years before my visit in 1996. Patrick and I hired a car and drove there to see if we could track down the place where he had died and the people who had taken care of him during his terminal illness.

Martin had always had a strong faith and, at some point in his Australian life, became a monk. He had joined a community in Queanbeyan on the outskirts of Canberra. He always referred to it as Queen Bee, and had talked of a man called Michael, and the Community of St Michaels. Martin was gay, and had contracted 'The Big A' (his phrase) while staying in Chang Mai, Thailand, and that was really all I knew.

One of my childhood heroes was Robin Hood. I remembered having a picture of an aging Robin, close to death, wearing a long white shroud, lying on a simple bed in an empty room, with a shaft of sunlight shining down through a gothic window onto his bed.

This vivid image is how I imagined Martin at his life's end, about to enter the eternal kingdom.

Driving round Canberra is a bit of a nightmare. The roads are very deceptive; you think you are driving in a straight line, but they are all very slightly curved, and you are actually circumnavigating the City.

"We're just going round in circles," I screeched, as my reliable map-reading skills, appeared to be failing. So we took in a few sites before finally coming across the exit for Queanbeyan.

We tracked down the district housing the church of St Michael where the priest, to our delight, had known Martin very well and told us of the whereabouts of the community we were seeking. In a cosy, suburban street with neat semi-detached houses and colourful front gardens, we found the house we were looking for. But, where were the shady cloisters...where the Gothic windows? A knock on the door produced the appearance of a little old lady, then a little old man, followed by another little old lady. When I explained that I was a great friend of Martin, they immediately welcomed us into the house and sent for 'Brother Michael'. Looking out of the front window, I could see a man emerge from a house opposite at some speed, and soon I was in the presence of the full group that made up 'the community', and the people who nursed Martin for many weeks before his death.

Their description of Martin's demise soon destroyed any 'Robin Hood' image I might have had. Clearly, he was part of their 'community' and had been cared for with love and loyalty, but he had not been an easy patient, making unreasonable demands on these sweet aging people, requesting certain specific pieces of music to be played over and over again. There was obviously some sublime Christian choral work he wanted to die to, but who knew when that would come about? It probably drove them all crazy, but they would never admit to that.

I felt strangely sad as I left this homely group of pensioners, and wondered how on earth the same Martin who had introduced me to his middle class world, his beautiful family home in Hatfield, who drove me round London in his little Morris Minor and whose house I shared in SE21, could be the same person who had died from AIDS in the upper room of a small suburban semi in 'Queenbee', New South Wales.

*****

Note to self: never form too strong an image in advance; reality can shatter your dream.

*****

Interlude

Sharing Martin's house with us, all those years ago in London, were two Australian actors appearing in Nöel Coward's *Sail Away* at the Savoy Theatre. I answered the phone one day to a man with a strangely familiar voice (could it be Coward himself?) saying: "Can I speak to Johnny, please?" and while we were waiting for Johnny to come to the phone, he asked me which part of London we were in.

"Tulse Hill," I said.

Then he confirmed his identity with one of his famous, quick-witted remarks.

"Tulse Hill?" he said. "Oh yes, I passed through there once on my way to Paris."

Scene 26

My Guernsey Roots

Is There Anybody There?

Patrick and I have spent many Christmases abroad. India, Egypt, Spain, Morocco, Germany, New York, New Zealand, Italy, Prague...and once on a Lesbian commune in the Red Woods of northern California. (Although Patrick was allowed in, for some reason Santa wasn't, so Mrs Claus delivered the presents!)

In 2009 I expressed a desire to visit Guernsey, so we made it our Christmas trip. My reason for choosing the Channel Islands was a hankering to link up with the land of my grandfather's birth. Henry Louis Brouard, my mother's father, was born in St Peter Port, but as a young man work was hard to find, so he ventured forth to England...Northampton, in fact, where he met Clara Walden. They married in August 1903, and my mother was born on the 20th of January, 1904. Hmm? They moved to Leicester to raise their family, where Henry became the local blacksmith, and I clearly remember his workplace where he made coach springs, with its roaring furnace and red hot steel which he hammered and shaped...and swore a good deal at the same time. Well, I had to have inherited that from somewhere.

We booked a room at the Imperial Hotel for the

Christmas period, so I could now begin a little research into the Brouard family tree. My mother had given me very little information, only that she had an aunt Adele (the one who married Ira Ozanne) a handsome woman who I believed to be childless, and who I had met once for tea at the Strand Palace Hotel. The only other relation I knew of was Mum's cousin, Lewis, who, in about 1953, had made a brief visit to our house in Leicester and had his picture taken with me in the back garden.

I visited the National Archives at Kew and found the 1911 census, which revealed some new details. My great grandparents, Caroline and Nicholas, had five children; my grandfather, Louis, two elder sisters, Alice and Marie…a younger one, Adele, then a younger brother, Nicholas. These people had all long since died, and I doubted if there was any remaining family in Guernsey, but since I had never been there it was worth one last effort to do a check.

I wrote a letter to the Island's most popular newspaper, asking if they would be kind enough to print it. In it I simply mentioned my grandfather with the family name, and said that the only other person I remembered was a man called Lewis Brouard, who would have been about 25 in the early 1950s. On the same evening the letter was printed I answered the telephone and a woman's voice said:

"I've just read your letter in the paper. My name is Margaret, and Lewis Brouard was my father."

I was amazed and delighted…goose bumps. I was actually talking to a blood relation I never knew existed until that moment. It transpired that Grandad's younger brother, Nicholas, was the father of Lewis, which meant that Margaret and I were second cousins.

It was an extraordinary feeling. My persistence in tracking down anyone who could develop my family story had paid off, and Margaret was, herself, almost in tears. We exchanged a few details of what we knew of the family background and arranged to meet up on the island at Christmas. When the meeting finally took place, we recognised in each other some physical likenesses, and we both had the same laugh. No, not our imagination. Patrick and Clive, her husband, and Claire, their daughter confirmed it. We laughed alike...and a lot.

We each brought with us a collection of photographs we had been hoarding for many years, and we both had the same large picture of our great aunt Adele, who I had thought was childless, but Margaret had some news that would change that belief. Then she produced a snapshot of her father with 'another' woman but had no idea who it was. She had found it in her mother's belongings. Was it an earlier (or secret) girlfriend? Another 'wife'? A love child? I looked at it, solemnly, and handed it back.

"That's me!" I said.

Her jaw dropped, then we both shrieked with laughter. It was the one taken by my mother in our back garden when he came to Leicester almost 60 years before.

Sad Tidings

The two further pieces of information Margaret supplied were both surprising and sad. She told me that Aunt Adele and her husband, Ira Ozanne had a daughter. I was excited to think there was another cousin.

"But she was adopted," said Margaret.

"So no blood relation there, then," I said.

"Well there is, actually," she said. "I meant that they gave her up for adoption."

The plot suddenly thickened. They named this girl Irene, and she went on to have her own illegitimate daughter called Anne who now lived in Tunbridge Wells. Anne, like me, had also searched for possible relations and had tracked Margaret down as I had, in Guernsey.

Anne, Margaret and I were second cousins, and on one wonderful occasion the three of us met up in London for a delightful lunch exchanging multiple stories of our various backgrounds. Sadly, this was to be our only meeting together. Margaret, when I first met her, had been stricken with cancer and gone through all the painful follow-up treatments. I went to Guernsey once more in 2010, and that was to be our last meeting. Although there were periods of remission, the inevitable came the following year and she died in 2011.

One of the saddest things she told me was that she'd had a younger brother, Peter Brouard who, while serving on H.M.S. 'Ardent' was killed in action on the 21st of May, 1982 on a rescue mission towards the end of the Falklands Conflict in the South Atlantic, aged 31. His body was never recovered. His only child, Mark, was born four months later.

5th Intermission

The 'Desperate' Replacements

Do you know the cartoon which shows a man and his dog? The man is saying: "Sit," and the dog is saying: "Why, is it bad news?"

Replacement No.12: (aged 46)

One day, when Patrick was away working in America, I received a telephone call from Julia Smith, a *BBC* television Producer, later to be the creator of *EastEnders*. She had employed Patrick to direct several episodes of the *BBC* series *Angels*.

"Are you sitting down?" she said.

A sudden fear gripped me. Had something happened to Patrick and she had been chosen to tell me the bad news?

"Er...yes," I said, grabbing the nearest kitchen chair.

It was clear from her next few words that she wasn't about to deliver the body blow I had dreaded, but to present me with a tricky situation, just the same. It appeared that one of the actresses in the current episode of *Angels*, now quite late on in rehearsal, had been dismissed (for reasons I never discovered) and could I take over the part of 'Staff Nurse Brindle'? In other words, get to the studio as soon as possible.

"But I've already played the part of 'Sister Muncey', quite recently," I said, knowing it was a *BBC* stipulation NOT to employ an actor in a different role in the same show within two years.

"Oh, that's alright," she said. "Nobody'll notice."

And she was quite right...nobody did. I believe the actress I replaced may have been Irish, so I may even have attempted her accent, just to give some variety to my performance but some time later, 'Sister Muncey' returned to the series, and I reappeared in the 'senior' role, but again...nobody noticed.

Replacement No.13: (aged 50)
In November, 1986 I went up for a French commercial to be made in Malaga. It was for a game very similar to *Scrabble*. I wore a dark green plaid suit and, at the time I had a slightly protruding front tooth (which I later had straightened). Then, acting out the scene, I remember being very animated, with lots of excitable facial expressions, as I 'won' the game. The sort of thing I do standing on my head (now that really would get a laugh) but, I heard nothing.

Three weeks later, just before Christmas, I was singing with my lovely Actors' Choir at St Paul's, Covent Garden, and at the end of the service I made my way home, only to find my answer machine flashing like the Aurora Borealis. This was very unusual, so I sat down with pen and paper to note each call. The first was from a film company asking if I could get on a plane to Malaga tomorrow morning at 9am. The second was my agent telling me that they had made a mistake in the casting and wanted ME for the board game 'ad'. There were two more calls regarding costume and make up, and yet another from my agent…"it's really urgent." How to exist without a mobile!

I responded as quickly as I could, putting some minds at rest by agreeing to be on the plane to Malaga the next day. The costume designer wanted to be sure I was who she thought I was, by describing my audition costume, and asking if I had a slightly protruding front tooth. It appears that, at the casting session, they had videoed us in a different order to the list of names on the call sheet. They always thought they had chosen me, but the name attached to my picture was that of another actress who had subsequently been flown out to Spain, only to be greeted with the awful news that she was not who they expected to see, and after an over-night stay, would be flown back to London. We actually crossed in the air and on landing I was whisked off to the location and was filming within an hour of my arrival. This debacle was soon doing the rounds of the casting directors, and ever since that day I have noticed that we often hold our written name up during 'the Ident', or the name is clearly shown on the screen below our picture.

Replacement No.14: (aged 63)
In the year 2000 I was asked by an *OSC* chum, who was directing an all-female production of *Richard III*, if I would play 'Queen Margaret'. I knew the part was wonderful, although I would not be anyone's first choice, not even my own, so I turned it down. He approached me again, explaining that I would be a great asset to the company with my experience, especially of Shakespeare, but once again I turned it down. I just didn't want to be in it.

By this time, of course, he had to look elsewhere to find someone willing to take it on, and did, BUT after a short rehearsal period, she left the production. Why was it proving so hard to cast this great part? Probably because it was coupled with 'Lord Stanley' with quick costume changes involved, and that the play was being performed from cue scripts. Not all the actors were trained for this, and although they were rehearsing without the full script in their hands, there would be a prompter on stage throughout the performance. Enough to terrify any actor unfamiliar with the *OSC* training.

Well, I was finally dragged, kicking and screaming into this production, which, for me, was fairly nightmarish from beginning to end. We played it for a week in a barn of a church in north London, with appalling acoustics and, without doubt, it received one of the worst reviews for a play I have ever read. One critic, adversely described, not only the production, but all the off stage sound effects, most of which were not part of the show, and the fact that the doors were locked at the interval so there was no escape. The review was appalling and hilarious at the same time but happily, neither I, nor my two 'characters' were mentioned. When rumours of "moving to another venue" hit my ears, thoughts of "over my dead body" sprang rapidly to mind.

Scene 27

Shakespeare In Jordan

Being in the Right Place

People often ask: "How on earth did you get to do that? You lucky thing."

Well, I can assure you that most jobs are months, if not years, in the making, as was the case with our three visits to Jordan with *OSC*. During our time of public demonstrations in London, one of our actors, Philip Bird, drew our attention to the possibility of playing in the Great Hall at Hampton Court where Shakespeare and his fellow actors had performed. Our enthusiasm was rewarded with permission to perform for a select invited audience, for one night only.

The time allotted was not enough for a full-length play, so Patrick adapted parts of 'the History plays' and called it *Margaret of Anjou*. It was terrific, and in the audience was a man who was responsible for putting together performances by British artistes in Jordan each year. And so it came to pass, when we followed this up, that the *OSC* was invited to present one full-length play for two performances at the Jerash Festival in the height of the summer of 1997.

Dream Parts (me aged 60)

If our presentation was supposed to be spontaneous where the actors didn't know what the play was about or how it ended, we would need to have two casts; but we were restricted to 17 individuals, including Patrick (a non actor) and me as the prompter (on stage throughout the play). All the actors would have to learn two parts, a different one for each performance, but that still left us an actor short. There was only one solution. I would have to play 'First Fairy' AND 'Starveling' in both performances. We got round this by Patrick subbing for me on the book when I was 'acting'.

Alternating between the two roles, with the necessary costume changes and prompting between scenes was so exhausting, I was going on stage for a rest! Although I had been teaching all the guidelines for years, this was to be my first attempt at it and I can tell you, it is a bit unnerving…to say the least. When we were invited again the following year, Patrick and I decided to send a company alone (without us) as a way of checking that this stuff could be done by actors who we trained up in the techniques, without us nursing them through it. By now we had Simon Purse in place as the prompter and their *Twelfth Night* was a great success.

The third year brought another invitation to the Jerash Festival; this time we chose the less well-known play *The Two Gentlemen of Verona*. This slightly puzzled the producers who wanted to know if this was a play by Shakespeare. They accepted our assurance, but asked if we could supply them with a synopsis of the story, since the audience, like them would be unfamiliar with the play? "No," was Patrick's immediate reply, and he stuck to it. On the first night the wholly Arabic audience not only loved it, but totally understood what was going on, especially Julia's description of "life as a woman in a man's world."

"It is the lesser blot modesty finds, women to change their shapes, than men their minds."

The audience responded collectively with a knowing:

"Aaahhh."

I did make a small contribution by playing a madrigal singer in a quartet and particularly enjoyed rehearsing the song in my dining room. We were introduced to Queen Noor before the show and she was given special cushions to sit on.

*****

Note to self: add to list: never travel without a blow-up cushion.

*****

We had our final invitation to the Festival in 1999 and decided to do our first 'tragedy'. *Romeo and Juliet* was the choice, and because this play requires a large cast, once again I was called upon to act. Having played 'The Nurse' in Crewe some years before, when I hadn't a clue about how to act Shakespeare, the frightening memory hung in my mind, so I plumped for 'Lady Capulet' on the grounds that I (just about) looked young enough to play Juliet's mum.

The conditions at the 'theatre' were horrendous when we arrived to set up, and there seemed to be no furniture at all backstage. The stalwart, Nick Day, rose to the occasion and cleaned out the disgusting loo, then announced that he had found a stool in one of the dressing rooms but, unfortunately, it was not the sort you could sit on. He then proceeded to sweep the stage, and wash it down, set out some silver (foil) platters and, having shopped in the City beforehand, supplied loads of wonderful local food for us all in our hour of need. What a star!

Just before the first performance a sand storm developed; you could see it coming across the city towards the Artemis Steps, part of the temple where we were performing. We actors had the presence of mind to shelter underneath the stage, but it dumped itself all over the set, leaving a thick film of sand for us to wade through. It was eight o'clock at night and 40 degrees centigrade and, in a supreme effort to look youthful, I was in a full length Elizabethan style dress with tight fitting corset, plus a wig and quite heavy make-up. In almost unbearable conditions we took on the show as if everything was perfectly normal, even when the Imam's prayer chant started up from the local mosque during the 'balcony scene', Juliet was totally unfazed.

Comparison with the First Folio of *Romeo and Juliet* and a modern edition of the play throws up some very interesting contrasts. I'm only going to reveal one here, but it is something that you can only discover by working on the play the way we do with the *OSC*. It concerns the very opening which you might think starts with the 'Chorus' speech.

"Two households, both alike in dignity...etc," which goes on to outline the play, and that the two star-crossed lovers kill themselves at the end. This speech does not appear in the Folio version at all, so we didn't include it in our production.

There is another short 'Chorus' speech a little later on, which is fairly innocuous and it was suggested that we might also leave that out. Patrick was insistent that there must be a reason for it, because it's in the Folio, and only in the performance did we discover why it was there. The speech comes just after the big Capulet party, with dancing and revels, and this 'Chorus' speech perfectly covers the scene change to set up the balcony for the lovers' tryst. We only realised this by doing the play the way it was originally performed, when they were just being practical.

There is a very interesting link here between this play and the modern, musical version, which is *West Side Story*. Jerome Robbins, the brilliant choreographer, had put together some amazing dance sequences, including an opening routine reflecting the 'Chorus' speech of two households. The show opened in Philadelphia, but was not getting the expected praise. A 'play doctor' was sent for and after one performance he said:

"Cut the first number."

"But that is Jerome Robbins' best number in the show," the management declared.

"Nevertheless...it gives the whole story away. You're telling the audience that it ends tragically... and believe me, they don't want to know before they've even seen it."

They agreed to cut the number, it transferred to Broadway and *West Side Story* became the great hit it is today.

*****

Note to self: the Elizabethan actors would have altered things for good theatrical reasons.

*****

No-mad Travelling

It had been established each year that the Company's payment for the two performances at the Artemis Steps would be a hotel with full board in Amman, followed by a trip round Jordan in a modest coach with a driver/guide, which would include Wadi Ram, Aqaba, Petra and the Dead Sea. A night sleeping under the starts in the desert was amazing and when the sun came up from behind a rock, it was like a radiator had been turned on at full blast. One actor decided to 'go for a walk' at dawn, but wandered down the wrong Wadi leading to emergency tactics of sending a local second jeep out on a search. Arriving in Aqaba, Patrick was mistaken for William Shakespeare by a newspaper vendor, and the news spread fast that the famous English playwright was in town.

The highlight of anybody's worldwide travels would surely have to be Petra, and I've been there three times! The first sight of The Treasury takes your breath away...nothing prepares you for it, because you cannot believe that it is carved out of the rock, but looks for all the world like a building. Inside this temple is a space which produces the most exquisite acoustics. We couldn't resist singing our signature tune: "Pass time with good company," which reverberated round the chamber, beautifully harmonising with itself.

There is a lot of walking to get through in Petra, and the occasional donkey ride was more than welcome, but I resisted the trek up to the Monastery. I'm not sure whether the poor donkey that heehawed its breathless way up to the top with Patrick on board, made it to see another day. We explored areas we hadn't visited on previous trips and at one point we were faced with a choice between edging ourselves round a huge rock on a narrow ledge, or a two mile detour. Patrick naturally chose the rock and made it look reasonably easy. There was now no real alternative for me and I hung on for dear life, straining every sinew, 'encouraged' by Patrick urging:

"Come on, darling, you can do it."

This was probably the nearest I came to...well, we won't go there.

Dead Sea Scrolls

Floating in the thick salt water, perfectly balanced enough to lie back and learn your lines from a cue roll sounds like paradise but is actually quite hard to do. If you can balance yourself carefully, without getting any of this vicious liquid in your eyes, then it is bliss. The agony, if you do, I will leave to your imagination, and I should know because I suffered; so the third year I watched as the rest of them waded in and, as if standing upright but actually floating, they linked hands and sang a reprisal of the *OSC's* song *Passtime*. Was it my imagination or were they singing 'Bath-time' with good company? After the salt water, we covered ourselves in Dead Sea Mud, showered down, swam in the gorgeous hotel pool then, sipping cool drinks, watched the sun go down through the silhouetted palm trees. Patrick and I toured Israel once when he went there to direct *A Chorus of Disapproval* (in Hebrew) and floated in the Dead Sea from the other side. I preferred the Jordan side for many different reasons!

I know that I am not the first person to have done all these things, but with the added joy of being with a large group of actors who have bonded through an emotional working experience and enjoyed this 'free' journey through one of the great spectacles of the Middle East, you realise that some experiences are simply unique. You couldn't buy this camaraderie with all the money in the world, and you certainly couldn't buy these memories.

A Crying Shame

We realised that this would be our last visit to Jordan, so five of us hired a people carrier, driver and guide and spent a week touring Syria. I cannot begin to tell you how sad I feel at what has happened in that glorious country since our visit. To see newsreels of the destruction of the cities and desperation of the people is unbearable for me. Even the Crac de Chevalier, a crusader castle situated on a remote hill surrounded by flat desert for miles around, and in such good nick that you could imagine Richard the Lionheart had just ridden away, was attacked and left considerably damaged. When, during our visit to this magnificent, yet isolated castle, we had reached the tippy top to survey the miles of desert yonder, there was sudden scream of delight from a young woman hurtling towards me with:

"Chrissie!!"

She was already upon me, with her arms round my neck, before I could draw her away to see who it was.

"Belinda," I shrieked. "What the..."

It was only the daughter of my best friend, Jan, one of 'The Coven'.

"What a small world."

The city of Aleppo was a magical place, especially the souk - the most wonderfully colourful market, now in ruins. No tourists, probably for years, will see the whirling dervishes in Damascus, the ancient ruins at Palmyra, and the wonderful Roman amphi-theatre at Bosra. I raved about Syria as being one of the most beautiful and interesting countries I had ever seen. It is a senseless tragedy.

Scene 28

The Great Globe Itself

No Pillars of Wisdom

If you are unfamiliar with Shakespeare's Globe Theatre in London, let me tell you it is a monstrous problem for the actors, because there are two thick round pillars holding up the stage roof, which have to be constantly manoeuvred. I christened the space between the two pillars 'the valley of death' and we trained our actors to place themselves anywhere but on that line. In fact, we insisted that they try to place themselves on diagonals, so that the audience could see at least one person's face during a duologue. Whenever I see a play there now, it is guaranteed that the actors will mostly play out front (ignoring the audience round the sides) and treat the pillars like a proscenium arch.

Interlude

There was a lot of dispute at the Globe about where the pillars should be, and the decision was taken, by the academics, to put them down stage...so blocking some of the audience's view of the actors. At a conference to discuss all this, Felicity Kendal, a member of the Globe Directorate, stood on the stage and announced that:

"I've toured Shakespeare all over India, in all sorts of arenas, and I can tell you that no group of actors would have agreed to this arrangement."

Even though all the actors on the directorate agreed with her, the academics overruled this point of view. They felt that the roof should come to the front edge of the stage, as the actors would not want to get wet, and the weight of the roof meant the pillars had to be kept in their current badly sight-lined positions.

Merely Players

Because of Patrick's long-standing relationship with The Globe, the *OSC* were given the opportunity to perform there for one night only during the summer season. Our first booking was Monday the 1st of September, 1997, the day after the death of Princess Diana! Undeterred, we played *As You Like It* to a full house; the groundling area being packed, and although it was a long evening, the reception at the curtain call was tremendous.

Today's actors rehearse each production for several weeks, so an 'on stage' prompter would be thought of as amateur in the extreme, but with the *OSC*, as in Shakespeare's day, we needed a prompter on stage throughout the performance. I am the only person to have filled this role for a full-length play at the Globe, and I did it three times. I loved doing it; I felt part of the cast and I never felt nervous before a performance although, given the fact that it was totally unrehearsed and that the actors knew nothing but their own lines, the task stretching ahead should have frightened the life out of me. There is a quote from an Elizabethan letter writer, which goes, 'The Performance was not so good tonight, me thought I heard the prompter more often than the Actors'. Because the audience knew the actors hadn't rehearsed the play together and were living on a knife edge, once the first prompt came (which it inevitably did) they were able to relax in the knowledge that we were not cheating and the actors really didn't know what was going to happen next.

As He Liked It

We make many delicious discoveries when actors only have a cue script and have absolutely no idea of the 'arc of the play'. They spend the whole time just listening for their cues and discovering what the play is about as they go along. For example, when 'Rosalind', dressed as a boy, has a long scene teaching 'Orlando' how to woo a woman, and 'Celia' is on stage all the time, but has practically nothing to say. Many modern directors send her off, or have her read a book, or lie in a hammock (I've seen that twice)...BUT...she does eventually have a line. So, the actor playing 'Celia' in a cue script production has to stay attentive in order to hear her cue, because she has no idea when it is coming, or who is going to say it. Our 'Celia' strode around the stage, following the others wherever they went. The impression was that she was eaves-dropping, which 'Rosalind' found somewhat annoying, and 'Orlando' wondered why she always seemed to be 'hanging around', but she was simply waiting to hear someone say her cue, which was "Pray thee marry us."

Her relief at eventually hearing it caused her to hesitate slightly before delivering her line: "I cannot say the words," which, of course, got a huge laugh.

With no rehearsal or ability to time the perform-ance, it was clear by the first interval that we were going to overrun by miles, and the message came from the management that we would have to cut the play. Well, working this way, you CANNOT DO that, so the decision went out to have three, five-minute intervals only, and we came down just before eleven o'clock. Well, the audience just LOVED it. A 'first' for them, and most of the actors, some of whom enjoyed it a little bit too much. It's called over-indulgence, and who could blame them, but we were all thrilled with our numerous discoveries.

Not surprisingly, some people were sceptical about our methods, working from cue scripts and having no rehearsal of the play, and explained our success by saying that modern actors would know the play 'well enough' to muddle through. Well, our 'Orlando' had never seen the play or read it, and was as surprised by the ending as anyone in the audience. There were still some who couldn't believe this was the way the original actors worked, so the following year we chose *King John* which is unfamiliar to both actors and audiences. Again, our process worked fine, the play went wonderfully well, and there were none of the predicted rail crashes, or things grinding to a halt. The doubters (fewer of them by now) then said that the original actors would have known the English history about King John well enough, and that would have allowed them to 'muddle through' again. We knew that this process worked and that it was not necessary to know the background and history of a play to perform it, so the following year we chose *Cymbeline*, a play that no-one knows well, or knows its history. And, yes, it still worked...triumphantly.

The Skies Opened

Cymbeline presents one or two major challenges. In one scene the Folio stage direction says: Jupiter descends in Thunder and Lightening, sitting upon an Eagle: he throws a Thunderbolt.

How to get this effect with virtually no rehearsal time, except on the day, was tricky. Some of the clever actors made a wonderful eagle with a vast wingspan and fixed it to the end of a ten-foot pole. They would then raise the eagle to meet 'Jupiter' as he appeared from the 'skies'. We hired Kirby's Flying Ballet to install a pulley in the roof of the stage. There were two trap doors already built into the ceiling at the Globe, which were beautifully painted over with sky and cloud effects so that on cue, the 'clouds would part' and 'Jupiter' would descend through the traps and be lowered in on a pulley.

All the research suggested that there was only one pulley for this manoeuver, there is even a demonstration of this in the Exhibition under the stage at the Globe. Of course, when we arrived at the theatre on the day, Kirby's had installed two pulleys and the technician explained:

"Well, you see, you need two pulleys or else he'll just go round and round."

"I know," said Patrick. "Nevertheless, I only want one pulley," knowing it was all they had at the original Globe. After a second attempt to persuade Patrick, the guy shrugged, gave up and left just the one pulley. And so it came to pass, that when 'Jupiter' was lowered in on one pulley, he slowly began to go round in a circle.

Patrick, alerted to this confusion over the pulleys, had said to the actor:

"Whatever happens, make sure the audience believe that it is what you, 'Jupiter', wanted to happen.

It all worked out rather well, with him cheerfully

waving and addressing each section of the audience, as he slowly twirled around. The end was even better because, when he instructed his eagle to ascend, "Mount Eagle, to my Palace Christalline", the stage hands started hauling him up and the actors on stage continued with their dialogue. Just as they said: "The Marble Pavement closes, he is entered," was the exact moment when the stage hands, above, were replacing the trap door through which 'Jupiter' had just disappeared. We hadn't rehearsed this (no, we really don't rehearse) but, to our great relief, it worked perfectly on the night.

*****

Note to self: Why be surprised? After all, it would have taken just as long to haul 'Jupiter' up 400 years ago as it does today.

*****

The final scene has 17 actors on stage at the same time, each with lines, but having no idea where their cues might come from. You could say there were some very bemused people up there concentrating like mad, with their ears pinned back straining to pick up their cues; and a challenge for me as prompter, too, I can assure you. The effect, of course, is that all the characters appear to be 'really interested in what's going on'. This scene was hilarious as more than a dozen revelations were acted out in quick succession, enjoyed enormously by the audience. I think this was the highlight of all our experiments.

Our demonstrations were simply meant to recreate the conditions of the original Elizabethan actors at the Globe and, hopefully, to learn something about the building. We never intended them to be compared with modern productions, and we certainly never intended any form of competition, but Mark Rylance, the Globe's artistic director at the time, never accepted that our actors could genuinely perform to a high standard without knowing the 'arc of the play'. He truly believed that actors needed to know what a play was about and how it concluded, and he voiced his opinion to Patrick by saying that he thought the audience were laughing at the actors, rather than with them.

We had presented a comedy, a history and a romance, and would have relished the opportunity to complete our cycle of plays by presenting a tragedy the next year, but with Mark feeling so strongly that our Company appeared to be making light of the presentations, we were, henceforward, banished from the Globe, and that was that.

We did have the opportunity to present a tragedy the next year with *Romeo and Juliet* in Jordan, which I have already chronicled. Back in England we performed it at a venue in Surrey, and we also gave our wonderful actresses an opportunity to work as 'A Boys Company' and perform *A Midsummer Night's Dream* there, too. We learnt a huge amount about 'women playing men' from this experience, especially about their hair, which would be a great asset to any 'all female' company playing 'men', should they wish to avail themselves of our discoveries.

I know that *The Dream* never fails to amuse, but when a girl, playing a boy, plays 'Starveling' as a 'gay' tailor, the results are hilarious. The actress, preparing this role in private, and taking all the clues from the text, decided that 'Starveling' remains fairly aloof, with very few lines. When he is given the part of Thisbie's mother in *The Most Lamentable Comedy and Most Cruel Death of Piramus and Thisbie*, he preens and beams with sheer pleasure. The actress also sported a hairy chest wig - a first, I believe? We always allowed our actors to decide how their character should look, so long as it comes from the text. This was a wonderful example of inventiveness when you trust your actors and let them fly.

Ain't That the Truth?

My thoughts on the question of 'Who wrote Shakespeare?' are these. William Shakespeare's genius was not just his brilliant use of words and his creation of wonderful poetry, but the way he structured these words in order to help his fellow actors. What we have discovered from working with cue scripts, which we know his actors did, Shakespeare understood their task. He put everything they needed to know into their lines...and their lines only. He was clearly a man of the theatre and there seems to be no other contender with a similar claim to the authorship of these great plays.

But, here's another thought. If someone other than Shakespeare wrote the plays credited to him, all his fellow actors would have known the truth...and all of them would have been expected to keep the secret? Speaking as an actor...some hopes!

Scene 29

Around The World In 40 Days

Finding a Spouse

One of my close friends from The Actor's Choir was Lynn Webster. She and her journalist husband Rod Oram shared several Christmases with us in London and New York. When they emigrated to New Zealand we only got to see them, with their daughter Celeste, when they returned to the UK for holidays.

Then we were invited to help celebrate their Silver Wedding Anniversary in 2001. The Invitation read 'A 2001 Spouse Odyssey'...their plan was to have a party of 'couples' for Christmas and/or New Year for which they would hire a large house on Omaha beach north of their home city of Auckland. We accepted with joy and used the occasion to visit other places both before and after their party.

Rod and Lynn had married on September the 11th, 1976, which meant that their 'Silver Wedding' was on the very day of the Twin Towers disaster in New York; except that they were totally unaware of it until they woke up on September the 12th. Being in New Zealand tends to mean that many things that happen in the world, especially in America, happened yesterday.

My old flat mate in the 1960s, Jenny McNae, had emigrated to Perth over 40 years before and carved out a good acting career for herself, mainly in theatre. Although she had been back to England a few times, we had never seen her new home. Now was our opportunity, with the excuse of 'the Silver', to see her and the famous city we had heard so much about. Jenny hosted us royally, and we even spent a day at The WACA, Perth's famous cricket ground.

Our overall impression of Perth was that it would be wonderful for the outdoor life, sun, sea, sand and sailing, but culturally, not a lot goes on, especially when you are used to London's theatres and art galleries. If you look at an atlas Perth is very isolated, almost as near to Singapore as Sydney, and surrounded by desert. Just a bit cut off.

On to Melbourne for a couple of days, complete with trams decorated for Christmas, Santa in sunglasses and red shorts and a most enjoyable *Singing in the Rain* at the beautiful Regent Theatre. Then on to Auckland and another first...Christmas on the beach! Not the actual dinner I hasten to add, that was very English traditional fare eaten under a canopy in the garden, but we did get to build sandcastles and bathe on December 25th; Patrick's long-term ambition. We were taken by our hosts on a divertissement to the tippy top of the North Island where we saw the biggest, widest tree trunk in the world. One public convenience was decorated in brightly coloured tiles throughout, including the roof garden, which was fertilized by the output of the building itself.

On Boxing Day we hired a car and travelled south, taking in the amazing glowworm caves at Waitomo, silently gliding under the most starlit sky you'd ever seen, then on to Wellington. Leaving the car there, we took the ferry to Picton, picking our way through a channel of small islands, then boarded the first of two magnificent rail journeys.

Picton to Christchurch hugs the east coast of the South Island for the first half, and sea life is evident, especially from the open observation coach. The next day we took the spectacular Alpine Line through Arthur's Pass National Park. Gorgeous waterfalls, canyons and colourful wild flowers at the highest point where we stopped to roam around. This day trip to Greymouth over on the west coast, allows less that an hour in the town, but you could do that easily, including both sides of the street. It is a blissful train journey, almost too much for one day, but we were alarmed to see some of the passengers sleeping through all these wonderful vistas. The reason? They were mostly students on holiday from the Orient but, although I'm sure they intended to enjoy the scenery, they found the nightlife of computer games the evening before had taken its toll. The really sad thing was that, even when they woke up, they carried on playing their screen games. Ah well, what you don't see, you don't miss, I guess. The timing of our round-the-world trip didn't allow us to visit the famous mountains, Milford Sound, Dunedin or Queenstown, but, well, what you don't see...etc.

These two railway journeys are considered to be among the best in the world, and I can see why. On our return to Picton, we fell into conversation with a charming, elderly woman who was venturing 'abroad' for the very first time, to visit her sister in the North Island. I mean, she had never before left the South Island of New Zealand in her life! I had to ask her several times to confirm this.

We picked up the car again in Wellington and drove to Napier, which was destroyed by an earthquake and fire in 1931, and rebuilt in 22 months.

Because this was the early '30s, and so many buildings were replaced, it is now the art deco capital of the world. It is quite remarkable and very beautiful. From there to Rotorua and the fascinating geysers, back to our chums in Auckland for fond farewells, then a flight to Rarotonga in the Cook Islands.

This was supposed to be a week of blissful sunbathing, snorkelling and generally messing about in boats. Didn't quite turn out like that. Less sun than expected for one thing, very sketchy transport, fleapit cinema (yes, bites and all) and very boring food. The only truly enjoyable treat was the discovery of a Brit who had settled out there with his family and had transported a railway engine and tender from Poland to Rarotonga, via New Zealand. He had made a clearing in the forest, laid some track, and charged a few pence for anyone to ride to and fro about 100 yards. His young daughter served tea, which came in genuine tin railway mugs, and homemade 'train shaped' gingerbread, for whoever turned up. It was surreal.

I never really felt that the island was big enough to take a jumbo jet, never mind the runway at the bijou airport, and leaving in the middle of the night during a rainstorm was as uncomfortable a feeling as you could imagine. This was the plane that would take us to Los Angeles, where we would, mercifully, change carriers for the next leg to New York.

The Second Family

Ah, New York! Almost a second home by now. There are even shopkeepers who greet us with, 'Hi, guys, glad to see you back', especially the man who sells us *The International Guardian* every day. We have been visiting New York on a regular basis, mainly to run workshops on Shakespeare, since the early 1980s, and for much of that time have been fortunate enough to be hosted by 'The Margots'. Let me explain. Margot Stephenson, a veteran screen and theatre actress who died in 2011 aged 98, inherited a brownstone in The Village, close to Washington Square when still quite young. With her husband, Val Avery, an actor best known for his many cameo film roles, occupied the top four apartments of the building, together with their daughter (also Margot) with a spare apartment for - um - guests, renting out the other four floors.

The Margots became great fans of Patrick - especially his work on Shakespeare - and offered him the spare room whenever he was in town. I was with him on most occasions and when we expressed the hope that we were not intruding, 'big' Margot insisted:

"Oh, you're family."

We have spent both Christmas and Thanksgiving with them. Val being an excellent cook with his Armenian roots and a kitchen to rival that of any professional chef. Once, 14 of us sat down for the turkey roast and pumpkin pie, and the wine flowed. A robust time was had by all, especially one guest called Sylvia Miles, famous for playing 'the lady with the dog' in *Midnight Cowboy*, and nominated for the Best Supporting Actress Oscar! Talking to Val the next day, we commented on his 'lively' friend who made us all sit up and take notice. His analysis?

"Goddam pain in the ass!"

This bolthole was a life saver as far as we were concerned. It is quite unthinkable that we could have made so many visits on the modest fees earned from the workshops. On this particular visit Andrea, one of young Margot's friends, was working for Nathan Lane who was playing the lead (the Zero Mostel part in the film) in *The Producers*. By way of a coincidence, Zero had been best man at Margot and Val's wedding at Caxton Hall in London when the happy couple were working in the West End.

Tickets for the Broadway show were at a premium, and couldn't be bought for love nor money, but Matthew Broderick, the co-lead, was taking a break and Nathan was not too keen on the understudy. Not keen enough, apparently, to release his house seats to anyone he knew, so Andrea secured them for us. They were $100 each, but in the centre stalls with an excellent view. We adored it. With one more hop over the pond, our circumnavigation of the world was complete.

Scene 30

Exotic Gatherings

The Big Game

In 2001 Patrick was invited to Nairobi to train the directors for a television soap opera (Kenya's first) but realised that the actors also wouldn't be experienced in 'soaps'. He then came up with a brilliant idea and offered to go out there for three weeks to train both actors and directors in soap opera techniques, before working on some scripts to put a showreel together. They bought the idea at once, which meant Patrick would go out to Nairobi four weeks ahead of me and I would join him for the filming and we could give ourselves an adventure afterwards.

His employers would pay all Patrick's expenses and a fee, but I would pay my own airfare, and arrange bookings for our post-filming holiday. I spent a week in the hotel and joined him on location every day to watch and see if there were any great differences shooting in Kenyan conditions. It was their winter in August, so normal temperatures, but the local people were clearly not used to such invasions of their pavements and shop fronts. They stopped everything they were doing to watch these strange happenings, open-mouthed. One interesting discovery was that most of the actors lived in shanty towns, with no maps and no postal deliveries. The introduction of the internet meant that, for the first time ever, they had an address (an email one) and could be contacted directly by mobile phone.

*****

Note to self: what to us is an annoyance on a crowded bus is a life-line to those in a crowded shanty town.

*****

The one thing we simply had to experience was a Safari. Trailfinders did the business, as usual, and sorted out a tented lodge in the Masai Mara, but if we wanted to do a hot air balloon trip we would need to book it locally. The lodge we found seemed pretty good value, and our accommodation was (indeed) a tent with windows and doors you zipped up at night - a magnificent colonial style affair with one of those showers where the water comes straight down from a round metal head as big as a dinner plate. That was wonderful enough, but when we met up with our guide for the big game search, he showed us into a jeep with a canvas roof and roll up windows, and a rifle on the seat next to him - er - just in case. We were his only customers, so we sat there, raised up behind him, feeling (if not looking) for all the world like Robert Redford and Meryl Streep in *Out of Africa!* Bliss it was in the afternoon.

We saw all the big game, except the leopard - a rare sighting apparently. The wildebeest and zebra happily mingling alongside each other, herds of elephant, giraffe, buffalo, loads of deer and monkeys (various) lions, of course, and best of all...cheetahs. Our guide, Mousa, was terrific at knowing where to find a spectacle, and led us stealthily towards a recently caught prey, probably a hyena, being devoured by a cheetah. We were but yards away, listening to the gnawing sounds and, nestling nonchalantly in the background, was a flock of vultures, biding their time, just waiting to swoop on their next meal.

Oh, it was all marvellous, but we had to contain our smugness at the sight of other tourists being driven through this wilderness in white vans, totally enclosed except the a gap in the raised roof to stand and look through. I actually did feel sorry for them as they gazed longingly at us. How could we have been so blessed?

We found a hot air balloon company and booked it - "hang the expense," as my mother used to say - for an early morning flight over the Masai Mara. When I say early, we were up, showered, breakfasted, journeyed, given all our flight instructions and standing in the wicker basket underneath a brightly coloured spherical dome before sunrise. Then...lift off! As we began to rise so did the sun. What timing? What followed had to be one of the highlights of any traveller's experience. It was just thrilling; to see two lions moving slowly round a group of wildebeest in a pincer movement, waiting to entrap one and pounce. Looking down directly over a group of elephants in a small forest of trees, and many other spectacles. Then landing (ok, on our sides) to find a full champagne breakfast waiting to be served at tables and chairs, on a hillside with views to die for. The Land Rovers had tracked our flight with all the necessaries, and spare seats to drive us back to base. If you ever get the opportunity, don't balk at the price, it's worth every penny.

Back in Nairobi, with one free day before leaving the city, we met up with a couple who had provided facilities for the training course, and they offered to take us on a trip to the Rift Valley. Wow, yes, please. The history, the heat, the villagers, families and children who shied away from having their photographs taken, till I offered them £5.00 for a goat bell. This sits on our mantlepiece along with other minute holiday trophies. Just the sound of that bell brings it all back, every time.

To recover from safari-ing and all these strange new experiences, we took ourselves off to the coast for a couple of days to the island of Lamu, just a few miles from the Somalian border and probably out-of-bounds for tourists these days. One of the hotel outings offered to us was a short boat trip to a beautiful beach with perfect sand...you know the sort...the hotel's own beach bar, cultivated flowerbeds and hammocks. We two, a man from Australia and the boatman pitched up on the beach, pulled the boat on to the sand and made for the bar. Taking the orders for lunch we were asked:

"Pizza, ok?"

"Yes, pizza's fine, thank you."

Then, off to give the hammocks a test-run. An hour later we spot sight of a boat arriving alongside ours, and walking up the beach we see the waiter from the hotel carrying our lunch!

Back home with our memories, trophies and midge bites, we totted up the total sum of costs for the round trip. Patrick's fee, minus my airfare and the holiday, and we had made a profit of £13.09. A bargain for an exotic holiday, since we had simply done our usual trick of taking advantage of a job abroad to go sightseeing.

Riding high

My niece, who had been flown round the world by her employer for a number of years, announced that she had 32,000 air miles that she couldn't possibly use, and would we like to take them off her hands? They were BA air miles, with up-grading to business class possibilities, so we studied the British Airways map of routes and saw that we could make our first visit to South America by going either to Rio, or Lima. Recent news had revealed that Rio was very popular with Brits, and therefore was full of fish and chip shops. So, we settled for Lima.

I then read, quite by chance, that an old railway line had been opened up again and that, once a month, it took locals and tourists from Lima to Huancayo, some 16,000 feet up into the Andes. A journey of some twelve hours climb up the side of the mountains with, as you can imagine, spectacular views. Conveniently, 'Journey Latin America' had their offices in Chiswick, a stones throw from my house. I asked whether they could book us on to this train (which they didn't even know about) and arrange a trip to cover that train, plus Cusco, Machu Picchu, Lake Titicaca, Lima and back to London in a two-week visit? Because of work commitments we couldn't leave the UK before the 23rd of July and we had to be back by the 8th of August, to be sure to make an important 100th birthday party on the 10th.

JLA did the business. There was only one of the big train trips in that period and they managed to book us on to it. Everything else slotted in nicely. We flew BA to Madrid and picked up the Iberia flight to Lima, business class all the way. After one day looking

round Lima then, on the 26th, we began the big one.
Very comfortable seats with a table. Really good food,
and plenty of it, amazing views, and a nurse with an
oxygen cylinder on wheels moved through the
carriages. Although I had suffered from asthma
earlier in my life, I am relieved to say that I didn't
need the oxygen - even at 16,000 feet! In 2003, this
was the highest passenger railway line in the world.

Staying in Huancayo for three days helped us
acclimatize, and I spent my 67th birthday trolling
round this extraordinary township, almost in the
clouds. The pronunciation of Huancayo, I should tell
you, is as if the 'Hu' sounds like 'Wh'; and our tour
guide announced that he was extremely proud to be a
native of Huancayo, adding:

"I come from a long line of Huancas"

Umm...don't we all?

Back down the mountain on the same train for one
further night in Lima, then a flight to Cusco, again
high in the mountains. This beautiful place had so
much to offer in the way of buildings, art, culture and
a delightful hotel with a courtyard café open to the
sky.We made a couple of local interest trips, then took
the train to Machu Picchu. From all accounts, we were
very wise not to have considered the Inca Trail. A bus
wound its way up the hillside with hairpin bends that
stopped your breath and then suddenly, there it was,
that famous 'shaped' mountain, which I had seen
pictured in many travel books. There is a narrow,
steep pathway winding through it all the way to the
top, and I'm sure the views would have been spectacular, but we decided to stand and look at it through
our binoculars...and, yes, you could just see people
waving from the top. The story of the building of this
phenomenal city in the 15th century is quite extraor-

dinary, and the modern discovery of it, in 1911, just as amazing. An overnight stay in the village meant that we could go back the next day and wallow once more in this incredible spectacle.

Our next train journey along the top of the mountain range where farmers dressed in traditional Peruvian costume worked the land, brought us to Puna, with plenty of 'Llama Alerts' and from there by bus to Lake Titicaca. Well, you just have to go there, don't you? We took a boat trip out to the islands built on reeds. Yes, really. They just renew the reeds all the time and somehow it solidifies and floats. Whole communities exist on them perfectly happily, generation after generation. The children draw very sophisticated pictures of the life around them which we bought to bring home as souvenirs. One remarkable feature anchored in the water, is an iron gunboat, used to police the lake against armed smugglers in the 19th century. Since the watery borders were hard to control, they bought this iron warhorse built, as it so happens, in Chiswick. 'Gunboats R Us!', perhaps? Having had it shipped out to Peru, they were faced with the problem of how to get it up to the lake. They had to carve it up into 2,000 bits and transport it, piece by piece, on mule trains, then reassemble it at the lakeside. It took them eight years before it was finally rebuilt and launched.

The last leg of our trip was the journey back to London, which seemed straightforward enough. JLA had given us a leeway of two and a quarter hours in Lima, between our flight arrival from Puna and the London flight departure. Sitting in the airport lounge at Puna you could see a vast expanse of sky with very little activity. Planes to and from Puna were pretty spaced out and ours was the next departure. We just had to wait for the plane to arrive from somewhere else first. As the minutes ticked by, well past our time to leave, I began to get a little anxious as I stared out into the cloudy void. Nothing. I went to the desk clerk and explained that we had to make a connection at Lima; could she contact them and get a message through that we were temporarily stranded in Puna, and may well be late checking in. No response; if she understood me at all, she clearly thought it was a ridiculous request. Back to the window; still nothing.

Even when I think of it now, the situation is gut-wrenching; Patrick sat looking extremely calm and unconcerned, reading a book. An hour went by; I could think of nothing but, if we miss our flight home a) it will cost a fortune and b) we will probably miss the 'special birthday' because it was only the day after tomorrow. The two-hour mark was just upon us when: out of the clouds I spot a black thing moving. At least the pilot knew the urgency of the situation as I have never known a plane land, deposit its 200 passengers and luggage, load up with us and take off in a space of 20 minutes. Then, it was due to make another stop before Lima! Finally, we landed there, disembarked, dashed to the carousel, waited for the luggage, dashed to the check in and:

"Sorry, the flight is closed."

It was time for the Mongolian visa tactic all over again. Down on the knees, clenched fists, beg, beg, beg, tears, anything to get on the flight. All explanations of late arrival from Puna, plus the urgency of our need to get back to London seemed to work... *RADA* be praised, again. Check-in clerk grabs our bags, labels them, throws them on the moving belt and turns to us with:

"I'm afraid your seats in Economy have been

reassigned, I shall have to put you in Business Class."

There IS a pot of gold at the end of the rainbow.

The Big Day

Patrick's Mum's 100th birthday party was a triumph, hosted by a granddaughter's family, with a big marquee, a paddling pool for the children, a sumptuous lunch, and many amusing tributes delivered, including a piece of doggerel I wrote on the plane. It was the 10th of August 2003 when the temperature appropriately reached 100 degrees for the first time in England since records began. Betty lived for another five and a half years!

The Big Party Games

It was all my fault. We were going great guns with the *OSC* in 1996, running training workshops on Sunday afternoons and building up a large core company of actors. My 60th birthday happened to land on a Sunday that year, so I decided to celebrate with an elaborate party, and managed to book the beautiful medieval hall in Lincoln's Inn, with its famous wooden ceiling. I booked caterers, and ordered three magnificent cakes celebrating the diverse elements of my life.

The invitations went out to around a 150 friends and relations, an event which would include an opportunity to take part in a 'cue script' scene. They may not be actors at all, never mind familiar with our ways of presenting Shakespeare. Were they willing to have a go? A goodly number took up the challenge and the results were hilarious. The *OSC* actors did a 'showcase' from a Thomas Middleton play *No Wit, No Help Like a Woman's*, which I prompted, of course. I joined in with the *OSC* 'troupe' of singers rendering suitable madrigals, and Patrick hosted the proceedings, although he was directing *Brookside* in Liverpool either side of the event. Exhausting, but the whole day was the best fun imaginable.

Not to be outdone on his 60th in October 2001, Patrick came up with an equally large-scale plan. This time we hired the Isleworth Town Hall, which had an adorable old-fashioned music hall type stage, a little set of steps up to it, and a pair of red curtains that swished across at the turn of a wheel. Patrick wanted to give everyone a full blow-out three course meal, and serve a huge variety of beers instead of the usual red and white wine. That took some organising before we even started to arrange the entertainment, which was to cover his directorial achievements in theatre and television.

We hired a large screen and projector and I showed up in scenes from his first play for the *BBC*, *The Land of the Living*, and his most recent - an episode of *Casualty*, with me as a 'bag lady', what else? The real joy on the screen that night, though, was the contribution from our American friends. They had spent weeks going round Manhattan filming local people and many friends, including bus and tube train passengers, who all said: "Happy Birthday, Patrick" to the camera. It was beautifully put together, and included the 9/11 aftermath, and was accompanied by some evocative and atmospheric New York music.

Patrick's first job back in England, after graduating with an MFA from Boston University, was stage-managing a strip club in Soho. His elder brothers were horrified at the time, then asked if he could get them tickets, but he left to go on tour (and meet

ME) before this could be arranged. The party's stage show began with a real 'stripper', who we dressed in Elizabethan garb, arranged to be easily removed bit by bit (to Perry Como's *Magic Moments*) until the final garment was completely removed. No-one could quite believe what they'd seen, thinking it would have stopped...a little bit earlier! This was followed by a performance of *Skinhead Hamlet* by Richard Curtis. Here's the first scene...

> Enter Hamlet followed by Ghost:
> Ghost: "Oi! Mush!"
> Hamlet: "Yer?"
> Ghost: "I was fucked!"
> Exit Ghost.
> Hamlet: "O fuck."
> Exit Hamlet.
> It continues in this vein.

The stage show was rounded off with my very own rendition of *Why Am I Always the Bridesmaid*, which was the first solo performance Patrick saw me do after the *Oliver!* tour. Then he grabbed a ukelele and sang *It's Foolish but It's Fun*, a song written in the year of his birth. I was still in a side room changing out of my comedy 'bridesmaid' frock, when I heard my name being called. "Ozanne! Get in here." Patrick had quickly changed to a guitar and was about to serenade me with *I'll be Loving You, Always*. There were tears.

'Extra' Arrangements

At the beginning of 2011 my heart sank slightly when there were mutterings of another event to celebrate Patrick's 70th on Sunday October the 30th. He was thinking in terms of introducing the younger members of his extended family to the film world. Just have a get-together and 'shoot' the party. Sounded simple, but I suspected it wouldn't stop there and even though it was very early days, I started to investigate suitable venues, and once the numbers grew to include relations, actors, friends and neighbours, we were looking at well over a hundred.

Since the idea was to make a short film during the event, Chiswick Town Hall was not only round the corner, but had the perfect facilities, so we went in to ask: "How much?" Never mind how much, this was April and weekend bookings for the autumn were already being snapped up; we were just in time to get a Sunday at the end of October! This place is very used to film units, so the idea of the full location catering team, complete with double-decker bus, adapted into canteen seating arrangements would give our guests an extra thrill. Even some of our actors had never filmed on location and experienced these joys. As it happens, after a long search, we found the perfect suppliers and the location lunch was sensational.

The theme of the Party was to be a Hogwart's Old School Reunion. The venue had one 'great hall', and a smaller one, where all the children could be entertained by a face painter and a magician. We even found a man with a 'Dumbledore' act. We set out four long table arrangements with a flag and cake at one end to represent the four 'houses crests'. We asked all our guests to wear one of the four 'house colours' and, as Hogwart's alumni they would, of course, also be 'extras' in the film.

The idea was that two actors, in exotic costumes, would have conversations with the 'extras', about their true opinions of their various teachers. These scenes would be cleverly 'edited' to seem that they were criticising Patrick, and a rough cut would be shown to the audience at the end of the party...and a 'fine cut' DVD sent to everyone afterwards. Patrick got his current film students to do the shoot and editing, with two great nephews on boom and clapperboard - thrilled was not the word - while he ran around giving instructions to the 'extras' and shouting: "Quiet! Quiet!" to them from the balcony. This highly amused those who had never been anywhere near a film set before in their lives. A friend asked me: "It all looks exhausting for him. Do you think Patrick's enjoying this?"

"Are you kidding?" I said. "He's like a pig in shit."

The whole occasion was acknowledged by most as a unique experience, but neither of us has threatened such a monumental manoeuver ever again.

"That's all, folks!"

Scene 31

To Be Replaced

Foreign Parts

The downside of being a 'freelance' can mean total uncertainty about what happens next…if anything. At each New Year, Patrick and I look in our diaries to see what is in store. Usually there are a number of work bookings in the UK and often something pencilled in for a trip abroad. Sadly, 2014 was looking bleak with nothing new on the horizon, apart from a small operation on my big toe in February and a handful of regular workshops for Patrick.

The upside, on the other hand, is that the phone can ring and lead to something new and entirely un-planned. In this case, on the 2nd of January, 2014 an email came through that was to change the year quite dramatically. It was from a young woman called Svetlana Punte, who was a first assistant director with a film company based in the Latvian capital of Riga. The story was that a colleague of hers had attended Patrick's 'Hand's On' film directing course in London some while back, and returned to Riga raving about it and saying, 'We must all go over there and do this course'. Realising that the expense would be enormous, she wondered if Patrick could come to Riga and how much would he charge?

In all the years we have been together, I have rarely known Patrick to turn down an opportunity of work anywhere, especially abroad, and more especially to a place as yet unvisited.

"Let's try to make this happen," he replied.

His modest demand would be for them to fly us both over, we do the two-day workshop, look round Riga, and fly home. All expenses paid, and that would be the fee. We went in April and they clearly loved us.

"Would you come back again to do a screen acting workshop in, say, late July?"

Without hesitation, we said:

"Yes."

It is fair to say that the first workshops were not well attended. In fact, they would have made very little money (if any) from the paying customers, but they had high hopes of attracting more people, especially actors, in July. This is when the Russians visit Latvia in huge numbers, mainly for the purpose of sunning themselves in Riga Bay. It is a hundred mile long curve of golden sands, and although it is glorious, it is so covered with bodies as to obliterate the sand altogether. Russians, having very little 'summer type' coastline, have dominated the Baltic coast, especially this Latvian shore, for many years, and they own most of the beautiful houses near the sea.

Sadly, the advertised screen acting workshops had once again not attracted the numbers they had hoped for...not surprising in the unexpected heatwave, so the company concerned were to make no profit. This enterprising group, however, had recently set up a 'females only, sex therapy workshop' (to save marriages). This had wives queueing round the block to learn how to use sex aids, and enough money was made to bring us over again.

As in April, they had booked our air flights to and from Riga, covering a five-day July weekend, which would include my birthday on the 28th, and they promised to give me a party. As on many occasions in the past, we have tried to use a working trip to visit other places (at our own expense, of course) and this time we chose St Petersburg, having never been there, and we loved it. Then, shortly before the trip, a new challenge was proposed. The film company (our hosts) had been asked by two Russian producer/script writers, Vasashlav and Denis, to film a pilot for a new sitcom, and could they suggest a European director to take it on. The dates fitted perfectly so long as we could extend our stay for an extra eleven days! The chance to direct a Russian sitcom in Latvia was irresistible and, naturally, Patrick said "Yes."

They did host a party for me on the 28th in the hotel roof garden for a select number, which included the two Russians and our film company team...nine in all. Thinking about this back in England, we had wondered what we might bring to the party, and we found a box of eight party crackers with a musical theme. Paper hats, of course, English jokes, which proved to be impossible to translate, and a set of tin whistles, each with a different note in the C scale - perfect for *Happy Birthday to You*. The hats were numbered 1 to 8, and a musical score printed in numbers for a dozen or so popular tunes with a little baton for the conductor (Patrick) to point to each whistler. Madness! About the best ice-breaker in the world. We were all reduced to childish shrieks and the champagne flowed.

The next day we all went round to the film producer's apartment to meet the sitcom leading lady and, believe it or not, out came the tin whistles again, more Madness! After several renderings of *Happy Birthday*, and much jabber-jabbering in 'foreign', a game of 'hide and seek' was set up, not easy in an open-plan area where there *is* nowhere to hide. I was sitting down watching this childish hilarity, when someone threw a blanket over me, and Patrick was urged to hide behind an open umbrella. What was it all about? My lasting memory of this will be the sight of an elderly Russian Oligarch, in suit, collar and tie, disappearing head first under a two-seater sofa.

The famous hotel bedroom
On our first visit to Riga, we stayed in the Old Town and very nice it was too. Then...crash, bang, wallop! Because the sitcom was being shot on the outskirts of Riga, we were housed midway between the Old Town and the location. Not quite the boon docks, but...it meant that we would be wholly reliant on their 'pick-up' transport system and I might be left for hours on my own in the hotel. Fortunately, I had this 'Tome' to be getting on with.

The temperature was in the upper 90s for the whole two weeks, and we were shown to a room, which was called 'The Junior Suite' and was, the receptionist assured us, the most sought after room in the hotel. It was sweltering and there was NO air conditioning. The east and south-facing walls were all glass and one of them had no curtains, or fitments for them. The sun was beating down straight onto the bed, and without hesitation we returned to reception.

"But this is the most asked for room in the

hotel...etc."

"But there's no air conditioning."

"It is same through all hotel."

"But there's no curtain at the window."

"No, there has never been curtain at window, and we cannot put one there."

We protested, and begged for another room...at least, to look at another room.

"Oh, no, we are completely full," then after a long pause,"...well, there is room 402, but it is terrible."

We decided to take it for one night. It was terrible, but *did* have curtains; then next day, the film company sweet-talked the manager and, for extra money I'm sure, secured for us 'the best room in the hotel' - 604. Hurrah! This one had 'LUX' on the door and was probably the only room with air conditioning this side of Moscow.

Upon entering room 604, the cooler air certainly registered. It was produced from a noisy box on the wall and stayed on all the time at around 17 degrees. There was a small desk, just big enough for a laptop and table lamp, with a completely empty fridge underneath, leaving a small gap for your knees. The sunny side of the room was all window, but thankfully curtained, with several hooks missing, especially the ones at each end (know what I mean?) and because of the constant heat and sunlight we kept the curtains closed the entire time, although I had to use some emergency safety pins to join them all together.

*****

Note to self: never travel without safety pins.

*****

At least three light bulbs were missing, there were only two pillows, no cupboard space and NO wardrobe at all...just a few hooks on the wall and three lonely hangers! Our un-hangable clothes we threw over the back of the sofa, so much for 'luxury'. An enormous television screen, with nothing decent to watch, and a DVD machine we couldn't connect to the TV. One decent News channel meant I could keep abreast of the worldwide wars, but I was shocked to learn that the Latvians (well, those we were working with) never watched the news programmes, at all. The door keycard refused to operate after two or three goes, so it was a constant trek down to the lobby for replacements. This appeared to apply to all the rooms.

Unfortunately, the bedroom alcove also housed the connecting door to the bathroom and this had a large glass panel in it, throwing the morning (4am) light straight on to the bed, so we solved this by sticking a large black carrier bag over the door panel with masking tape, which did the trick.

*****

Note to self: add masking tape to the 'never travel without' list.

*****

Even a top sitcom designer would be pushed to come up with a worse bathroom than that in Room 604. An enormous jacuzzi almost filled the room but - "You must not use it; black water will appear from jets," - and there was no shower, or bath tub. There was a shower head on a low fitment which extended enough for a leg wash, but all this was very awkward, not to say somewhat perilous since the floor of the jacuzzi had two levels, and a number of large water outlets to manoeuvre your way round. We belligerently fixed the showerhead on the wall with the good old masking tape, and within a few days a maintenance man had drilled some holes and made it permanent.

Since I was still feeling quite shaky on my pins, as a result of the recent toe operation, I decided that a cat lick and a promise (as my dear old mother used to say) over the washbasin would have to suffice. On further inspection of the bathroom, my plans for a strip wash were also full of obstacles. The space between the jacuzzi and the wall, which housed the washbasin, was only about 60 centimetres wide, and this was reduced by the presence of a thick towel rail in the shape of a double 'S' bend and was scalding hot day AND night. Did I mention that there was a monstrous heatwave going on outside?

The final feature in the bathroom, living up to the hotel's reputation to annoy the hell out of the customers, was the loo. It worked well enough, but the bog paper holder was fitted to the wall just behind your left elbow...when seated. It was the sort with a curved metal attachment covering the top of the bog roll; you know the one? Aagghhh! We simply removed the paper and put it on the floor so that the maid could dutifully return it to its rightful place every day. Everything you could get wrong in a hotel room; they managed it. Oh, and browsing through the hotel facilities book I came across... 'Bathhouse Complex'...and the following message.

Our hotel offer You clean Your organism in sauna on the terrace, which include sauna, jacuzzi and hall with a fireplace. The meeting woth friends and relatives will be memorable!

(Hmmm, I bet.)

The food in Riga was marvellous (compared with St Petersburg) and most evenings we would eat in the hotel restaurant, but the orders took ages to arrive. One evening Patrick had to go off to visit a location, so he reckoned on being away for about 45 minutes. I waited a bit, then went along to the restaurant and ordered our main courses. He was considerably longer than expected, arriving back with an extraordinary story.

The location was a flat on the 7th floor of a large and disgusting tenement block, from the outside, anyway. Think The Gorbles, 1930. Along with the cameraman, sound guy and designer, he checked out the flat, then they all crammed into the lift again to go down but after three seconds it clunked to a halt. Mobile phone to the rescue, BUT the maintenance man could take 20 minutes. They were actually in the lift (bodies touching) for nearly an hour. Even with that delay, Patrick appeared at the dinner table... before the dinner!

For safety's sake, and for shooting in the apartment the next day, we were restricted to one person at a time in the lift. There were at least 25 cast and crew with all the necessary equipment, but as Patrick said: "This is just today's problem. There always is one."

And this was my shoot day. They needed an older pair of hands for Grandma, and when Patrick suggested mine, they said they had thought of that, but didn't like to ask. Ahh.

We found a huge 'glass' ring, which looked great, and could be worn by whoever eventually played the part. Oh, needless to say, Grandma's lines were all off camera and spoken by Denis, since I was to be replaced later by 'famous Russian actress'. Anyway, I don't hold out great hopes for my hands and feet making the final cut either, in this Russian sitcom!

Apart from Grandma's flat, the rest of the sitcom was being filmed at a Fitness Club. I went in there every day to watch some of the action, but since it was all 'foreign' I didn't really know what was going on. There were loads of 'extras' being used in the gym, the pool and the cafeteria and Patrick gave one of them a tiny note.

"When I say 'Action' I want you to laugh. And... ACTION!"

Nothing.

"CUT!"

He carefully repeated the instruction through the interpreter. Again...nothing! He went back to the 'extra'.

"When I say 'action' I want you to laugh. What's the problem?"

"Well," says the Stanivslaski-influenced wannabe. "I have to get into the mood."

"Oh, you want some motivation? Right, well how about this? When I say Action! You fucking-well laugh, OK?"

I spent the rest of the time trying to keep cool and catch up on writing my memoir. It had been a gruelling four-day schedule, but Patrick was lauded at the Wrap Party and praised for his organisation and speed. He was asked if he would like to direct the next 29 episodes, but politely turned it down on the grounds that he had directed one and that:

"Doing any more would just be a chore, really. But, if you were to offer me something else..."

"Well, we have this feature film..."

"Ah, now you're talking."

On our final day in Riga, editing completed, Sveta took us on a site-seeing tour of the Old Town, but we arrived ten minutes late for an organ recital in the Cathedral and the gate was closed. Sveta left us to wait with other hopefuls and went to the gate. We could see her talking to a woman inside, then she signalled to the two of us to go through, and the gate was closed behind us. At the end of the concert we wondered how she had managed it.

"Did you tell her I was an important film director from England?" said Patrick.

"No," said Sveta. "I told her that my Grandma and Grandpa had trouble walking, and that was why we were late."

Scene 32

More Eastern Promise

Dulwich College, Singapore?

2014 was still to hold a few surprises. An unlikely trip to the Far East was to materialise in late October. This was a recruitment drive for the Central Film School where Patrick had worked as a teacher over the past six years, and it hoped to attract new students from Asia. I was to be included in the trip, not only because he wouldn't go without me, but that I do make a contribution to the masterclasses on 'screen directing and acting'. At the time I was suffering from adverse effects of an operation on my foot, which had caused much leg pain, and a wheelchair was provided for me at all the airports and on our first flight to Singapore we had to change planes at Qatar.

I was intrigued to see what this 2022 World Cup host city looked like. Well, of course, I didn't get to see that, but the airport was a revelation. Vast areas the size of several football pitches, full of empty seats, hundreds and hundreds of them, as far as the eye could see. All this was built to accommodate the (expected) fans. The heat outside was fierce and I couldn't imagine how the players were going to survive it and stay upright. In my wheelchair I was elevated to the body of the Dreamliner aircraft by a forklift truck. Wonderful.

We were to stay in Singapore and Bangkok for one week in each place, with business class travel, five star hotels and a bit of spending money. It wasn't the first time I had travelled in this elevated section, but *Qatar Airlines* 'business class' is something else. There were just four seats across the wide-bodied fuselage…well, not so much a seat as an apartment…you kind of 'moved in'. On one handset, there were 14 push buttons controlling the seat's ability to adjust the back, the individual leg rests, the arm rests and, best of all, vibration buttons for a back and bottom massage. When the seat levelled out as a bed, I was supplied with a mattress, pillows, pyjamas, socks and eyeshade. The cushioned earphones completely obliterated the engine noise, so the experience was spookily silent and smooth. The food was marvellous and could be ordered at any time. Altogether, it was like relaxing in a private nursing home; I almost found myself calling out 'nurse!' as the air hostess walked by.

In Singapore, we led one 'workshop' for the very young students, ten or eleven-year-olds, at Dulwich College! This was, indeed, a sister college of the one in south London. Of course, they were not going to be interested in recruitment for a film course for adults in London, and were somewhat mystified by our training programme.

Having no children of my own, I tend not to take too much interest in school protocol, but this was a learning curve (Singapore rules?) Teachers must never talk to the children in the corridors, or playground, or anywhere except the classroom, or on the playing field. They must not make any bodily contact with the children, other than (possibly) a formal handshake. All these rules were made to reduce any possibility of parents making claims of abuse. How sad, I thought, that we have come to this through fear, following the reporting of a handful of cases and newspaper scare stories. I think it's horrible.

Before all these restrictions were made known to Patrick, his regular screen acting class was soon overstepping the rules, and urgent messages were being passed to me to tell him 'not to...get so close to the children, not push two children close together to demonstrate a good two-shot, and his film clips must not show any kissing, even of a platonic nature.' The teacher in charge was threatening to stop the class. What's with these people? After 50 minutes the session was wrapped up and the children were sent away pronto, and we felt that it was probably the most unrewarding event, both for us and the students.

The whole thing was a total mistake. We should never have been taken to teach such young children, but it had been arranged as a desperate last minute booking as all the others had fallen through. You could be forgiven for thinking: "What does it matter, it was only an hour, and the rest of the week was yours to enjoy." Funnily enough, it doesn't work like that. We have enjoyed dozens of 'holidays' on the back of a paid job, but we have always felt that the work done was good and appreciated. "You've changed my life," is a regular phrase we hear after a workshop, so the reward for 'good job done' is the holiday you feel you have earned.

Oh, we did a few camp things. Like being taken to dine at the top of the tallest hotel, an eight course gourmet 'taster' meal, where each dish is minutely described beforehand - delicious and very expensive, I'm sure. Then a friend, who lives in Singapore, took us to a really homely buffet-style open-air place on the riverside, cheap and cheerful with jugs of beer... fantastic! Patrick pushed me round the orchid gardens in a hired wheelchair, and we travelled by local buses to China Town and Little India, but it never quite felt like we deserved all this luxury.

The hotel (in my opinion) was five-star pretentious rubbish. We had access to the Club Lounge, where cocktails and nibbles were available in the early evening. Overhearing the conversations of the other guests was deeply depressing. They talked about nothing but MONEY and finance. Bankers, yachtsmen, the whole motley bunch, boring for the world. Not surprisingly, we felt we didn't fit in. We tried to visit the Raffles Hotel as a token of old-world luxury. There was a handsome, be-turbaned Indian gentleman at the main entrance, which quickened my heart beat, but when he raised his arm, pointed his finger and instructed us to go round the side of the building, I knew we were not being recognised as the favoured elite. Instead we were restricted to the garden area and some unused indoor rooms, expected to give visitors a taste of the 'old colonial'. We chatted briefly to a group of women with their sketch pads, recording former glories for the folks back home. My hopes of sitting on a soft sofa in a magnificent lounge with morning coffee and a plate of delicacies, was shattered by the 'Private - Residents Only' sign at the entrance.

Harrow School, Bangkok?

We had a very similar experience in Bangkok, although our audience was a grown up one, as they were senior students at Harrow School! Yes, a sister school to the one in north London. What is going on? The teachers seemed to have no knowledge of how films are made, and little appreciation of the talent required to act in them; and this was the arts department! They had been asked to supply a camera that would link to the monitor, so that the class could see what we were filming. They presented us with an ordinary photographic camera. We discarded that, and made the best of things by using a lap top instead but, of course, everything appeared to be reversed on the screen. How any of these students could procure enough knowledge to go on to 'film school' in England, from this inadequate introduction, heaven knows.

Interlude
Between us, Patrick and I have sat through hundreds of short films, mostly made by students or wannabe film directors, and have come to the conclusion that there are two things wrong with them: a) they're too long; and b) they're much too long.

We tried to use our stay in Thailand by venturing into the unknown, and not do the touristy things. We tried the local eateries, and specially liked the one where they were spit-roasting a whole pig on the pavement outside. There were local markets where I trusted I would be buying my next summer wardrobe; those lovely soft, thin cotton things but, alas, most of the clothes were no different to those in London's Oxford Street.

We took a train going north towards the ancient capital of Thailand, and I had hoped we would be travelling into the hills, with beautiful scenery and views of Bangkok through the trees. I couldn't have been more disappointed really. It was flat all the way, passing light industry and squalid living conditions. In order to see all the ancient monuments and temples, we hired a taxi. This was a small van-type vehicle, which we had to climb in and out of a dozen times. I was almost more exhausted than if I had walked between the sites. There was a gigantic Buddha in a completely horizontal reclining position (as if taking a nap) and a temple devoted to the worship of cocks; beautifully painted cockerels everywhere. A few colourful memories, and a return trip to England in sumptuous luxury, but always a feeling that we hadn't really earned it.

Endeavouring to make a modest impression on the natives of Bangkok, I had delved into the Thai language survival kit phrasebook, and on page 17, I came across 'small talk' with the following information, exactly as printed...

The first word to be memorized by any student of Thai is the 'politening syllable' of khrap. Whenever you speak Thai to a stranger in Thailand your sentence or phrase should end in khrap. By muttering this lightest of syllables you will gain much. No catastrophe will befall you if you don't observe this convention; however, when you do, you will be perceived as polite and civil, rather than abrupt and aggressive. If your conversation is a long one (let's be ambitious) you can drop the khrap after a few lines. Throughout this phrasebook, you may assume that there is an invisible khrap after every phrase.

6th Intermission

The Last Replacement

Replacement No.15: (aged 77)

I have said many times how, being a freelance, a phone call can send you off in an unexpected direction; and so it did, in the autumn of 2012. Patrick and I were in Toronto presenting workshops and were about to travel to New York for a further ten days in America, when Hurricane Sandy hit the Eastern Seaboard. All planes, trains and roads were out of action; we simply couldn't get there. A further three days at *The Holiday Inn* was not a problem, but getting a reasonable flight out of Canada to the UK occupied our every moment. We realised that we would have to forfeit a large chunk of our return fare, and spend even more to get home, although there could be some insurance compensation later. Eventually we discovered an airline, which just travelled twice daily between Toronto and the UK, and we managed to secure two seats at a reasonable price.

We got back to London a week before planned and, during that week I was sent for two commercials and, unbelievably, got them both! This rare occurrence meant that I would have some exposure on television and, as it turned out, my brief two-second appearance in a Peugeot commercial (*Gary's Cat*) gave me an opportunity to do a mail out to over 80 casting directors, which triggered an instant re-sponse. From 17 casting sessions I got five jobs, none of them very grand, but there was one audition for the feature film *The Harry Hill Movie* - but I *didn't* get the part.

A month later I was travelling down to Guildford to see a friend in a play, when my phone rang. My agent!

"You remember that Harry Hill film you went for?" he said. "Of course I do," I said.

"Well, they liked you very much, but decided to go with someone else who they thought looked better for the part."

"How nice of them to let me know I didn't get it," I said.

"Well, it's a bit more complicated than that," he said. "They want to know if you're free tomorrow."

As it happened I was.

"They're thinking of re-casting. Could you stand by till mid-day? It's not an offer as yet, but if you don't hear by 12 o'clock, they'll stay with the other actress."

Now, what do you do in those circumstances? Well, I'll tell you what you do...you wait in, and hope.

So, there I was at ten to twelve, listening to *Test Match Special*, as you do, when the phone rang.

"You've got the job!"

After discovering that the money was fixed and non-negotiable, I got a second call, this time from the location.

"Is it alright if a car picks you up in twenty minutes?"

My driver swiftly navigated two motorways, depositing me in what looked like a disused airfield in Surrey. The film unit, consisting of prefabricated offices, trailers for make up, wardrobe and actors, and mobile catering vans, had encamped in a small corner of this vast empty wasteland. I was marched at some speed to the office to fill in health forms and sign a contract, then to wardrobe and make-up. I had my own suite in a trailer with my character's name on the door, 'Mrs Pickford'. There was a bed, wardrobe, fridge, shower and loo. My costume was already hanging up and I was asked to get into it as quickly as possible. Then, over to the make-up trailer, only to find a photograph of the actress I was replacing propped up in front of the mirror. It appears that, in addition to attending a cast read-through, a music call and recording, she had also appeared in the background of a shot, so a major attempt was being made to make me look as near to that image as possible. Apart from my being slightly taller (at four foot eleven that doesn't happen very often) and having a rounder face, I shaped up pretty well. With the addition of two wigs, on the front and back of my head, a grey frizzy mass with a mauve woolly beret plonked on top, a ghastly pale blue anorak and disgusting beige slacks, I looked a bugger, and that is how most of the cast and crew saw me throughout the filming. No wonder nobody recognised me at the wrap party! In fact, on the final filming day when I met up with all the actors and was standing next to Matt Lucas, he turned to me and said:

"Oh, hello, I sat next to you at the read-through."

None of the cast seem to be aware that I was a 'replacement'. Ah well.

From the make-up trailer I was whisked off to a leafy suburban street where the crew had already set up my scene, and because they had been working till midnight the day before, this was the first shot of the day. It also meant that lunch would be taken at 5 o'clock and I was, by this time, seriously hungry. Remember?

To go back to my audition, I had been sent a script for the two scenes featuring 'Mrs Pickford' with one line to learn. Mrs P was Harry's neighbour whose dog had died. Harry and his nan (being played by Julie Walters) see her walking along the pavement pulling a breezeblock to which she has attached a dog lead, then she stops abruptly and utters her one line.

When it came to the filming, I was briefly introduced to the director, Steve Bendelack, shown where to walk, then: "Action!" I walked along the pavement pulling my 'dog'…then: "Cut!" After several 'takes' during which the breezeblock mostly refused to stay upright, we got it. But, I hadn't said my line. They couldn't have forgotten about it, surely?

It was about 3 o'clock by now and we all repaired to the house which some crazy family had turned over to the film unit, and where Julie, seeing me searching for food, offered up her biscuits. Bless. A crumb, anything. The dinner, when it finally came, was about the worst location food I have ever encountered. However, when you're starving…

I was then approached by the director and a guy with an *iPod*, who told me that I wouldn't be needed again till about half past nine, because they had to shoot my next scene in the dark. And there was me thinking I was finished for the day.

"What…er…next scene is that?" I asked.

"The one where you sing a couple of solo lines in

the general company song." he said. What?! This was complete news to me. Nobody had even asked me if I could sing! I CAN sing, as it happens, AND read music, but I was to see no music that day. I simply had to learn it all from a recording made by the cast and try to copy what the previous artiste had sung. At least the words were on that day's call sheet but, alas, no dots.

Apart from the much longed for, though regrettably unappetising dinner, I spent the rest of the daylight hours standing in front of the long mirror in my trailer, playing and replaying the song. It sounded like, and indeed was supposed to be, a spoof of a big cast number from *Les Misérables* with individual contributions from each featured character. This was the first time I realised, by the way, that 'Mrs Pickford' was regarded as a featured character.

At one point I found myself staring at my reflection and thinking, all those years of belting out old time music hall numbers at 'The Green Man' are paying off at last, because that was exactly what was required here. I should point out that the recording, which was the only thing I had to learn from, threw up some difficulties. The four lines preceding mine were sung by two different characters, with different rhythms and in different keys. This meant that I would have to listen to the playback through an ear-piece, which would be faded out just before my entrance, then come in on cue with no accompaniment. Piece of piss.

At the point of no return, I was taken to the same back street where I went over the music yet again with the sound engineer, to get levels and so on. At this point the director joined us to see how I was doing, and after belting it out a few times, he seemed quite happy to go for a take. So, there I was: ten o'clock at night, in the open air, standing on a box, holding a breezeblock, in the dark, in the rain, singing solo, unaccompanied, straight into the camera lens, belting out part of a song I didn't know and had never heard all the way through...and having to pitch my note and pick up my rhythm on cue and in silence. Nothing to it, really.

After about ten 'takes' I heard the magical words: "That's a wrap for Christine," followed by a round of applause from the crew, a big hug from the director, who offered some not unwelcome praise, but I felt almost jetlagged by this time, and could only respond with:

"You do realise, I was out of work this morning?"

Encore

2016 (Age 79)

After many years, when I thought my sitcom days were well and truly over, a casting director came through and offered me a part in a new one by Ben Elton called *Upstart Crow,* which was to be recorded in a couple of weeks time. No interview required, just 'are you available and interested?' You bet I was.

Like so many of my 'acting job' stories, this one came with its share of misunderstandings. I was booked to play a witch, but which witch? The script, as emailed through to me, had 'First Witch' with some single lines, and two other witches who spoke in chorus with the 'First Witch'. Then confirmation came from the casting department that I would be 'the witch with the lines'. Naturally, I took this to mean 'First Witch'.

I turned up, lines learnt, for a read through and found a pile of printed scripts on the table. I took one and opened it, only to discover that the 'First Witch' (the one with the lines) was now called 'Hecate' and from the cast list I saw that somebody else was playing it! I had a quiet word with the producer, just to let him know that I was a little disappointed at being misled. He was very apologetic (he seemed to know nothing of the misleading information) and really hoped I would stay. Of course I would stay, but I felt much happier having made my point, and later I was given a solo line and, on leaving, an enormous bunch of flowers.

It was lovely to be back in the world of sitcom, but on the second day I was approached by the other witch who asked:

"Are you really 79?"

"Who told you that?" I said.

"Nobody," she said. "I looked you up on Wikipedia."

Amazingly, four of the things I have talked about in this memoir had just manifested themselves in one acting job. A *BBC* sitcom, Will Shakespeare, a 'coven' and, after a week of working with several popular and very well-known performers, 'the generation gap' became alarmingly apparent.

After a while I was able to chat with some of the better known actors individually, mostly about their work. Although I could have bored them all to death with my anecdotes, and dear reader, you should know, I have learnt over the years that name-droppings from 'unknown' actors are brownie point losers, so I kept my lips severely sealed.

While the company were sitting round waiting to start a 'line run', Harry Enfield began to reflect amusingly on the direction his career was going, and what his future might be. It then occurred to me that, one day this group of actors could all be in my position, surrounded by a bunch of celebrated artistes half their age, who wouldn't be at all sure who they were, and care even less about what they'd done. It quite cheered me up!

*****

Note to self: fame can fade, but memoirs improve with longevity.

*****

Epilogue

2016

Obituaries fascinate me. Not necessarily in any morbid way, but simply to read about the life of someone who gets a full-page spread, with photographs, in a national newspaper. If it is an actor I have known and worked with, of course, it will be fully scrutinised for any links to my own life and work, but if they are of advanced years, they will not be known - at all - to the many young actors I teach and talk to. I once began a story about the actor Steve McQueen, of *The Great Escape* and *The Magnificent Seven* fame and was suddenly aware of a sea of blank faces; they didn't know who I was talking about. Oh, you don't either? Please get the DVD a.s.a.p.

So, what is fame, and how long does it last? Actually, it must be quite tough for those who live beyond their fame and become an 'unknown' again, but as the pantomime sprite states in her sad little ditty entitled *Nobody Loves a Fairy When She's Forty.*

> *If I can't do all I could*
> *I'm satisfied, because...*
> *I'd rather be a 'has been'*
> *Than I would a 'never was'.*

There are two phrases I try not to use.'If only...' and 'I wish...'. Whatever you have done, you cannot undo, and, as Shakespeare might say, "there's an end on't". I also believe that luck, chance, accident, coincidence and serendipity, are merely words we use to describe an unpredictable or inexplicable set of circumstances, but they are merely things happening in a certain order which appear, in some way, to be significant. Whether the results of these apparently weird occurrences are good, bad, helpful or disastrous, it's the way life is, so we should just get used to it.

Reflecting on this book, however, I would like to ponder what might have happened to me had John Fernald's prediction come about. If, during the eight years after graduating from *RADA*, I had been taken up by an influential agent, done really well in the comedy field and become something of a household name by the age of 30, the rest of my life would have been very different indeed.

For a start, I would not have joined the *Oliver!* tour as a chorus girl, and I wouldn't have met Patrick on that tour which, let's face it, changed my life. The most likely scenario would have been a career in sitcoms, maybe even having parts written for me. There were, in fact, two parts written with me in mind, by well-known writers, but when it came to the casting they were not consulted, and the parts went elsewhere. I could have been taken up by the *Carry On* team; plus prominent roles on stage in plays by Alan Ayckbourn, Ray Cooney and the like; the Joan Sims route, maybe. Sadly, I recall her saying that she never thought she would end up living alone in a bed-sit in Kilburn.

But my type and style of comedy performance may, with time, have become old fashioned, and I would have been unable to make the transition into shows like *The Green Wing; The Thick of It* and *W1A*. It is more than likely that I would have been featured as a regular in a soap, the Wendy Richards, Barbara Windsor route, and in my later years doing pantos and touring endlessly in pot boilers and Agatha Christies, with my 'well-known' character's name in brackets along side my own...plenty of routes to follow there! The possibility of my doing any classical theatre would have been a faint one indeed.

I would most probably never have married or had a permanent relationship (my gut feeling) but would hopefully have made enough money to live independently, and gone on sunshine holidays with chums. But, in order to maintain the fame and the income, I would have had to work continuously and would never have known the thrills of all the exotic experiences that have come my way.

Sailing in a friend's yacht on the Chesapeake Bay, dining at Sardis, visiting Petra three times with a hand-picked cast of actors, sleeping under the stars at Wadi Ram, sitting at the prompt desk on the Globe stage, in three separate productions, a tin whistle version of *Happy Birthday* (to me) led by a Russian Oligarch, in Latvia, being hosted by a famous Japanese film star at her home in Tokyo, Patrick and I doing a book signing for the university faculty in Southern Utah, plus the Atlantic crossing on the QEII, in exchange for two lectures and the extraordinary journey from Beijing to Moscow on the trans-Siberian railway.

Then there were the magic moments from *The Original Shakespeare Company* actors. Richard Cordery's 'Dromio' describing the geography of a grotesque woman, Mark Burgess ordering a Pizza before 'The Man from Pisa' arrived, David Ferry's creation of 'Gremio' as a cross-dresser and Nick Day's 'Bottom' in his death throes. There were so many times when I thought I would burst with joy. The same feeling you get, as an actor, after a perfectly timed laugh. It's called 'getting a belter' and it's a wonderful feeling.

So - I did NOT achieve early fame, and I DID join the chorus and meet Patrick, which led to us both discovering the wonders of Shakespeare and the inevitable industry that goes with it. His willingness to work abroad when the opportunities came along led to the most amazing travels, all over America as well as the Far East. My on-going life as a jobbing actor led to the fifteen extraordinary 'replacement' stories I have chronicled. I never wanted to give up acting, I simply loved it, but I found a way of combining it with my hunger to learn more about... well, everything really. I had been denied further education after the eleven plus failure, but I learnt to take advantage of opportunities and squared up well to Patrick's spirit of adventure.

Am I a typical actor?

Have I experienced real hunger? Oh yes, especially in those early years. In the summer break between my two years at *RADA*, I had only 'ninepence' in my purse (and no savings). When I applied to the *BBC* for a job as a tea-lady at Broadcasting House, they put me on the 5th floor trolley service, with subsidised canteen meals, which kept body (and legs) together! Later, I became hungry for audiences to entertain, and now I crave good actors, to teach them all those wonderful instructions in Shakespeare's text. Something I could definitely have benefited from before attempting 'The Nurse' at Crewe.

Have I prepared my Oscar speech? You bet! Although I am probably no longer in the running for the 'Most Promising Newcomer' award, so my ancient scribbled notes have long since hit the dust.

'Unknown' I still am, and glad of it, otherwise there would be no book on the subject! I am proud to stand alongside my fellow 'unknown' actors, because they are brave and loyal, and tremendous fun to be with. I salute them and sincerely hope that the joy they have brought to their audiences over the years has also brought them pleasure and, above all, contentment. They all deserve a gong!

The latest 'unknown' territory on my life's travels has been writing this book. What started off as a record of work, especially the 'replacement' jobs, grew into an investigation as to what makes me tick, and I had to allow things to surface which might otherwise have stayed buried forever. This wasn't too painful, in fact it was most therapeutic and produced some really comforting revelations which I hope will be received favourably by those people most closely involved in my life.

Even more recently I have learnt that if you are an 'unknown actor' it is much more difficult to get a book published.

Finale

Thespians are particularly fortunate in that they don't have to retire at a certain age. They can carry on in a very useful capacity until they feel they can no longer remember how to do it. I was going great guns when, a few weeks before my birthday in 1996, I received an alarming letter from the Department of Work and Pensions informing me that I would be 60 on the 28th of July (as if I didn't know) and that I would be entitled to a state pension on reaching that date. I was, of course, grateful for the prospect of a constant, if modest, income and in addition to this I would become entitled to free NHS prescriptions, concessions at many art houses and ...best of all...a bus pass. Now called a Freedom Pass, this entitles me to free travel on buses, tubes and overground railway journeys throughout Greater London. I cannot imagine how I got to be so fortunate.

All this meant that, at long last, I would not be required to 'sign on' at the Labour Exchange... or whatever they call it now...so I turned up on the appropriate day to 'sign off'. I waited in a long queue, nothing new there, and finally found myself standing face to face with a complete stranger. I had become familiar with all the clerks at the Chiswick branch over the years, but this young man was a very new addition to the staff. I told him my name; he looked through a box of cards; he looked up blankly, so I repeated my name. Again he flipped the cards… nothing. I smiled and slowly spelt out my surname, feeling sure he was looking in the wrong place. He tried another box and failed yet again. We looked at each other for a few seconds, then with some degree of nonchalance, he asked:

"Have you signed on here before?"

With supreme confidence, I pulled myself up to my full four foot eleven and replied:

"I've given you the best years of my life."

> I once saw a house called:
> DUNROAMING
>
> I thought that I might call mine:
> DUNACTING
>
> But not quite yet…

Curtain Call

Ken and Ethel Smith: For inspired casting
Rita Barsby: For spotting the potential
RADA: For supplying the springboard
Kim Grant: For suggesting the *Oliver!* tour.
William Shakespeare: For additional material.
Patrick Tucker: For his total dedication to my project, his patience and skill in the face my struggle with computers, and his determination not to read a word of this book until it was finished. He came into my life at the first Interval; read the script; altered the plot and insisted on a HAPPY ENDING!

My thanks to **Peter Gutteridge** and **David Warwick** for their advice and guidance and to **Alan Curtis, Sally Hallam, Steve Nealon** and **Greta Scacchi** for their supporting roles. My special thanks to **Sir David Jason.**

I am most grateful to **KT Forster** and **Matt Trollope** at **Avocado Books** for their editorial and publishing services, and to **Jax Etta Elliott** for her eye-catching cover design.

Photo credits / permissions

Images from:
Dirty Linen, courtesy of Ed Berman, MBE
Carry on Nurse, courtesy of STUDIOCANAL Films Ltd
Six Dates with Barker, courtesy of ITV/Rex Shutterstock
Comedy Playhouse (front cover), courtesy of *BBC* Photo Library

The extract on page 346 is taken from *Lonely Planet Thailand Phrasebook* - ISBN: 0 908086 57 1

Photographers:
Mark Browne, Christopher Davies, Forge Productions, Malcolm Gerard, George Kelman for *The Leicester Drama Society*; Simon Purse, Tim Reder, Leslie Roberts, Frank Sproston, Nicholas Toyne and Malcolm Venville. Larisa Dizdar for 2015 headshots.

Every effort has been made to trace copyright holders of photogrpahs and other material in this book. The author will be happy to rectify any omissions at the earliest opportunity.

About the Author

CHRISTINE OZANNE is an actress who has worked in all areas of the entertainment industry since graduating with an Honours Diploma from *The Royal Academy of Dramatic Art* in 1958, at the age of 22. Her work includes roles in Weekly Repertory and West End theatres, television drama series and serials, 20 situation comedies, 60 commercials and 12 feature films.

Christine, with her partner, Patrick Tucker, founded and ran *The Original Shakespeare Company* and mounted 28 productions world-wide, including three separate plays at Shakespeare's Globe theatre in London. Together they have travelled extensively, both with their Company and teaching programmes in numerous colleges, drama schools and universities including Cambridge and Yale. They have written four audition books together, plus *The Actor's Survival Handbook*.

Comedy was always Christine's strong point in performance, which began in 1958 with her film debut in *Carry on Nurse*, and has continued up to 2016 when she appeared in the *BBC* sitcom, *Upstart Crow*. She is an avid theatre-goer, has a passion for cricket and adores maps. This is Christine's first solo attempt at writing, and she has loved every moment of it. **ChristineOzanne.com**

Index

64528658R00195

Made in the USA
Charleston, SC
01 December 2016